D1686804

ecpr PRESS

political trust

why context matters

Edited by
Sonja Zmerli and Marc Hooghe

ecpr PRESS

© Sonja Zmerli
and Marc Hooghe 2011

First published by the ECPR Press in 2011

The ECPR Press is the publishing imprint of the European Consortium for Political Research (ECPR), a scholarly association, which supports and encourages the training, research and cross-national cooperation of political scientists in institutions throughout Europe and beyond. The ECPR's Central Services are located at the University of Essex, Wivenhoe Park, Colchester, CO4 3SQ, UK

All rights reserved. No part of this book may be reprinted or reproduced or utilised in any form or by any electronic, mechanical, or other means, now known or hereafter invented, including photocopying and recording, or in any information storage or retrieval system, without permission in writing from the publishers.

Typeset by AnVi Composers
Printed and bound by Lightning Source

British Library Cataloguing in Publication Data
A catalogue record for this book is available from the British Library

Hardback ISBN: 978-1-907301-23-0

www.ecprnet.eu/ecprpress

ECPR – Studies in European Political Science

Series Editors:
Dario Castiglione (University of Exeter) and
Vincent Hoffmann-Martinot (Sciences Po Bordeaux)

ECPR – Studies in European Political Science is a series of high-quality edited volumes on topics at the cutting edge of current political science and political thought. All volumes are research-based offering new perspectives in the study of politics with contributions from leading scholars working in the relevant fields. Most of the volumes originate from ECPR events including the Joint Sessions of Workshops, the Research Sessions, and the General Conferences.

Books in this series

The Domestic Party Politics of Europeanisation: Actors, Patterns and Systems
(ISBN: 9781907301223)
Edited by Külahci Erol

Interactive Policymaking, Metagovernance and Democracy
(ISBN: 9781907301131)
Edited by Jacob Torfing and Peter Triantafillou

Perceptions of Europe: A Comparative Sociology of European Attitudes
(ISBN: 9781907301155)
Edited by Daniel Gaxie, Jay Rowell and Nicolas Hubé

Personal Representation: The Neglected Dimension of Electoral Systems
(ISBN: 9781907301162)
Edited by Josep Colomer

Political Trust: Why Context Matters
(ISBN: 9781907301230)
Edited by Sonja Zmerli and Marc Hooghe

Please visit www.ecprnet.eu/ecprpress for up-to-date information about new publications

contents

List of Figures and Tables	vii
Acknowledgements	xi
Biographies	xiii

Chapter One: Introduction: The Context of Political Trust
MARC HOOGHE AND SONJA ZMERLI — 1

Chapter Two: Measuring Political Trust Across Time and Space
SOFIE MARIEN — 13

Chapter Three: Falling or Fluctuating Trust Levels? The Case of the Netherlands
MARK BOVENS AND ANCHRIT WILLE — 47

Chapter Four: Winners, Losers and Three Types of Trust
SONJA ZMERLI AND KEN NEWTON — 67

Chapter Five: Trustworthy States, Trusting Citizens? A Multilevel Study into Objective and Subjective Determinants of Political Trust
TOM VAN DER MEER AND PAUL DEKKER — 95

Chapter Six: Political Trust and Distrust In Post-Authoritarian Contexts
RICHARD ROSE AND WILLIAM MISHLER — 117

Chapter Seven: Corruption, the Inequality Trap and Trust in Government
ERIC M. USLANER — 141

Chapter Eight: Dissatisfied Democrats, Policy Feedback and European Welfare States, 1976–2001
STAFFAN KUMLIN — 163

Chapter Nine: Evaluations of Welfare State Reforms in Germany: Political Trust Makes a (Big) Difference
EVA-MARIA TRÜDINGER AND UWE BOLLOW — 187

Index

list of figures and tables

Figures

Figure 2.1:	Solution confirmatory factor analysis	19
Figure 2.2:	Solution confirmatory factor analysis with imposed constraints	23
Figure 2.3:	Trends in trust in political institutions in the Nordic countries	28
Figure 2.4:	Trends in trust in political institutions in Southern Europe	28
Figure 2.5:	Trends in trust in political institutions in other established democracies	29
Figure 2.6:	Trends in trust in political institutions in new democracies	30
Figure 2.7:	Trends in satisfaction with government in the Nordic countries	32
Figure 2.8:	Trends in satisfaction with government in Southern European countries	33
Figure 2.9:	Trends in satisfaction with government in the other established countries	34
Figure 2.10:	Trends in satisfaction with government in new European democracies	35
Figure 1,	Appendix B: Solution Confirmatory Factor Analysis (2006)	39
Figure 2,	Appendix B: Solution Confirmatory Factor Analysis (2004)	39
Figure 1,	Appendix C: Solution Confirmatory Factor Analysis with Imposed Constraints (2006)	40
Figure 2,	Appendix C: Solution Confirmatory Factor Analysis with Imposed Constraints (2004)	42
Figure 3.1:	Satisfaction with cabinet and with government performance 1995–2008	51
Figure 3.2:	Trust in cabinet 2003–2010	52
Figure 3.3:	Trust in cabinet, political parties and parliament in the Netherlands 1997–2009	53
Figure 3.4:	Agreement with negative statements about politicians and political parties in the period 1977–2006	54
Figure 3.5:	Percentage of respondents who are satisfied with the way democracy works in the Netherlands 1974–2009	54

Figure 3.6:	Trust in cabinets (national government) in the Netherlands compared with the other EU members 1997–2008	56
Figure 3.7:	Satisfaction with the way democracy works in the Netherlands and consumer confidence in the Netherlands 1974–2009	60
Figure 3.8:	Confidence in the economy and trust in cabinet in the Netherlands February 2007–July 2009	62
Figure 6.1:	Variations in trust within and across nations	125
Figure 6.2:	Trends in political trust 1993–2004	126
Figure 8.1:	Welfare state benefit generosity	171
Figure 8.2:	Satisfaction with democracy and unemployment benefit generosity at different unemployment rates	178

Tables

Table 2.1:	Solution confirmatory factor analysis	20
Table 2.2:	Testing for cross-cultural equivalence in trust in political institutions	23
Table 2.3:	Trust in political institutions in Europe	26
Table 1,	Appendix A: European Social Survey – Completed Questionnaires	38
Table 1,	Appendix C: Testing for cross-cultural equivalence in trust in political institutions (2006)	40
Table 2,	Appendix C: Testing for cross-cultural equivalence in trust in political institutions (2004)	41
Table 3.1:	Short- and long-term explanations for the flux in political trust	58
Table 4.1:	Distribution of social and political trust	75
Table 4.2:	Mokken scale analysis, twelve trust items, pooled data	75
Table 4.3:	Nonparametric correlations between social trust, political trust and socio-economic and attitudinal items	78
Table 4.4:	Nonparametric correlations between three types of trusters and socio-economic and attitudinal items	79
Table 4.5:	Linear regression, political trust index with particular and general social trust as predictors	80
Table 4.6:	Linear regression, political trust index with three types of trusters as predictors	81

Table 4.7:	Logistic regressions, particular trusters and general trusters	82
Table 4.8:	Logistic regressions, particular trusters and general trusters with two types of political trust as predictors	83
Appendix 1:	Countries included in the analyses, WVS 2005–7	88
Table 5.1:	Determinants of trust in parliament	105
Table 5.2:	Bivariate correlations of intermediary factors with contextual determinants and with trust in parliament	106
Table 5.3:	Explaining contextual effects on political trust	109
Appendix 1:	Countries, objective characteristics, and average levels of trust in parliament	113
Table 6.1:	Trust in political institutions	123
Table 6.2:	Combining contextual and individual influences on trust. Multilevel model of institutional trust	129
Appendix A:	NEB surveys in the analysis	135
Appendix B:	Coding of variables	136
Table 7.1:	Determinants of public service deterioration in transition countries: State Failure Data	149
Table 7.2:	Determinants of service interruption in transition: Aggregate models from BEEPS 2005	151
Table 7.3:	Determinants of service interruption in transition: Individual-level models from BEEPS 2005	153
Table 7.4:	Determinants of trust in government (LiTS data)	157
Table 8.1:	Multilevel models of satisfaction with democracy	173
Table 8.2:	Multilevel model of satisfaction with democracy	177
Table 9.1:	Acceptance of welfare state reforms: old-age pensions	198
Table 9.2:	Acceptance of welfare state reforms: health care policy	199
Table 9.3:	Acceptance of welfare state reforms: family policy	200

acknowledgements

Most of the chapters in this volume were first presented either during a panel on political trust at the ECPR General Conference in Potsdam in September 2009 or the workshop on the same topic at the ECPR Joint Sessions in Münster in March 2010. The editors especially thank all participants of the workshop for a week of lively and high quality discussions that helped to shape the overall argument in this volume.

Financial support for the language editing and assistance during the editing process was generously provided by the Goethe-University Frankfurt am Main. In particular, Cordula Schöneich's knowledgeable and thorough correction and formatting input is highly valued. The editors also thank Mark Kench of ECPR Press whose thoughtful, kind and patient support contributed considerably to this volume in its published version.

| biographies

UWE BOLLOW is a Research Assistant at the Department of Political Systems and Political Sociology at the University of Stuttgart. He recently completed his thesis on the role of ambivalence in the evaluation of welfare state reforms.

MARK BOVENS is Professor of Public Administration and Research Director at the Utrecht School of Governance of Utrecht University in The Netherlands. His research interests include political trust, democracy and citizenship, and public accountability. His latest book (with Deirdre Curtin and Paul 't Hart, eds) is *The Real World of EU Accountability: What Deficit?*, Oxford UP 2010.

PAUL DEKKER is Professor of Civil Society at Tilburg University and Head of the Participation and Government research unit of the Netherlands Institute for Social Research | SCP. Among his (co-)edited books are: *The values of volunteering* (Springer, 2003), *Politiek cynisme* (Synthesis, 2006), *Civil society* (Aksant, 2009), and *Civicness in the governance and delivery of social services* (Nomos, 2010).

MARC HOOGHE is Professor of Political Science at the University of Leuven (Belgium) and the University of Lille (France). Recently he has published on electoral reform in Belgium (*West European Politics*, 2011) and behavioural consequences of political trust (*European Journal of Political Research*, 2011).

STAFFAN KUMLIN is Associate Professor at the University of Gothenburg and Research Fellow at the Institute for Social Research, Oslo. Kumlin studies political behaviour and European welfare states and is the author of *The Personal and the Political: How Personal Welfare State Experiences Affect Political Trust and Ideology* (Palgrave-Macmillan, 2004), as well as articles in journals such as *British Journal of Political Science*, *Comparative Political Studies*, *Comparative Politics*, and *European Journal of Political Research*.

SOFIE MARIEN is a Post-doctoral Researcher at the Department of Political Science at the University of Leuven. Research interests include political trust, political participation and representation. Previously, her work has been published in *European Journal of Political Research*, *Government and Opposition*, and *Political Studies*.

WILLIAM MISHLER is Professor of Government and Public Policy at the University of Arizona and Co-Editor of *The Journal of Politics*. A specialist in democratic theory, he teaches and writes on public opinion, political representation, and the dynamics of citizen support for political parties, leaders and regimes. He is the author or co-author of eight books, the most recent of which is *Popular Support for an Undemocratic Regime: the Changing Views of Russians* (Cambridge University Press, spring 2011). He also is the author of numerous articles and chapters in most of the leading political science journals including the *American Political Science Review, American Journal of Political Science, The Journal of Politics, British Journal of Political Science, Comparative Politics, Comparative Political Studies*, and *Legislative Studies Quarterly*.

KEN NEWTON is Professor Emeritus at the University of Southampton and Visiting Professor at the WZB, Berlin. He was Executive Director of the ECPR for ten years and has recently published work on the mass media, trust, democratic innovation, participation, and comparative politics.

RICHARD ROSE is Professor of Politics at the University of Strathclyde. Since 1991 his *New Europe Barometer* has conducted more than one hundred nationwide sample surveys about mass response to transformation in seventeen formerly Communist countries. His latest book, with William Mishler and Neil Munro, is *Popular Support for an Undemocratic Regime: the **Changing** Views of Russians*.

EVA-MARIA TRÜDINGER is a Researcher at the Department of Political Systems and Political Sociology at the University of Stuttgart. Her research interests and recent publications focus on public opinion about policies and about the European Union and questions of political psychology.

ERIC M. USLANER is Professor of Government and Politics at the University of Maryland. His recent books include *Corruption, Inequality, and the Rule of Law* (2008), *The Moral Foundations of Trust* (2002), and *Segregation and Mistrust* (under contract, in progress). In 2010, he was the Fulbright Distinguished Chair in American Political Science at Australian National University and he is also Senior Research Fellow at the Center for American Law and Political Science at the Southwest University of Political Science and Law, Chongqing, China.

TOM VAN DER MEER is Assistant Professor of Political Science at the University of Amsterdam. His interests encompass political trust, citizen participation, electoral volatility, and ethnic diversity. He has published on these topics in edited volumes and various national and international journals such as *American Sociological Review, Comparative Political Studies, European Journal of Political Research, European Sociological Review*, and *International Review of Administrative Sciences*.

SONJA ZMERLI is currently Acting Professor in Comparative Politics at the University of Mannheim. Her research interests focus on social capital, political trust, political participation, welfare state regimes and inequality. She has published in several edited volumes and international journals such as *American Behavioral Scientist, European Political Science, European Political Science Review*, and *Public Opinion Quarterly*.

chapter one | introduction: the context of political trust

Marc Hooghe and Sonja Zmerli

Recent election results suggest that political incumbents are facing an uphill struggle in quite a few Western democracies. The most obvious example might be the May 2010 general elections in the United Kingdom that ended thirteen years of Labour government, leaving the party with only twenty-nine per cent of the vote. If there is one general trend in recent election results in Western Europe, it is that governing parties tend to lose votes in favour of the opposition. In various countries, populist and anti-system parties, too, seem to be on the rise. The most telling example here might be the result of the September 2010 elections in Sweden, a country that usually, and rightly, prides itself on a strong democratic political culture. In those elections, the extreme right Swedish Democrats won 5.7 per cent of the vote and entered Parliament. For most Swedes, this was quite a shock, as the extreme right had been virtually absent from the recent political history of their country. Developments in Eastern Europe, however, are by no means more encouraging. Although a number of Central and Eastern European societies have been experiencing democratic rule for twenty years or more, political trust has neither attained levels comparable to those in established democracies, nor are these societies less prone to extremist voting behaviour.

A number of authors have interpreted these election results as a symptom of a more structural political malaise and of disenchantment with liberal democracy as we know it. It is claimed that there is a lack of connection between citizens' political preferences and the way political parties and political decision-makers work. This is not a recent concern. As early as the 1960s a number of authors argued that Western political systems no longer adequately represent the preferences of the population and thus cause citizens to lose confidence in the system. Four decades ago, authors also decried what was called the crisis of the current system of liberal democracy. For the United States in particular there is abundant empirical evidence for this rather pessimistic outlook on contemporary politics. First, there is a structural trend toward declining levels of voter turnout as fewer US citizens care to participate in elections. Apparently, a growing number of eligible voters in the US no longer feel that their current two-party system adequately reflects their preferences and opinions (Franklin 2004; Blais 2006). Secondly, observations show that political trust has been declining in the US since the early 1970s. This not only refers to the president and government in general, but also to other elements of the political system, such as Congress or political parties. It is clearly a phenomenon that affects political institutions across the board.

This decline in political trust has important social and political consequences. It has been argued that low levels of political trust are one of the main reasons why the United States has not yet developed an elaborate system of social protection and social services as found in most other Western societies (Hetherington 2005). Developing such a system involves government agencies assuming a larger role in, for example, managing health care systems or pension plans. If, however, people strongly distrust these agencies to use their new authority wisely, this may fuel opposition against plans to develop a more comprehensive social security system. Indeed, some of the recent opposition against the health care reform plans under President Obama's administration can be traced back to feelings of distrust toward 'big government'. The impact of political trust goes even further. A number of recent studies have demonstrated that low levels of political trust are associated with illegal or risk-taking behaviour, like the illegal use of alcohol or drugs (Lindström 2008). Other studies show that low levels of political trust are associated with a greater willingness to condone various forms of illegal behaviour (Marien and Hooghe 2011). In both cases, the underlying logic seems to be that if citizens feel the authorities can no longer be trusted, there is less reason to comply with social norms or with the laws of the country. While earlier studies have demonstrated that the presence of generalised social trust has important positive effects on the functioning of society, the associated literature suggests that political trust, too, can have more or less comparable social outcomes.

These studies demonstrate that political trust does remain an important resource for liberal democracies. In recent years, a number of authors have argued that trust in the political system has been overrated in the academic literature. They assert that citizens should in fact be able to distrust their political leaders (Inglehart 1997; Norris 1999; Rosenvallon 2008). This claim reflects a structural transformation of public attitudes in liberal democracies. Especially among younger age cohorts, respect for authority has eroded and a more critical outlook on political decision-makers seems to prevail. With the traditional linkage mechanisms between citizens and the political system disintegrating, voting patterns have become much more volatile and voters rely less on ideologically-structured cues to make up their minds about politics and politicians. By itself, this more critical outlook can be seen as a positive development in a mature and healthy democracy, as indeed citizens are expected not to simply accept the authority of office-holders, but to scrutinise their actions. This does mean, however, that among this group political trust by itself would be lower. Almost all available studies document a positive relationship between a person's level of education, political knowledge and political sophistication on the one hand, and their political trust on the other hand (Newton 2007). While there is empirical evidence for the rise of a new generation of 'critical citizens', they are not necessarily distrusting citizens. While it is assumed that citizens should display a critical attitude towards political office-holders, support for the principles of liberal and democratic government has in general only tended to grow in Western societies. Studies by Ronald Inglehart and others have indeed amply demonstrated that public support for authoritarianism, or a rejection of the fundamental principles of liberal democracy, has been on the decline in Western democracies for the last few decades.

There is a relatively strong consensus in the literature about the importance of political trust. Much less agreement, however, can be found about the theoretical status of the concept, its actual meaning, the causes and the consequences of political trust.

The theoretical status of the concept of 'political trust' remains highly dubious. Some authors would even argue that it does not make sense to talk about 'trust' at all when analysing citizens' attitudes toward the political system. The notion of trust implies specific knowledge about the likelihood of trustworthy behaviour by someone else. For example, based on my previous experiences and my field knowledge, I can decide whether or not to trust a neighbour or colleague. Following this logic, it could be argued that the concept of 'political trust' as such is meaningless (Hardin 1999). As we usually do not have sufficient information about the trustworthiness of leading politicians or about civil servants in general, we lack the ability to decide whether or not we will trust the 'system'. We might still develop other attitudes toward the political system, but from this perspective they should not be seen as falling under the category of 'trust', which is seen as a form of experience-based encapsulated trust. Following this line of thinking, political trust appears here much more as a kind of general expectation that on the whole, political leaders will act according to the rules of the game as they are agreed upon in a democratic regime. Whether or not this expectation is experience-based does not make a difference then.

This view of political trust can be related to a notion that was already developed in the 1960s by David Easton (1965), who assumed that the attitudes of citizens toward the political system function as a source of diffuse support for the system. Even if citizens do not agree with a certain decision made by the political elite, they are still willing to support the regime in general and to comply with its decisions. Political trust means that the legitimacy of the political regime is acknowledged and that there is a high degree of willingness to accept the decisions of politicians and government agencies. Thus this notion rather refers to a general recognition of authority and a benign attitude towards political institutions. It is clear, therefore, that political trust should be distinguished from other, much more intense forms of trust. At best, political trust is a very thin form of trust, and it should rather be seen as the expectation that political actors generally behave in a fair manner. This expectation that democratic procedures will be followed is closely related to the concept of legitimacy, and as such it can indeed function as a form of diffuse support for the political system as a whole.

The origins and determinants of this attitude, however, are far from clear. The most straightforward assumption would be that political trust is developed as a reaction to the perceived performance of the political institutions. From a rational point of view, it can be expected that citizens will display higher levels of political trust in institutions that deliver, compared with regimes that do not succeed in reaching clear policy goals. Indeed, political trust tends to correlate quite strongly with government performance, to the extent that performance can be measured in a more or less objective manner. This correlation, however, does not explain the causal mechanisms at work.

The argument that political trust should primarily be seen as a reaction to the performance of government institutions creates further problems. First, not all citizens directly experience how these institutions work. For example, most citizens have very little first-hand experience with the way the courts in their home countries operate. Nevertheless, they will have some perception of the trustworthiness of these institutions. If political trust was really experience-based, there would be more 'don't know' and missing answers relevant to those institutions where respondents have less direct experience compared to those institutions that they do experience directly. This, however, is not the case. Most surveys show that respondents simply answer all the items on the political trust scale with very little variation across the different items.

A second problem is that the experience perspective also implies that we should observe significant differences across institutions. For example, I might have a very favourable perception of the way the local administration functions, as I have had only good experiences with this administration. My experiences with political parties, on the other hand, are far less positive. If my trust judgment depended on actual experience and performance levels, we would observe great variation in my responses to the various political institutions as not all of them reach equal levels of output and performance (Fisher *et al.* 2010). This, however, proves not to be the case, as the political trust scale in most surveys is strongly one-dimensional. Put another way, if respondents have a rather favourable view of political parties, they most likely have a positive attitude to their parliament, the police, the courts and other political institutions as well. To some extent, this might be attributed to a form of cognitive laziness. Since respondents do not take the trouble to carefully consider for each and every institution separately whether or not it is trustworthy, they simply make up one overall judgment for all institutions that more or less represents their general feeling towards the system. However, if the one-dimensionality of the political trust scale was the result of insufficient information or political sophistication, we should find that the dimensional structure of the scale is not the same across different groups in the population. We would then observe that those with little political interest or political knowledge simply lump all elements together (and this would lead to a one-dimensional scale), while those with high levels of political sophistication actually make the effort to judge individual institutions separately. Again, however, this proves not to be the case. Among those with high levels of political sophistication, the one-dimensional structure of the scale is just as strong as among those with low levels of political sophistication. This means that the judgments made on the political trust scale are not necessarily based on the actual performance of individual institutions, but rather reflect a kind of general assessment of the prevailing political culture within a country. This culture is indeed shared by all institutions, as it is a characteristic that is tied to the political system as a whole. It is difficult to imagine a system, for example, where the police would be highly corrupt while the courts are completely trustworthy. Corruption is usually so pervasive that a condoning attitude towards bribery usually extends to all political institutions rather than being limited to one or a few. Thus, political trust can be considered as a general assessment of the political culture in a country that guides the behaviour of politicians and civil servants alike.

By conceiving political trust as an assessment of the political culture in general, we can also explain the observed stability of this attitude. At least with regard to Europe, all the available evidence suggests that political trust levels remain relatively stable across the continent. While the Scandinavian countries, in general, enjoy high levels of political trust, they are much lower in Southern and Eastern Europe. What is more, they tend to remain lower. Despite the fact that most countries in Central and Eastern Europe became parliamentary democracies more than two decades ago, political trust levels remain structurally lower than in the more established democracies of Western Europe. This stability of political trust also supports the fact that trust levels do not reflect the performance of government institutions in a direct and straightforward manner. If that was the case, political trust levels would have been considerably more volatile in Central and Eastern Europe given the political transformations there.

It makes sense, therefore, to consider political trust in a much more comprehensive and qualified manner than in earlier research. Context clearly makes a difference in the development of political trust. It is not only the political culture in general that matters in understanding political trust, but also historical traditions and the way politics and the economy work. The complex interplay of these elements makes it extremely difficult to deliver straightforward answers about the future development of political trust in European societies. Thus far, trust levels have remained rather stable in Europe, but this stability can by no means be taken for granted. Economic and cultural changes might easily challenge this stability any time.

Structure of the book

The issue of political trust is approached from several perspectives. In the first chapters, we look at empirical evidence describing the nature and evolution of political trust. We then go on to explore how political trust can be explained and what elements seem to have the strongest influence on the level of trust. More specifically, we take a comparative approach and ask why people evaluate the trustworthiness of political institutions the way they do. Another focus of the empirical comparative studies in this volume is post-communist societies and countries in transition. The extent to which support of welfare state reforms is at the origins of, but also subject to, political trust is explored in the concluding chapters.

To commence, Sofie Marien takes a cross country approach to investigate the construct validity of a one-dimensional concept of political trust. Observing that political trust has previously been studied as a one-dimensional as well as a multi-dimensional concept, she draws on the four recent waves of the European Social Survey to explore the dimensionality of political trust in established and new democratic societies. Although some authors oppose a one-dimensional conceptualisation of political trust, arguing that people make distinct trust judgments when assessing the trustworthiness of political institutions, others suggest that citizens' evaluations of the performance of individual political institutions are closely related. Using confirmatory factor analysis, Marien demonstrates that the objects of political trust typically measured in population surveys, such as trust in parliament, politicians, political parties, police, and the legal system, do indeed load on a single dimension and that this one-dimensional conceptualisation of political trust holds for all European democracies alike. She then proceeds to determine to what extent the general concern about decreasing levels of political trust is effectively substantiated by current European trends. According to Marien's findings, however, there are no general and persisting declining trends with regard to political trust, except for a very limited number of countries. Distinct differences can be observed in the levels of political trust between established and new democracies. Not only does political trust turn out to be lower in new democratic societies, but it is also significantly more volatile, which is assumed to be due to insufficient institutional performance in those countries. In conclusion, while contextual factors do not impact on the way political trust is measured as a one-dimensional concept, they significantly determine the level of political support.

A close inspection of the trends in political trust in established Western democracies and an investigation of the underlying factors are the focus of Chapter 3 by Mark Bovens and Anchrit Wille. In the light of a myriad of studies that maintain a widespread trend of declining political trust in the United States, the authors conclude that Western European societies do by no means experience any such continuous and irreversible decline. Although sharp drops in political trust were observed in countries such as Belgium, the Netherlands and Germany, the figures soon returned to their original high levels. As Bovens and Wille argue, these developments can be attributed to an increasing volatility of political opinion, which results from structural factors that explain long-term changes, on the one hand, and factors related to short-term trends on the other. A better informed, politically more interested but less aligned citizenry, national governments facing the challenges of globalisation, as well as the pervasiveness of the media and the internet, with their ensuing tendencies of democratisation, all reflect reactions to long-term changes. Short-term trends, by contrast, reflect in particular fluctuating levels of consumer confidence, individual perceptions of political processes and an upsurge of dramatic events or crises. Given the extraordinary sharp decline in political trust in the Netherlands at the beginning of the twenty-first century, Bovens and Wille take a comparative approach to analyse the trends there. Their empirical findings are based on various Dutch population surveys and several waves of Eurobarometer surveys. They, unequivocally, suggest persistently high levels of political trust that might experience short-term drops, but yet provide the basis for the legitimacy of political decision making.

In Chapter 4, Sonja Zmerli and Ken Newton take on a broader perspective on trust by attempting to explain how different sorts of trust, i.e. political, particular and general social trust, relate to each other and to elucidate what sorts of people in what sorts of circumstances express trust in other people and in political institutions, and why. Their empirical results based on the most recent wave of the World Values Survey and comprising twenty-two democratic nations around the world reveal distinct patterns of trust and sketch the social, economic and political characteristics of different trust groups. As a result, these findings open up a set of

introduction: the context of political trust | 7

related questions about the connections between different forms of trust and the structural characteristics of modern societies, most notably their wealth, income equality, the quality of their political and civil institutions, and the heterogeneous nature of their populations. As Zmerli and Newton argue, particular social trust is the foundation on which general social trust and political trust are based. However, particular trust is a necessary but not sufficient cause of general trust, and both particular and general trust are a necessary but not sufficient cause of political trust. So-called 'winners' in society, those with money, socio-economic status and education, who are happy and satisfied with their life and in good health and who view the political system as giving them a chance of being on the winning side of society, are the most likely to extend their willingness to trust people they know personally to those they meet for the first time, or who are unlike themselves, and to political institutions. One of the main theoretical implications is that particular trust, or in-group trust, is not incompatible with general trust, or out-group trust, and that the heterogeneous nature of modern societies and low levels of general and political trust are not necessarily connected. The practical lesson, however, suggests that the larger the 'loser' percentage in the population, the lower the trust levels are likely to be. As a consequence, a growing share of those who perceive themselves as the 'losers' in society can pose a serious threat to social cohesion and political stability.

In Chapter 5, Tom van der Meer and Paul Dekker explore which aspects of the relationship between citizens and the state determine political trust. Presuming that political trust is a relational concept, they argue that former research failed to take the mediating links between political institutions and citizens into account. Instead, these studies either focused on specific features of political institutions or on individual characteristics. Van der Meer and Dekker, by contrast, extend established theoretical and empirical research designs by investigating the mechanisms that affect citizens' attitudes to and perceptions and evaluations of political institutions. Thus, their study aims at re-testing traditional models with regard to which contextual characteristics explain political trust, as well as at expanding an understanding of the macro-micro mechanisms that link context factors and political trust. Their principal argument is that citizens assess the trustworthiness of political institutions by evaluating four central features: competence, care, accountability and reliability. The authors' analyses are based on the first wave of the European Social Survey (ESS) and a set of country-specific indicators and multi level regression techniques. The main contextual factors affecting political trust that van der Meer and Dekker identify are corruption, the type of electoral system, and what seems to be the economic and political underperformance shared by all post-communist societies. As for the linking mechanisms between political institutions and citizens, the assessment of competence and care appear to be of particular relevance. However, as the authors point out, the ESS dataset provides only a limited set of useful variables. As a consequence, the empirical testing of their assumptions remains partly incomplete. In conclusion, van der Meer and Dekker suggest several solutions to counter these shortcomings in future research.

On the basis of a time series analysis covering the time span from 1993 to

2004 and encompassing sixty-seven New Europe Barometer surveys in fourteen post-communist countries, Richard Rose and William Mishler, in Chapter 6, run multilevel analyses and test theories that aim at explaining the variability of political trust in different national, temporal and social structural contexts. In particular, they address the question: to what extent can societies that were socialised under communist rule 'learn' to trust political institutions that have proven to be trustworthy over time? Reaffirming the conceptualisation of political trust as a relational entity, Rose and Mishler's empirical findings depict distinct between-country differences in the levels of political trust and provide additional empirical evidence for the assumption that trustworthiness of political institutions is assessed through macro-political and economic performance, but concomitantly mediated at the micro-level by value-laden attitudes and perceptions of individuals. As a consequence, their results suggest that macro-institutional theories advocating direct pathways of influence need to be complemented by the insights into the complex interplay with mediating micro-level factors. Most importantly, the authors conclude that the notion of a fatal legacy of socialisation under communist rule that continues to inhibit the development of political trust is a myth. As they argue, changes in trust do not require decades or generations of re-socialisation in order to transform a national political culture. Although the effects of institutional and economic performance are contingent upon mediating individual attitudes and perceptions, citizens can 'learn' to trust as they accumulate experience in how they are governed. In the same vein, however, political institutions can also generate political distrust in as much as they are ineffective and prone to corruption. Given the persistence of corruption in a number of Central and Eastern European societies, the prevalence of low levels of political trust is certainly rather the outcome of bad performance than of an insurmountable communist legacy.

In Chapter 7, Eric M. Uslaner elaborates on this effect of corruption, by elucidating its origins and consequences in transition countries. As Uslaner lays out, corruption affects rules of fairness, privileges some people over others, acts as an extra tax on citizens, leaves less money to invest in public goods, slows economic growth, and leads to ineffective government. In contrast to most theoretical accounts that attribute corruption to institutional deficiencies, the author offers an alternative explanation. According to his line of argument, corruption stems from an unequal distribution of resources and reinforces greater inequality. Uslaner describes this self-perpetuating process as the 'inequality trap', where inequality leads to low levels of generalised trust, which in turn results in more corruption, and then to even more inequality. In addition, inequality and corruption lead to lower levels of service delivery, such as electricity or water supply, which aggravate inequality. Based on data from the 2006 Life in Transition Survey conducted in twenty-eight transition countries, Uslaner provides empirical evidence for the detrimental effects of inequality, corruption and insufficient service delivery: low levels of trust in government, tax evasion, and weak infrastructure. While the link between corruption and trust in government is straightforward, with citizens distrusting their leaders whom they believe to be dishonest, the link with inequality is less direct – through economic evaluations more generally. Notwithstanding, the individual assessment of the trustworthiness of government is also contingent on citizens' socio-economic background and as such Uslaner's findings resonate well with the empirical insights of preceding chapters. The wealthy take up a moral stance on government and judge it more by its level of corruption. The less well-off, by contrast, want government to get involved in reducing inequality and judge government performance more by how well leaders have steered the economy rather than by how honest they are.

In the final two chapters, the relationship between political trust and the welfare state is examined. In Chapter 8, Staffan Kumlin explores the effect of welfare state policies on political trust. While there exists a wide range of studies pertaining to the welfare state or political support, both strands of literature go mostly unrelated. By contrast, Kumlin argues that welfare state retrenchment and its ensuing less generous policies may engender increasing numbers of dissatisfied democrats. Unlike most 'policy feedback' studies that address the ramifications of policy outcomes, Kumlin assumes that dissatisfaction with democracy can arise from attention to the policies themselves. In a cross-country study, the author investigates the repercussions of benefit generosity in three realms of social security: pensions, sickness insurance and unemployment insurance generosity. Empirical analyses are based on Eurobarometer surveys from 1976 to 2001, cover eleven Western European countries and also comprise macro-level indicators. Applying multilevel regression techniques, Kumlin discloses the extent to which systematic measures of benefit generosity account for within-country over-time variation in democratic dissatisfaction. However, the impact of the three tested types of social security benefits differs considerably as only less generous unemployment benefits appear to be a universal generator of democratic dissatisfaction. Interestingly, these effects can be observed across broad groups in Western Europe and are thus *not* contingent on individual employment status, socio-economic background or value orientations. With higher unemployment rates, however, citizens' attention to public expenditures and budget deficits associated with unemployment benefit generosity increases. As Kumlin's 'visible costs hypothesis' suggests, positive effects of generous unemployment benefits become weaker as unemployment rates increase. As a consequence, generous benefits can lose their beneficial impact if they go along with high unemployment rates and associated costs.

While the preceding chapters implicitly acknowledge the importance of political trust as a promoter and stabiliser of democratic societies, Eva-Maria Trüdinger and Uwe Bollow, in Chapter 9, investigate whether political institutions and actors do indeed benefit from politically trustful citizens. More specifically, the authors explore the ramifications of political trust or the lack thereof for the support of welfare state reforms and their implementation. They examine which effects political trust exerts on people's evaluation of reforms in three sub-domains of the German welfare state that has undergone significant changes during the last few years: pension, health care and family policy. They hypothesise that politically trustful citizens are more supportive of their government's decisions and actions and, as a consequence, also more supportive of welfare state reforms. This holds even (or particularly) true when people themselves are confronted with material or ideological losses. Based on a German population survey carried out in 2007, Trüdinger and Bollow test these assumptions and arrive at several far-reaching conclusions. First, being politically trustful affects the evaluation of welfare state reforms in all three policy domains. Thus, the greater the stock of political trust, the easier it is for governments to legitimise the implementation of new policies. Secondly, their empirical evidence suggests that material and/or ideological costs moderate the influence of political trust on reform evaluations. Thirdly, these moderating effects, however, are contingent on the type of policy domain. While the relevance of material costs for the influence of political trust prevails with the assessment of pension reforms, ideological costs moderate the impact of political trust on the evaluation of health care reforms. Assessments of changes in the realm of family policy, by contrast, are affected by political trust that is moderated by material and ideological costs alike. In sum, Trüdinger and Bollow provide substantial evidence for political trust as a cultural resource that can potentially be exploited by politicians to back up welfare state reforms and identify specific circumstances under which political trust is likely to guide policy evaluations.

References

Blais, A. (2006) 'What affects voter turnout?', *Annual Review of Political Science*, 9: 111–25.
Easton, D. (1965) *A Systems Analysis of Political Life*, New York: Wiley.
Fisher, J., van Heerde, J. and Tucker, A. (2010) 'Does one trust judgement fit all? Linking theory and empirics', *British Journal of Politics and International Relations*, 12(2): 161–88.
Franklin, M. (2004) *Voter Turnout and the Dynamics of Electoral Competition in Established Democracies since 1945*, Cambridge: Cambridge University Press.
Hardin, R. (1999) 'Do we want trust in government?', in M. E. Warren (ed.) *Democracy and Trust*, Cambridge: Cambridge University Press.
Hetherington, M. (2005) *Why Trust Matters: Declining political trust and the demise of American liberalism*, Princeton: Princeton University Press.
Inglehart, R. (1997) *Modernization and Postmodernization*, Princeton: Princeton University Press.
Lindström, M. (2008) 'Social capital, political trust and experience of cannabis smoking', *Preventive Medicine*, 46(6): 599–604.
Marien, S. and Hooghe, M. (2011) 'Does political trust matter? An empirical investigation into the relation between political trust and support for law compliance', *European Journal of Political Research*, 50(2): 267–91.
Newton, K. (2007) 'Social and political trust', in R. Dalton and H.-D. Klingemann (eds) *The Oxford Handbook of Political Behaviour*, Oxford: Oxford University Press.
Norris, P. (ed.) (1999) *Critical Citizens: Global Support for Democratic Government*, Oxford: Oxford University Press.
Rosenvallon, P. (2008) *Counter Democracy: Politics in an age of distrust*, Cambridge: Cambridge University Press.

chapter two | measuring political trust across time and space

Sofie Marien

Introduction

The level of trust citizens have in their political system has been the object of extensive academic and public debate. The dominant view is that contemporary democracies are experiencing a large-scale crisis of confidence. In 2008, only 30 per cent of US citizens trusted their government, while this was more than 60 per cent in the 1960s (American National Election Studies 1958–2008).[1] However, a number of studies have provided evidence that does not support and even contradict this pessimistic proposition (Klingemann and Fuchs 1995; van de Walle *et al.* 2008; Hooghe and Wilkenfeld 2008). In effect, while there is evidence of a structural trend towards lower political trust since the 1960s in the United States, there exists no conclusive evidence of a general decline in political trust in Europe (Lipset and Schneider 1983; Catterberg and Moreno 2006; van de Walle *et al.* 2008). Besides the distinct cross-national trends, the inconsistent findings are also often due to the operationalisation of political trust. A range of measurements have been used, including support for particular policies, evaluations of the politicians in office, trust in political institutions and trust in the political system.

Citizens' trust can relate to distinct objects of the political system: its current authorities, the political institutions, the values and principles or the political community (Easton 1965; Dalton 2004). In empirical research, this issue is often not taken into account: trust in one object is measured and labelled 'political trust' or one measure includes trust in several objects. Nonetheless, distrust in the political system has different implications than distrust in the politicians in office (Anderson *et al.* 2005). A critical attitude towards the politicians in office is generally considered to be a normal and healthy part of a democracy. Citizens can easily 'throw the rascals out' and replace them with politicians they perceive trustworthy by means of elections (Klingemann and Fuchs 1995: 2–5; Anderson *et al.* 2005). However, citizens should be able to put (some) trust in the democratic procedures and institutions. This kind of trust, which relates to Easton's concept of *diffuse support*, acts as a reservoir of support on which a system can fall back when *specific support* for a particular policy measure or prime minister is lacking (Easton 1965). Moreover, it has been argued that trust in the democratic procedures and institutions also influences the willingness of citizens to commit public resources to public policy ends, to accept and comply with political decisions and to engage

---

1. See http://www.electionstudies.org/nesguide/toptable/tab5a_1.htm.

in politics (Hetherington 2005; Dalton 2004; Marien and Hooghe 2011).

The nature of trust in political institutions has also been the topic of debate. Institutional trust has been conceptualised and studied as both a one-dimensional and a multidimensional attitude. On the one hand, it has been argued that citizens use different criteria to evaluate the trustworthiness of different institutions (Fisher *et al.* 2010; Hibbing and Theiss-Morse 1995). As citizens develop distinct trust judgments, one should not simply add these different trust judgments into one measurement scale. On the other hand, institutions do not operate in a vacuum but are part of a political system with a particular prevailing political culture (Almond and Verba 1963). As a result, we could expect that citizens develop one comprehensive attitude 'trust in political institutions' that is shaped by the political culture of their country.

Our understanding of political trust is shaped to a large extent by research conducted on the United States. Comparative research has confirmed, but also modified these research results (Bélanger and Nadeau 2005). Cross-national research has enabled researchers to investigate the generalisability of trends and theories. However, this kind of research entails methodological problems not encountered in single country studies. In particular, cultural differences in the interpretations of questions or words can emerge. 'Trust' in the political system in an authoritarian country is likely to have a different meaning than 'trust' in a democratic political system. But even among democracies, every country has its own language, culture and political system. While this can invalidate research results – apples are compared to oranges – most scholars ignore these problems.

In this chapter, I will address several problems related to the measurement of political trust. The chapter begins with a description of frequently-used measurements of political trust and the problems with these. In the second section, the nature of institutional trust is investigated. Do citizens have one comprehensive attitude towards all political institutions or is institutional trust multidimensional? Subsequently, the issue of cross-cultural equivalence is addressed, i.e. I test whether trust in political institutions can be measured in a similar way across different countries. Then an overview of levels of trust in different political institutions is provided. Finally, recent trends in trust in political institutions and trust in the current government are presented.

Measuring political trust

A frequently used data source to analyse political trust is the American National Elections Studies. This study has questioned respondents' political trust from the 1960s to the present day. The questions are paraphrased here: 'Do you think you can trust the government in Washington to do what is right; does the government waste a lot of money; is the government run by a few big interests looking out for themselves; are most politicians crooked; do politicians know what they are doing?' However, the validity of these questions was already being criticised in 1974. Particularly noteworthy is the discussion between Arthur Miller and Jack Citrin in the *American Political Science Review* of 1974. Using ANES data, Miller argued that trust in the political system decreased sharply during the past years, Citrin refuted this conclusion, arguing that Miller was measuring trust in the current incumbents rather than trust in the political system (Citrin 1974; Miller 1974). At present, there is still substantial debate on the trends in political trust, its causes and consequences due to disagreement about the measurement of political trust. Pippa Norris (1999), for example, states that the extensive literature on decreasing political trust is based on an erroneous interpretation of the data at hand.

Besides these five ANES questions, scholars have also attempted to measure citizens' political trust by asking respondents how satisfied they are 'with the way democracy is working in [their country]'. Political trust is often measured using this wording of the question, especially in European empirical studies (e.g. in the Eurobarometer surveys, the European Value Studies and the European Social Survey). However, this measurement also conflates trust in the current authorities and trust in the principles of a political system. It is not clear whether this survey question taps a more generalised political trust judgment, a more specific judgment of the trustworthiness of the politicians in office or a respondent's state of mind at the moment. Still other empirical work studies political trust by focusing on citizens' trust in different political institutions. Citizens are asked how much they trust their country's parliament, government, political parties, the legal system, the police and so forth. Although this question is designed to tap into a more generalised form of political trust, this measurement also cannot rule out that respondents think about the people running these institutions when answering this question.

However, we can question whether it is possible at all to fully disentangle trust in the current authorities and trust in the political system and its institutions using survey questions. Some scholars state that a 'referent' is needed to obtain a valid measurement (Aberbach 1969). It is argued that citizens cannot assess the trustworthiness of political institutions without thinking about its current incumbents. Moreover, both forms of trust are clearly related. Citizens that have no trust at all in the political system will also distrust the current incumbents, and strong distrust in the politicians in office can spill over to trust evaluations of the institutions and the political system. This last measurement focuses on one part of the broader concept of political trust, i.e. trust in the political institutions. It does not assess trust in the political system as a whole. Nor does it assess trust in the democratic principles or values, nor in particular political leaders. The advantage of studying trust in one specific part of the political system is that it is clear what is being measured. The drawback is that only one part of the broader concept of political trust is measured. However, as political institutions play an important role in shaping a democratic society, we can assume that citizens' trust in these institutions is strongly related to citizens' evaluation of how they perceive a political system is performing.

Therefore, trust in political institutions is the focus of this chapter. Apart from these theoretical reasons, data on trust in political institutions in more than thirty European countries is available in the European Social Survey (ESS) datasets. In this chapter, I will not study citizens' trust in the principles or values of a democracy. The latter is (and remains) at a very high level within democracies. Democracy is considered among the overall majority of its citizens as the best system to govern a society (Klingemann 1999: 45). Whether these democratic principles and values are upheld in a democracy is an interesting question, but beyond the scope of this study. Trust in individual politicians, such as the current ministers or party leaders, is also interesting to investigate, but will not be my main focus, as distrust in the current authorities is generally considered to be a normal practice in a democracy. Nevertheless, some figures on satisfaction with the current government in several European countries will be presented at the end of the chapter.

The results of the ESS datasets 2002–2009 will be presented (Jowell *et al.* 2003, 2005, 2007, 2009). These datasets provide extensive and up-to-date information on trust in political institutions and, to date, four waves of high-quality survey data are already available. The data were collected biannually between 2002 and 2009 by means of uniform face-to-face interviews among representative samples of the population of more than thirty European countries (see Appendix A). Particular attention has been paid to the operationalisation of political trust, and a measurement report by the ESS researchers on the quality of the 'trust in political institutions' already reveals that the question has a high level of validity and reliability.[2] The question on trust in political institutions used in ESS is phrased as follows:

> Using this card, please tell me on a score of 0–10 how much you personally trust each of the institutions I read out. 0 means you do not trust an institution at all, and 10 means you have complete trust:
>
> – Country's Parliament
> – The legal system
> – The police
> – Political parties (from second ESS wave onwards)
> – Politicians

Trust in political institutions: one theoretical concept?

Institutional trust can be defined as the expectation that political institutions operate according to fair rules even in the absence of constant scrutiny. Trust in political institutions has been studied as a one-dimensional as well as a multidimensional concept. On the one hand, it has been argued that citizens use different criteria to evaluate the trustworthiness of different institutions (Fisher *et al.* 2010). As citizens develop distinct trust judgments, one should not simply add these different trust judgments into one scale of measurement. On the other hand, institutions do

---

2. The report can be downloaded from the ESS website: http://ess.nsd.uib.no/streamer/?module=main&year=2003&country=null&download=%5CSurvey+documentation%5C2003%5C10%23ESS1+-+Reliability+and+validity+of+questions%2C+ed.+1%5CLanguages%5CEnglish%5CESS1MTMManalysis.pdf.

not operate in a vacuum; they are all part of a political system with a particular political culture (Almond and Verba 1963). As a result, we can expect that citizens' judgments of the performance of various political institutions are strongly related to each other (Hooghe 2011). Consequently, citizens are likely to develop one comprehensive attitude of 'trust in political institutions', which is shaped by the political culture of their country. This general attitude influences their judgment of the trustworthiness of various institutions. By means of factor analysis, it is tested whether one underlying construct of 'institutional trust' exists that explains a set of trust judgments. This underlying construct cannot be observed directly – as with all latent variables – but its existence is inferred from the way it influences variables that can be observed (Brown 2006).

Confirmatory Factor Analysis (CFA) explores the variation and co-variation among the trust judgments of the different political institutions and identifies the number and nature of latent variable(s) that account for this variation (Brown 2006). I hypothesise that citizens' trust in political institutions is shaped by their general orientation towards the political system. Consequently, a one-factor measurement model is tested, whereby the observed measures of trust in the country's parliament, trust in the political parties, trust in the legal system, trust in the police and trust in politicians are conjectured to load on one latent factor, i.e. 'trust in political institutions'. The measurement model was estimated using the maximum likelihood method. Not all institutions were questioned in the first wave of ESS (2002–2003), therefore, the analyses were only performed on wave 2 (2004–2005), wave 3 (2006–2007) and wave 4 (2008–2009).[3] Given that the results are very similar, only the results of the last wave are discussed in this section. The results of the other waves can be found in Appendix B.

After specifying the measurement model, it is estimated and evaluated. To evaluate the fitted CFA solution, one has to study the overall goodness of fit, analyse specific points of ill-fit and look into the direction, magnitude and significance of the parameters. Several tests have been developed to evaluate whether the model provides a good description of the data. The indices of fit that I will use are the χ^2, RMSEA and CFI. I will report the χ^2 of the model as this is a classic goodness-of-fit measure. However, given the large sample that is used in the analyses, χ^2 is a poor measure as it generally rejects solutions based on a large N (Brown 2006; Reeskens and Hooghe 2008: 523). A better measure, and which is widely used, is the Root Mean Square Error of Approximation (RMSEA) as 'it assesses the extent to which a model fits reasonably well in the population (as opposed to

---

3. The analyses are limited to free democratic countries. The Freedom House Index (FHI) is a widely used indicator to assess whether a country is democratic by looking at the amount of political and civil liberties in the country. Several political and civil rights are lacking in some of the countries included in the European Social Survey. The Freedom House indices range between 1 and 7, where 7 is the lowest level of freedom. Based on this index in 2008, Russia, Turkey, Ukraine, Romania and Croatia were not included in the analyses – with combined Freedom House indices (political plus civil rights) of respectively: 11, 6, 5, 4 and 4. Given that the focus of this study is on European countries, Israel was also not included.

testing whether the model holds exactly in the population; cf. χ2)' (Brown 2006: 83). A reasonably good fit is operationalised as a RMSEA close to 0.06 or below (Hu and Bentler 1999). Finally, the Comparative Fit Index (CFI) will be used to evaluate the fitted CFA solution. The CFI ranges between 0 and 1. A reasonably good fit is operationalised by values that are close to 0.95 or greater. These cut-off criteria are reported by Brown (2006) based on several simulation studies of Hu and Bentler (1999).

The results of the Confirmatory Factor Analysis are visualised in Figure 2.1. The goodness-of-fit measures indicate that the estimated model provides a good approximation to reality. Institutional trust can be conceptualised as a one-dimensional attitude. The factor loadings reproduce the relation between institutional trust and the different trust judgments. A factor loading of '1' indicates a perfect relationship, while a value of '0' depicts that there is no relationship between the observed measure and the latent concept. Besides the variance accounted for by the latent concept, every measure also has its unique variance, which is labelled as the error variance. In Table 2.1 additional estimates of the parameters of the confirmatory factor analysis are reported. The test statistic tests whether there is a relationship between latent concept and observed measure, i.e. whether the factor loading is significantly different from '0'. The last column of Table 2.1 includes estimates of the explained variance of the observed measure, which can be considered as an indicator for its reliability. For instance, 80 per cent of the variance in trust in parliament can be accounted for by respondents' institutional trust. The remaining 20 per cent cannot be explained by institutional trust, but is 'unique variance'.

We can conclude that all items contribute significantly to the measurement of this latent concept. In effect, every factor loading is clearly above 0.30, i.e. the value that is commonly used to define a 'salient' factor loading (Brown 2006: 130). The contribution of trust in the police to the measurement of institutional trust is slightly smaller. In general, the factor loadings of the observed measures of trust in implementing institutions are lower than the factor loadings of trust in the institutions on the representational side of the political system. In summary, the measurement model indicates that all observed measures are inter-correlated because they are influenced by the same underlying construct, i.e. 'trust in political institutions'. For instance, trust in police is related to trust in parliament because they are both influenced by respondents' general attitude of 'trust in political institutions'.

However, there is some covariance between the two implementing institutions, the police and the legal system, due to sources other than this general attitude of 'trust in political institutions'. Therefore, the errors of these two measures are allowed to correlate. The police and the legal system are primarily responsible for the maintenance of order, and we can assume, in line with Inglehart's postmodernisation theory (1999), that citizens have a different opinion towards these order institutions than towards representational institutions. Likewise, citizens hold different expectations towards implementing and representational institutions. While political parties, the parliament and politicians are expected to be partisan, implementing institutions are expected to be impartial (Rothstein and Stolle 2008).

However, we should note that this is not always the case; for instance, the legal system is more politicised in the United States, e.g. judges are politically appointed and their party preference is often well known. Given these theoretical arguments and the covariance between these two measures, it can be useful, depending on the research question, to make a distinction between implementing institutions and institutions on the representational side of the political system.

Furthermore, a preliminary analysis showed that trust in politicians and trust in political parties also share variance that cannot be explained by the latent concept. Allowing an error correlation between these two items increases the fit of the model. At first sight, this correlation is less clear than the error correlation between trust in the legal system and trust in the police. We can speculate that this shared variance could be because respondents perceive political parties, and especially politicians, as less of an 'institution' than parliament, the legal system or the police. The assessment of trust in politicians and political parties might be influenced more strongly by the performance of the current incumbents than respondents' trust in parliament, the legal system or the police. In addition, politicians are routinely members of a political party. The mean value of, and the variance in, trust in political parties and trust in politicians are indeed very similar, which could indicate that citizens do not make a distinction between political parties and politicians.

A one-factor measurement model was also fitted to the survey data from ESS (2006–2007) and ESS (2004–2005). Similar results emerged from these analyses (see Appendix B). We can conclude that institutional trust can be conceptualised as a one-dimensional attitude. Citizens have one generalised attitude that influences their trust evaluations of specific political institutions.

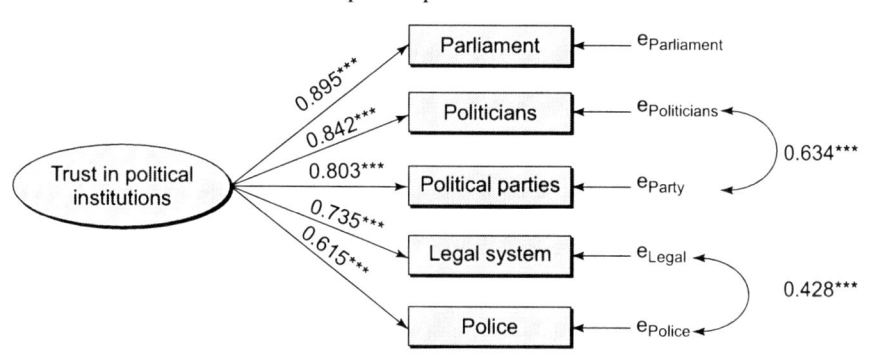

Figure 2.1: Solution confirmatory factor analysis

Notes: Standardised factor loadings resulting from a confirmatory factor analysis on the full sample.
Fit indices: $\chi^2 = 137.747$; $df = 3$; p value = 0.000; RMSEA = 0.034; CFI = 0.999; N = 39,764.
Source: ESS 2008. Twenty-two countries.

Table 2.1: Solution confirmatory factor analysis

Observed measures	Factor loading	SE	z test	Standardised factor loading	Standardised error variance	R^2
Trust in parliament	1.000	0.000	–	0.895	0.198	0.801
Trust in politicians	0.865	0.005	186.05 ***	0.842	0.292	0.709
Trust in political parties	0.815	0.005	174.26 ***	0.803	0.355	0.645
Trust in the legal system	0.850	0.005	163.71 ***	0.735	0.459	0.540
Trust in police	0.689	0.005	127.65 ***	0.615	0.622	0.378
Error variances						
Legal system – police	1.568	0.024	66.48 ***	0.428	–	–
Politicians – parties	1.128	0.018	63.34 ***	0.634	–	–

Notes: Variance latent variable 'institutional trust' = 5.301 (SE = 0.050). The marker observed variable is 'trust in parliament', which was fixed at 1.000. The last column includes estimates of the reliability of the observed measures (R^2). Composite reliability index of scale = 0.89. Variance in observed measures explained by latent concept = 0.61.

Source: ESS 2008. Twenty-two countries. N = 39,764.

Trust in political institutions in a cross-national setting

So far, the country-level context was not taken into account in the analysis. However, cross-national comparisons entail methodological challenges that should be addressed. In particular, cultural differences in the interpretations of questions or words can emerge. The European Social Survey pays particular attention to ensure an optimal comparability with regard to the operationalisation and cross-cultural validity of concepts in the participating countries. Nonetheless, even if all questions are translated adequately and the same method of data gathering is used, it is still possible that respondents with a different cultural background will react differently to the same measures. Using Multigroup Confirmatory Factor Analysis (MGCFA), it is investigated whether the general model that was developed holds true in all countries under study. In more technical terms, I test for the 'cross-cultural equivalence' of the 'institutional trust' scale. In particular, I test whether the same factor structure emerges in all countries.[4]

A Multigroup Confirmatory Factor Analysis on ESS (2008–2009) reveals a similar factor structure across the twenty-two countries. The fit indices indicate that the CFA solution has a reasonably good fit. In all countries, the five measures contribute significantly to the measurement of trust in political institutions. Trust in the police has the weakest contribution to the measurement of institutional trust in all countries, but the factor loading is still largely above the minimum requirement of 0.30.[5] In summary, the same pattern of factor loadings is found across the different countries. It is thereby possible to discuss institutional trust meaningfully in all countries. This kind of equivalence is labelled *configural equivalence*. Nevertheless, the magnitude of the factor loadings can differ across the different countries, which can make cross-country comparisons problematic. In a next step, it is tested whether the factor loadings are the same across the countries. Put another way – is the relationship between the five measures and the latent concept the same in all countries? Only if this is the case, can one unit increase in the 'trust in political institutions' scale in country X be compared to one unit increase

---

4. These countries include Belgium, Bulgaria, Cyprus, the Czech Republic, Denmark, Estonia, Finland, France, Germany, Greece, Hungary, Latvia, the Netherlands, Norway, Poland, Portugal, Slovenia, Slovakia, Spain, Sweden, Switzerland and the United Kingdom in ESS (2008–2009). Austria, Iceland, Ireland and Luxembourg were included in previous waves of the European Social Survey (see Appendix). The distinction between Eastern and Western Germany is still considered to be relevant in public opinion research (Zmerli and Newton 2008). Therefore, the analyses were also performed considering Eastern Germany and Western Germany as two distinct countries. These analyses led to similar results.

5. The measurement model was also performed on every country separately. This additional analysis showed that the measurement model in Cyprus gives a poor description of the data. The different results for the trust measurement may be caused by the conflict between the Greek and Turkish community in Cyprus. However, the case of Cyprus falls beyond the scope of this study as it calls for an in-depth investigation. The subsequent analyses were conducted twice: including and excluding Cyprus. The model fit was each time slightly better when Cyprus was excluded from the analyses, but the same pattern emerged in both cases. Therefore, I decided to keep Cyprus in the analyses.

in the 'trust in political institutions' scale in country Y. In order to test this, the factor loadings are constrained to be equal across the different countries. This test is called *metric equivalence* and is a stricter test of cross-cultural equivalence (Brown 2006).

The factor loading of some observed measures deviates from the general pattern in a number of countries. For instance, in Bulgaria, trust in the police has a stronger connection to institutional trust than in other countries. Put another way, the factor loadings do not reproduce the relationship between observed measure and latent concept well in all countries. The imposed constraints on the measurement model worsen the fit of the model to the data (see Table 2.2). In practice, full metric equivalence is often considered to be unrealistic (Byrne *et al.* 1989). Therefore, partial metric equality has been proposed as an alternative, which entails that at least two items of the construct possess measurement equivalence characteristics (Byrne *et al.* 1989). Some imposed constraints can be removed in order to improve the measurement model. One has to look at the nature of the constraint, the Modification Index (MI) and the Expected Parameter Change (EPC) in order to decide whether to relax a constraint. This is an iterative process. The constraint with the highest Modification Index and a substantial Expected Parameter Change is removed. Subsequently, the model fit is re-evaluated. This procedure is repeated until an additional modification does not make a substantial difference.

Table 2.2 shows the modifications that have been implemented in order to arrive at a better model. We removed the constraint on the factor loading of trust in the police in Bulgaria. This factor loading was constrained to equal 0.619; however, the connection between institutional trust and trust in the police is stronger in Bulgaria (Factor loading POLICEBG = 0.851). A one-unit increase in institutional trust in Bulgaria is associated with an increase in trust in the police of 0.851 units. By removing the equality constraint for trust in the police in Bulgaria, i.e. the factor loading can now be freely estimated, the model fit improves substantially: the χ^2 drops with more than 100 points, the RMSEA decreases from 0.068 to 0.065 and the CFI increases from 0.98 to 0.99. The equality constraints on the factor loadings of trust in the police and trust in the legal system in Finland are also removed. The connection between institutional trust and trust in the police and the legal system is weaker in Finland than in other countries (see the negative signs of the EPC estimates). In effect, a one-unit increase in institutional trust in Finland is associated with an increase in trust in the police of 0.462 units. Most of the modifications concern trust in the implementing institutions. In general, we observe that the connection between institutional trust and trust in the police and the legal system is stronger in the newer democracies than it is in established democracies. Overall, the connection between institutional trust and trust in parliament is rather strong. In Spain and Slovakia, however, the connection between institutional trust and trust in parliament is weaker than in other countries. Removing some of the equality constraints, the model demonstrates a good fit of the data (CFI = 0.993; RMSEA = 0.058). The final model is shown in Figure 2.2.

Table 2.2: Testing for cross-cultural equivalence in trust in political institutions

Model specifications	χ2	df	RMSEA	CFI	EPC	MI
Configural equivalence	397.742	66	0.053	0.997	–	–
Metric equivalence	1412.841	150	0.068	0.989	–	–
Free BG police	1292.412	149	0.065	0.990	0.185	113.535
Free FI police	1217.963	148	0.063	0.991	-0.150	76.453
Free FI legal system	1154.527	147	0.062	0.992	-0.153	65.558
Free SK police	1113.000	146	0.061	0.992	0.123	39.723
Free SK parliament	1080.068	145	0.060	0.992	-0.131	34.414
Free ES parliament	1044.826	144	0.059	0.992	-0.149	36.493
Free HU police	1019.571	143	0.058	0.993	0.108	24.152

Notes: Entries are the results of confirmatory factor analyses.
Three goodness-of-fit indices are presented (χ2 with degrees of freedom, RMSEA and CFI). The last two columns include the modification indices: The standardised Expected Parameter Change and the Modification Index.

Source: ESS 2008. Twenty-two countries. N = 39,764.

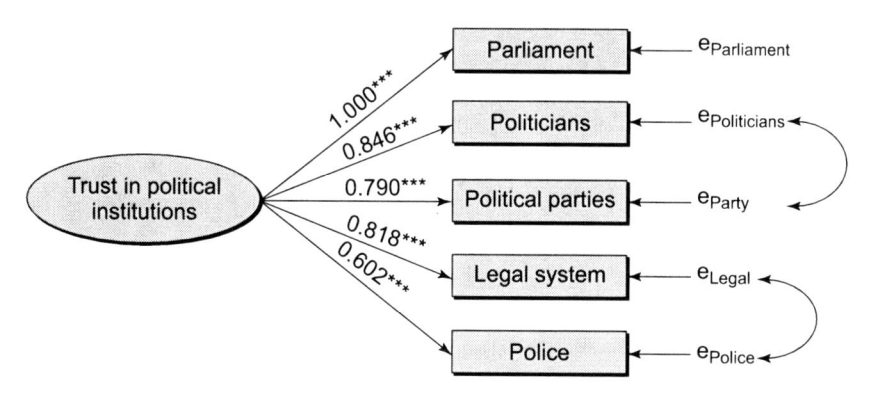

Figure 2.2: Solution confirmatory factor analysis with imposed constraints

Notes. Unstandardised factor loadings resulting from a confirmatory factor analysis in which the factor loadings are constrained to be equal across the countries (testing metric equivalence). Some constraints were removed (see Table 2.2). Fit indices: χ2 = 1019.571; df = 143. RMSEA = 0.058; CFI = 0.993; N = 39,764.

Source: ESS 2008. Twenty-two countries.

The same analyses were performed on ESS 2006–2007 and ESS 2004–2005 (see Appendix C). These analyses show that there is indeed a similar configuration of factor loadings across the different countries. In all countries, trust in the police has the lowest factor loading and thus the weakest relationship to institutional trust. As regards the tests for metric equivalence, some of the equality constraints also needed to be removed from ESS 2006–2007 and ESS 2004–2005 to obtain a better measurement model. We can observe a pattern in the applied modifications; the factor loadings of trust in implementing institutions are lower in the Nordic countries than in the other countries. In the newer democracies (Bulgaria, Hungary, Slovakia), the factor loadings of trust in implementing institutions are higher than in the other countries. The measurement models based on ESS 2006–2007 and ESS 2004–2005 have a slightly better fit than the model based on ESS 2008–2009 presented here.

From the analyses we can conclude that the 'institutional trust' scale is configural equivalent: a similar pattern of factor loadings emerged. Therefore, institutional trust can be meaningfully discussed in the different countries. The factor loadings are not entirely the same in all countries. In general, institutional trust has a stronger connection to trust in implementing institutions in new democracies than in more established democracies. It seems that citizens' expectations towards representing and implementing institutions differ more in established democracies. As stated already, implementing institutions are expected to be impartial, while representing institutions are expected to be partisan. It might be that citizens in newer democracies do not perceive implementing institutions as impartial but rather as political, and even as corrupt, as their representing institutions. This could offer an explanation for the stronger connection between the different trust judgments in new democracies. Therefore, some of the equality constraints had to be removed. After these modifications, the constrained model provides a good fit of the data.[6]

Trends in political trust

From the previous analyses, we can conclude that trust in political institutions can be analysed as a one-dimensional latent concept across different countries. A second part provides an overview of recent (trends in) political trust figures in Europe. Citizens' trust in a number of political institutions is described, and then recent trends in institutional trust and government support in Europe are outlined.

Table 2.3 includes citizens' trust evaluations of a number of institutions between 2002 and 2009.[7] The same patterns emerge in all waves of the European Social Survey: respondents' trust in implementing institutions is significantly higher than in representational institutions. Moreover, the difference proves to be

---

6. Several additional tests for cross-cultural equivalence can be performed, which constrain the factor intercept, factor variances and error variances (see, e.g. Brown 2006; Reeskens and Hooghe 2008).
7. Note that a comparison of the evolution of trust levels is not possible using Table 2.3, as different countries are included in each wave.

significant in all countries under study.[8] Political parties and politicians in particular receive low trust scores. Between 2002 and 2009, 10 to 15 per cent of the respondents indicated that they do not trust politicians and political parties at all (a value of '0' on an 11-point scale). Conversely, less than 8 per cent answered that they had no trust at all in the legal system, and less than 5 per cent indicated that they had no trust at all in the police. Table 2.3 also includes information on citizens' trust in two international institutions: the European Parliament and the United Nations. Trust in international institutions was not taken into account in the previous analysis, given that not all countries are a member of the European Union, which makes it difficult to compare the countries on this trust measure. Moreover, scholars are generally interested in determinants and consequences of trust in national political institutions.

International institutions enjoy more trust than most national institutions. Citizens have more trust in the European Parliament than in their national political parties or politicians. Moreover, respondents in half of the countries have more trust in the European Parliament than in their national parliament. Trust in the United Nations is also remarkably high. Particularly in new democracies, international institutions receive higher trust values than the national institutions. We can assume that most citizens do not have any direct contact with these international institutions and do not know much about them. In effect, fewer respondents are able to evaluate the trustworthiness of international than national institutions. In every wave of the European Social Survey, between 10 and 15 per cent of the respondents indicated that they do not know whether to trust or distrust the European Parliament or the United Nations. On the other hand, less than 4 per cent of the respondents do not know whether to trust or distrust their national institutions. Almost all respondents – 98 per cent – have an opinion on the trustworthiness of the police, which is the institution with which respondents were most likely to have come into contact. The number of missing values for international institutions is even larger in new democracies.

Self-evidently, it is important to distinguish countries that are not members of the European Union. In effect, a larger number of respondents in Switzerland and Norway are not able to form an opinion on the trustworthiness of the European Parliament. Thirteen per cent of the Norwegian respondents do not have an opinion on the trustworthiness of the European Parliament, while this is less than 1 per cent for the Norwegian Parliament. However, also in EU-member countries, the number of respondents that is unable to judge the trustworthiness of the European Parliament is substantial (especially compared to their own national parliament). In 2008, almost a fifth of the Spanish and Portuguese respondents indicated that they do not know whether to trust the European Parliament or not.

These figures conceal substantial differences in trust levels between the different countries. In the subsequent paragraphs, recent trends in political trust in

---

8. A t-test was conducted per country, showing a significantly higher level of trust in implementing institutions than in representational institutions in every country.

Table 2.3: Trust in political institutions in Europe

	2002		2004		2006		2008	
	Mean	N	Mean	N	Mean	N	Mean	N
Police	6.21 (2.46)	39,438	5.99 (2.51)	43,028	6.05 (2.49)	37,062	5.81 (2.58)	40,488
Legal system	5.42 (2.56)	38,793	5.15 (2.57)	42,401	5.24 (2.56)	36,495	4.98 (2.66)	39,868
Parliament (national)	4.94 (2.41)	38,380	4.54 (2.45)	42,300	4.63 (2.48)	36,335	4.29 (2.58)	39,804
Politicians	3.95 (2.29)	39,045	3.66 (2.33)	42,614	3.67 (2.34)	36,734	3.44 (2.37)	40,205
Political parties	–	–	3.67 (2.30)	42,284	3.70 (2.31)	36,526	3.46 (2.35)	39,975
European Parliament	4.76 (2.36)	34,689	4.60 (2.39)	37,974	4.66 (2.37)	33,253	4.60 (2.39)	36,868
United Nations	5.46 (2.49)	35,855	5.33 (2.50)	39,091	5.43 (2.43)	33,814	5.31 (2.46)	36,808
Representing	4.45		3.97		4.02		3.75	
Implementing	5.81		5.56		5.64		5.38	
Significance test	t-test: 134.424 df: 37,562	$p < 0.000$	t-test: 170.899 df: 40,811	$p < 0.000$	t-test: 157.723 df: 35,262	$p < 0.000$	t-test: 171.403 df: 38,682	$p < 0.000$

Notes: The means are presented. The scale ranges from 0 to 10. Standard deviations are in parentheses.

Source: ESS 2002, 2004, 2006, 2008.

Europe will be described per country. While political trust has strongly declined in the United States since the 1980s (Lipset and Schneider 1983; Hetherington 2005), such a declining trend was not found in Europe (Klingemann and Fuchs 1995). Recent trends in institutional trust and satisfaction with the current government in Europe are described using the four available waves of the European Social Survey. Only the twenty-three countries that participated more than twice in the survey will be analysed.[9] Unfortunately, trust in political parties was not questioned in the first wave of the survey, therefore this measure was not included in the 'trust in political institutions' scale. The latter includes trust in the country's national parliament, the legal system, the police and politicians. The four items were added into one scale, and for reasons of clarity, this scale was recoded to range between 0 and 10.

Trust levels are represented by region in order to gain a clear overview of the trends. Looking at the established democracies, the most striking observation is the stability in levels of institutional trust (Figures 2.3–2.5). The general pattern is quite common in research on political culture, with the highest values documented in Northern Europe, while the countries in Southern and Eastern Europe tend to have lower levels of trust. In Figure 2.3, institutional trust in the Nordic countries is shown. In general, the changes in institutional trust are small in these countries: on average, a change of 0.13 on an 11-point scale. The most substantial changes in institutional trust are documented in Norway and Sweden. In Sweden, institutional trust decreased from 5.88 to 5.45 between 2002 and 2004. In the following years, however, trust increased again to its 2002 levels. While institutional trust was found to be in decline in Sweden during the 1980s and 1990s (Holmberg 1999), no such general declining trend can be observed in the 2000s. Institutional trust in Norway decreased between 2002 and 2004, to increase again to its 2002 level in 2006. In Finland, there is a small significant increase in institutional trust from 6.3 to 6.4 between 2002 and 2004. In Denmark, none of the changes in institutional trust between 2002 and 2009 are significant. In summary, the changes in institutional trust are modest in the Nordic countries and might even be due to sample differences.

Levels of institutional trust are less stable in Southern Europe (see Figure 2.4). On average, the changes in institutional trust amount to 0.4 on an 11-point scale. In Greece, in particular, institutional trust decreased significantly from 5.2 in 2002 to 3.9 in 2008. In Portugal, trust in institutions also decreased from 4.2 in 2002 to 3.8 in 2008. Spain, the third Southern European country that was questioned multiple times, can also be found at the bottom of the graph. In Spain, trust in political institutions amounted to 4.5 in 2002 and increased slightly in subsequent years to 4.9 in 2004 and 4.7 in 2008.

---

9. These countries include Austria, Belgium, the Czech Republic, Denmark, Estonia, Finland, France, Germany, Greece, Hungary, Ireland, Luxembourg, the Netherlands, Norway, Poland, Portugal, Slovenia, Slovakia, Spain, Sweden, Switzerland, Ukraine and the United Kingdom. A trend line can be presented for Ukraine as it was included in the last three waves of ESS (2004–2008). Note, however, that Ukraine is not a free democracy according to Freedom House and the results should be read with caution.

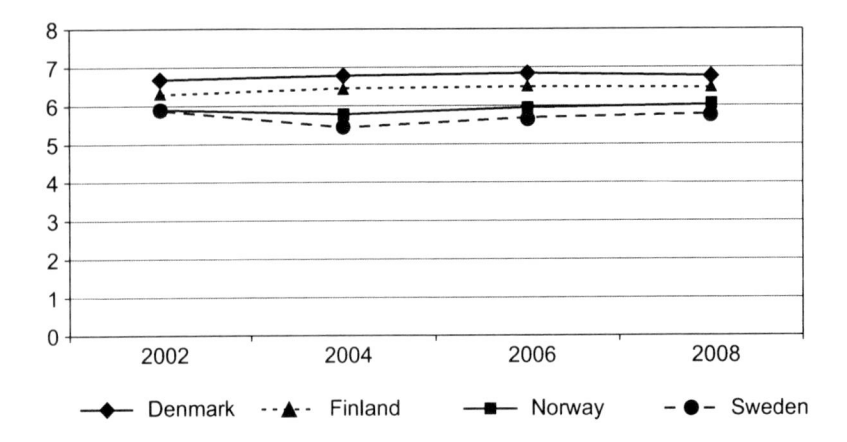

Figure 2.3: Trends in trust in political institutions in the Nordic countries

Notes: The means on the 'institutional trust'-scale are presented. The scale ranges from 0 to 10.
Source: ESS 2002, 2004, 2006, 2008.

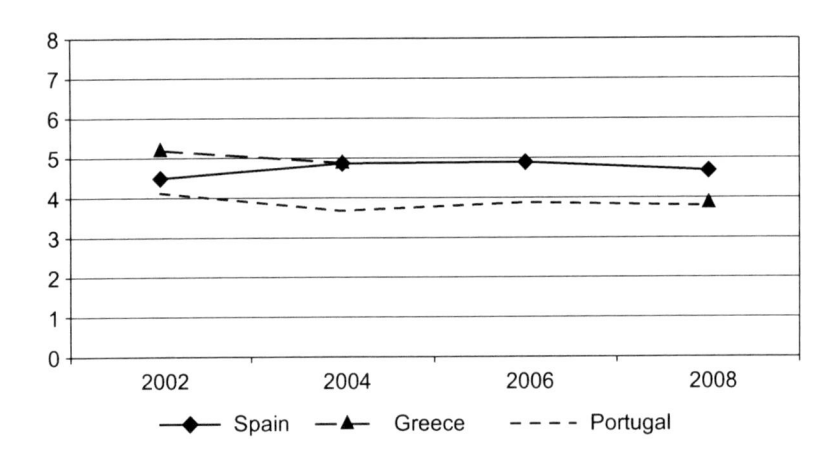

Figure 2.4: Trends in trust in political institutions in Southern Europe

Notes: The means on the 'institutional trust'-scale are presented. The scale ranges from 0 to 10.
Source: ESS 2002, 2004, 2006, 2008.

Next to Sweden, political trust levels were also found to be in decline in the Netherlands. Several scholars reported a strong decline in institutional trust in the Netherlands at the beginning of the twenty-first century (Bovens and Wille 2008; Hendriks 2009). Figure 2.5 reveals that this decline did not persist; institutional trust increased significantly in the Netherlands during the 2000s (from 5.3 in 2002 to 5.8 in 2009). In several countries, after an increase or decrease in trust, trust levels are restored to the original level in the following years. In effect, it is argued that public opinion has become more volatile as a result of different trends such as party dealignment, better informed citizens and a more sensation-seeking media (Bovens and Wille 2011). However, the variations in levels of institutional trust in established democracies are small (e.g. an average change of 0.1 on an 11-point scale for the countries in Figure 2.5). Trust levels remain relatively high in the Nordic countries, while trust levels in Southern Europe remain at a lower level. In general, the levels of trust in political institutions are also more volatile in the newer democracies in Southern Europe than in the longer established Northern European democracies.

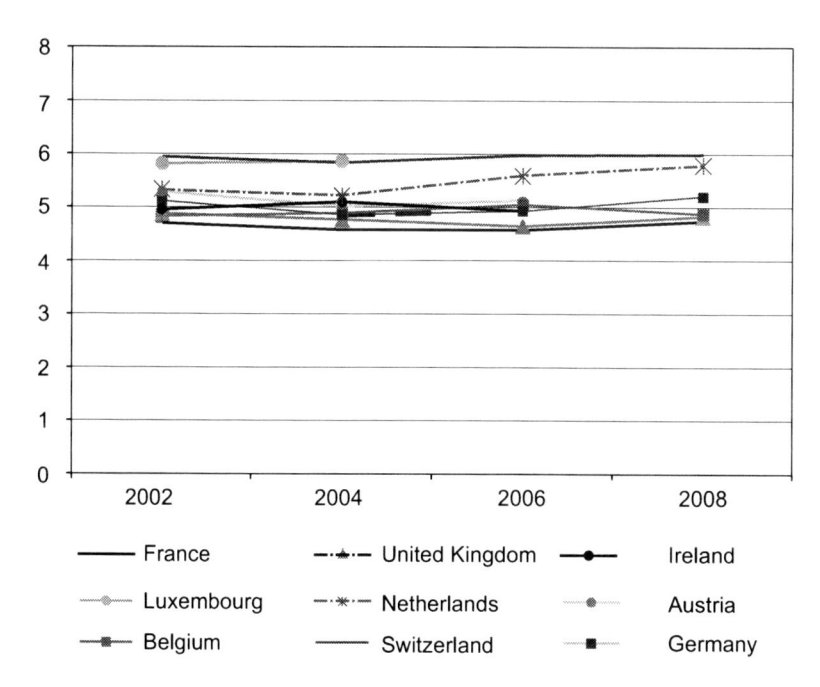

Figure 2.5: Trends in trust in political institutions in other established democracies

Notes: The means on the 'institutional trust'-scale are presented. The scale ranges from 0 to 10.
Source: ESS 2002, 2004, 2006, 2008.

A clearly different pattern emerges in the newer democracies in Eastern Europe (see Figure 2.6). First, trust levels are still substantially lower than in the established democracies. Estonia is characterised by the highest trust levels among the newer democracies, with an average score of 4.5/10 – which is still substantially below the average trust values in Western Europe. The lowest trust level is found in Ukraine, with an average value of 1.8 in 2008. Put another way, 26.5 per cent of the Ukrainian respondents indicated that they had no trust at all in any of the four institutions (parliament, legal system, the police or politicians).[10] Secondly, trust levels in new democracies are clearly more volatile than in more established democracies. We can observe significant decreases in trust levels in Hungary and Ukraine. In only six years, trust in political institutions declined almost two points on the 11-point trust scale in both countries (i.e. from 4.7 to 3.1 in Hungary and from 3.9 to 1.8 in Ukraine). On the other hand, trust levels increased in Slovenia and Slovakia (especially between 2004 and 2006). In Poland and the Czech Republic, we see that trust levels are restored to the original levels after a significant drop in trust between 2002 and 2004.

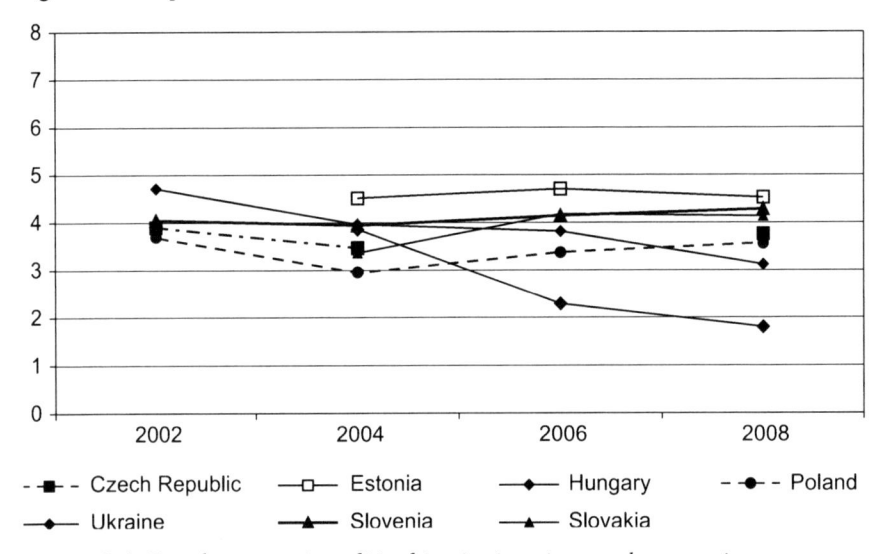

Figure 2.6: Trends in trust in political institutions in new democracies

Notes: The means on the 'institutional trust'-scale are presented. The scale ranges from 0 to 10.
Source: ESS 2002, 2004, 2006, 2008.

We can conclude that citizens' trust in political institutions in Europe has been stable over the past years. Institutional trust even increased in countries in which a general downward trend was documented during the 1990s or early 2000s. The analysis of trends in institutional trust in twenty-three European countries reveals that after a decrease or increase in trust, trust levels restore to their original levels in the following years. In newer democracies, institutional trust proved to be more volatile than in more established democracies. In Hungary and Ukraine, in particular, substantial drops in institutional trust were documented during the 2000s.

---

10. These results should be read with caution as cross-cultural equivalence tests show that institutional trust in Ukraine is not comparable to the other countries. Several political and civil rights are lacking in Ukraine, and therefore, it cannot be considered a free democracy, which makes comparisons with democracies difficult.

Institutional trust also decreased sharply in Greece during this period. However, in line with the trends in institutional trust that were reported in Sweden and the Netherlands, these findings more likely point at volatility than a persistent decline. These findings confirm the conclusion of Klingemann and Fuchs (1995) that there is no general declining trend in political trust in Europe. However, it also implies that levels of political trust in newer democracies remain rather low, and there are very few indications that levels of trust in these countries will rise substantially in the years ahead.

Satisfaction with the current government

In the next paragraphs, we will look into the trends in a more specific kind of political trust: satisfaction with the current government. Respondents were asked: 'Now thinking about the [country] government, how satisfied are you with the way it is doing its job?' A value of 0 indicated that they were extremely dissatisfied, while a value of 10 indicated that they were extremely satisfied. In 2008–2009, the average level of satisfaction with government amounted to 4.42/10 in established democracies and 3.19/10 in newer democracies (F = 2,316.922; p < 0.000). The cross-national patterns in this specific trust judgment are similar to the ones we observed in the more generalised institutional trust. But as we could expect from Easton's theory (1965), satisfaction with the current government is more volatile than trust in political institutions. In terms of government satisfaction, the Nordic countries are also at the top of the list, together with Switzerland and Luxembourg (see Figures 2.7–2.9). While satisfaction with government fluctuates more than institutional trust in Scandinavia, the fluctuations are rather modest, especially in comparison to the evolution of satisfaction with government in Southern and Eastern European countries (see Figure 2.8 and Figure 2.10).

In Southern Europe, citizens are in general less satisfied with how their government is performing than in the Nordic countries. However, in 2005, satisfaction with government was remarkably high in Spain and Greece, surpassing the satisfaction levels of their counterparts in Norway and the Netherlands. Government satisfaction significantly increased in both countries between 2002 and 2005. The increase in government satisfaction seems to follow the economic growth that Spain experienced during the 2000s. In effect, previous research has revealed that the economic situation is an important predictor for government support (Lockerbie 1993). Government support can also suddenly increase due to a dramatic event, which is called 'rally around the flag' in the literature (Hetherington and Nelson 2003; Gross et al. 2009). The terrorist attacks in Madrid on 11th March 2004 could have led to such a rally around the flag effect. The graphs indeed show a strong increase in satisfaction with government in Spain between 2002 and 2005 (from 4.3 in 2002 to 5.1 in 2005). In Greece, the alternation of the parties in office in 2004 and the organisation of the Olympic Games might offer an explanation for these high levels of government satisfaction in 2005.

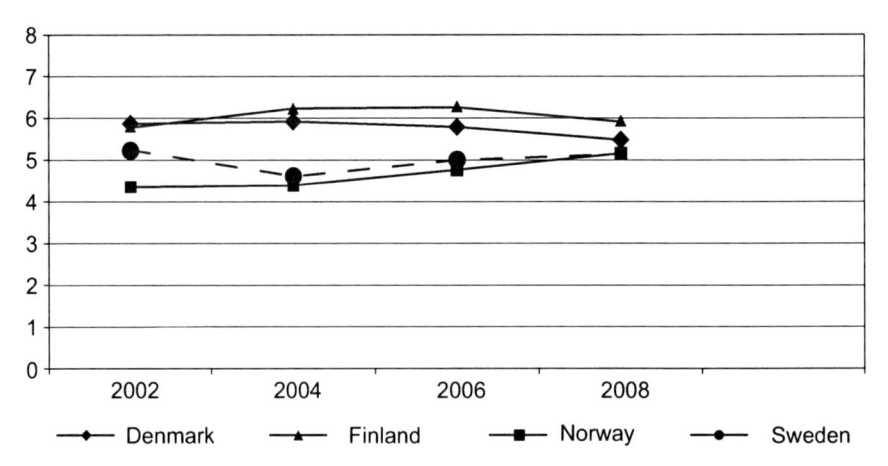

Figure 2.7: Trends in satisfaction with government in the Nordic countries

Notes: The means of citizens' 'satisfaction with government' are presented. The scale ranges from 0 to 10.
Source: ESS 2002, 2004, 2006, 2008.

However, in the second half of the 2000s, satisfaction with Greek government dramatically declined from 4.1 in 2002 to 2.7 in 2008. A quarter of the respondents indicated that they were extremely dissatisfied with their current government. Greece was confronted with an avalanche of political scandals in these years. Moreover, the government's plans to reform university regulation evoked several strikes and protests. The way in which the government handled severe forest fires also created the public perception of an incompetent, ineffective government. The general elections of 2007 revealed a widespread dissatisfaction with an increase in abstention of 2.6 per cent and a substantial increase in protest votes for three minor political parties (Mavrogordatos 2008). At the end of 2008, the Greek Government was confronted with the worst riots and unrest since the military dictatorship in 1974. The government failed to restore order promptly and the riots persisted for several weeks (Mavrogordatos 2009). Given the 2010 debt crisis and unrest, this declining trend in government satisfaction is likely to persist. Satisfaction with government also proves to be volatile in Portugal. In the beginning of the 2000s, satisfaction with government decreased. Portuguese politics was characterised by a series of scandals which led to numerous government reshuffles. In addition, the country was confronted with an economic recession and the government introduced severe austerity policies in public spending. However, by the mid-2000s, satisfaction with government increased gradually to its 2002 levels. At that time, the economic situation also slightly improved and the centre-right government was voted out of office and replaced by a new (socialist) government (Magone 2005).

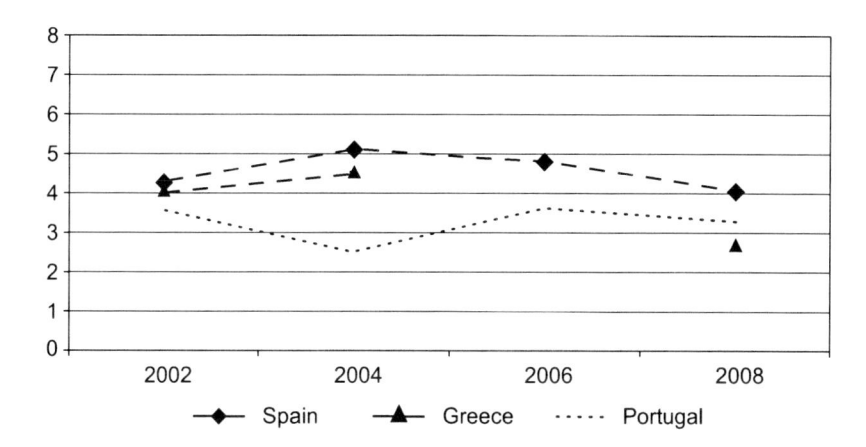

Figure 2.8: Trends in satisfaction with government in Southern European countries

Notes: The means of citizens' 'satisfaction with government' are presented. The scale ranges from 0 to 10.
Source: ESS 2002, 2004, 2006, 2008.

Satisfaction with government has also declined significantly in the United Kingdom and Belgium during the past decade. In the United Kingdom, satisfaction with the Labour Government gradually declined during the 2000s (see Figure 2.9). Satisfaction with government amounted to 4.38 in 2002 and dropped to 4.05 in 2006. In 2008, the average level of satisfaction with government only amounted to 3.60. Even the Labour voters were not satisfied with government in 2008, with an average level of satisfaction of 4.44. This might offer an explanation as to why the government could not secure re-election in the 2010 general elections. The next wave of ESS will show whether the alternation of power was able to reverse this declining trend in government satisfaction. In Belgium, satisfaction with the government reached its lowest level in the past decade (see Figure 2.9). The political and economic crisis seems to have exerted a strong effect on specific political support in Belgium. Satisfaction with government decreased from 5.18 in 2002 to 3.92 in 2008. However, these events do not seem to affect the more generalised kind of political trust, given the remarkable stability of trust in political institutions in Belgium we observed in Figure 2.5.

On the other hand, satisfaction with the current government has increased in the Netherlands. Previous research has documented a steep decline in satisfaction with government in the Netherlands at the start of the century. While approximately two-thirds of the respondents in 1998 thought the Dutch Government was doing a good job, less than a third of the respondents were satisfied with government at the beginning of the century (Bovens and Wille 2008). The ESS data show that this drop was only temporary; satisfaction with government was gradually restored from 4.24 in 2002 to 4.45 in 2004 to 5.44 in 2006, and eventually to 5.53 in 2008. Governments in Switzerland and Germany also received more support in

34 | political trust

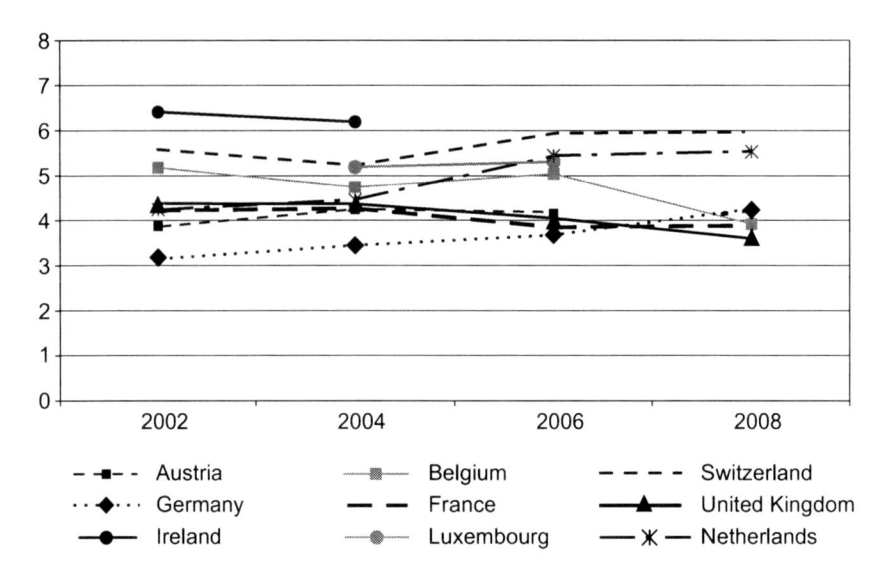

Figure 2.9: Trends in satisfaction with government in the other established countries

Notes: The means of citizens' 'satisfaction with government' are presented. The scale ranges from 0 to 10.
Source: ESS 2002, 2004, 2006, 2008.

2008 than they did in 2002, but these increases are rather modest.

Finally, the new democracies in Eastern Europe are characterised by substantial volatility in government satisfaction. In effect, only few governments in Central and Eastern European countries are able to secure re-election (Tavits 2005). Figure 2.10 shows a steep decline in government satisfaction in Hungary in the past decade. Satisfaction with the current government declined by three points on an 11-point scale (i.e. from 4.88 (2002) to 3.23 (2004) to 2.68 (2006) to 1.88 (2008)). In 2008, 37.4 per cent of the respondents in Hungary indicated that they were extremely dissatisfied with their government (i.e. value 0/10). Category 0 and 1 together include more than half of the Hungarian respondents. Figure 2.6 already showed that institutional trust also declined in recent years in Hungary. Ukrainian governments are also confronted with declining levels of government satisfaction. At the beginning of 2005, in the aftermath of the Orange Revolution, satisfaction with government amounted to 4.25 only to drop to 2.17 at the end of 2006 and to drop even further to 1.53 in 2009. Put another way, in 2009, 42.4 per cent of the Ukrainian respondents answered that they were extremely dissatisfied with their government. Three-fourths of Ukrainian respondents can be found in the lowest four categories. Decreasing levels of satisfaction with government are also prevalent in the Czech Republic and Estonia, but to a more modest extent. In Poland, satisfaction with government decreased between 2002 and 2004, but was restored to its original level in 2008. On the other hand, in Slovenia and Slovakia, satisfaction with the current government increased. In Slovakia, we see quite a substantial increase in satisfaction with the current government from 3.0 in 2002 to 5.0 in 2004 to 4.8 in 2008.

Similar trends emerge in institutional trust and satisfaction with the current government in some countries. While diffuse and specific trust have different determinants, there is certainly a spill-over between these two political trust measures. For instance, a corruption scandal can erode satisfaction with the current government as well as trust in the political institutions. In Hungary and Ukraine, strong declines in institutional trust and satisfaction with the current government were documented. On the other hand, the political and economic crisis does not seem to affect trust in political institutions in Belgium, while it strongly decreased satisfaction with the current government. Given that trust in the political institutions is less stable in new democracies, it is possible that the evaluations of the current government are more important for trust in political institutions in newer democracies than in established democracies. However, the calculation of correlations between measures of institutional trust and satisfaction with the current government show that the relation between these two is similar in established and new democracies (resp. 0.602 $p < 0.000$ and 0.572 $p < 0.000$). This correlation differs between the countries under study with the weakest association in Denmark (Pearson correlation = 0.333; $p < 0.000$) and Slovenia (Pearson correlation = 0.388; $p < 0.000$) and the strongest correlation in the Netherlands (Pearson correlation = 0.681; $p < 0.000$) and Bulgaria (Pearson correlation = 0.644; $p < 0.000$). But no clear cross-national pattern emerges.

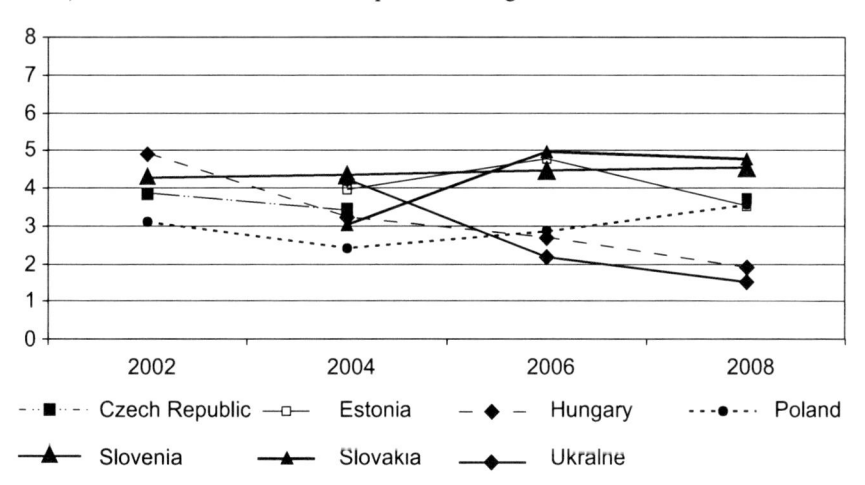

Figure 2.10: Trends in satisfaction with government in new European democracies

Notes: The means of citizens' 'satisfaction with government' are presented. The scale ranges from 0 to 10.

Source: ESS 2002, 2004, 2006, 2008. See Appendices.

Conclusion

Since the 1970s, it has been claimed repeatedly that democracy is losing legitimacy among its citizens resulting in an unprecedented confidence crisis (Crozier *et al.* 1975; Nye *et al.* 1997; Dalton 2004; Macedo *et al.* 2005). In the mid-1970s, Crozier *et al.* (1975: 159) for instance stated: 'Dissatisfaction with and lack of confidence in the functioning of the institutions of democratic government have thus now become widespread in the Trilateral countries.' Thirty years later, Dalton (2004: 1) repeats a similar message:

> Contemporary democracies are facing a challenge today. This challenge does not come from enemies within or outside the nation; instead, the challenge comes from democracy's own citizens, who have grown distrustful of politicians, sceptical about democratic institutions, and disillusioned about how the democratic process functions.

However, the evidence presented in this chapter clearly contradicts the claim that contemporary democracies are losing citizens' support. In effect, no general declining trend could be found in institutional trust among a wide variety of European countries in the past decade. Only in Greece, Hungary and Ukraine did institutional trust decline substantially in the past decade. More recent data is needed to ascertain whether this declining trend will persist. While institutional trust has decreased in some European countries during the 1990s and early 2000s (Klingemann 1999; Bovens and Wille 2008), this study also shows that institutional trust was restored to its original levels in the 2000s in these countries. Therefore, to date the only conclusion that can be drawn is that institutional trust is stable (especially in the more established democracies). These findings underline the importance of good operationalisation of political trust and of the study of political trust beyond the United States.

Throughout this chapter, the most outspoken difference in institutional trust is between established and new democracies. Not only is political trust lower in newer democracies, it is also more volatile. Nevertheless, the analyses revealed that institutional trust in new democracies could also be measured in a valid manner. A one-dimensional attitude, institutional trust, exists in all countries under study, providing strong support for the claim that institutional trust reflects an assessment of the prevailing political culture in a country. Institutional trust influences citizens' trust judgments of a broad range of institutions. While institutional trust influences trust in representative as well as implementing institutions, its influence on implementing institutions is smaller in established democracies. In new democracies, on the other hand, institutional trust influences representative and implementing institutions to the same extent. Put another way, citizens are distrustful of all institutions and hardly differentiate between (impartial) implementing and (partisan) representative institutions. Most likely, all institutions are perceived as political or even as corrupt.

While this study makes the necessary differentiations to the pessimistic claims that have repeatedly put forward, the results also show that citizens are rather critical towards political institutions and their government. Especially in new democracies, political institutions and leaders lack popular support. In Hungary, for example, 37.4 per cent of the respondents indicated to be extremely dissatisfied with their government. More than half of the Hungarian respondents gave their government a value of 0 or 1 on a scale from 0 to 10. Given the high levels of corruption in several of these newer democracies, it could be argued that low levels of trust in political institutions reflect an accurate assessment of the trustworthiness of these institutions. In established democracies, citizens might be dissatisfied with how their political system is performing, but they can have at least a reasonable expectation not to meet corrupt officials on a day-to-day basis.

Appendix A

Table 1, Appendix A: European Social Survey – Completed Questionnaires

	2002	2004	2006	2008
Austria	2,257	2,256	2,405	–
Belgium	1,899	1,778	1,798	1,760
Bulgaria	–	–	1,400	2,230
Switzerland	2,040	2,141	1,804	1,819
Cyprus	–	–	995	1,215
Czech Republic	1,360	3,026	–	2,018
Germany	2,919	2,870	2,916	2,751
Denmark	1,506	1,487	1,505	1,610
Estonia	–	1,989	1,517	1,661
Spain	1,729	1,663	1,876	2,576
Finland	2,000	2,022	1,896	2,195
France	1,503	1,806	1,986	2,073
United Kingdom	2,052	1,897	2,394	2,352
Greece	2,566	2,406	–	2,072
Hungary	1,685	1,498	1,518	1,544
Ireland	2,046	2,286	1,800	–
Iceland	–	579	–	–
Latvia	–	–	–	1,980
Luxembourg	1,552	1,635	–	–
Netherlands	2,364	1,881	1,889	1,778
Norway	2,036	1,760	1,750	1,549
Poland	2,110	1,716	1,721	1,619
Portugal	1,511	2,052	2,222	2,367
Sweden	1,999	1,948	1,927	1,830
Slovenia	1,519	1,442	1,476	1,286
Slovakia	–	1,512	1,766	1,810
Ukraine	–	2,031	2,002	1,845

Appendix B: One theoretical concept

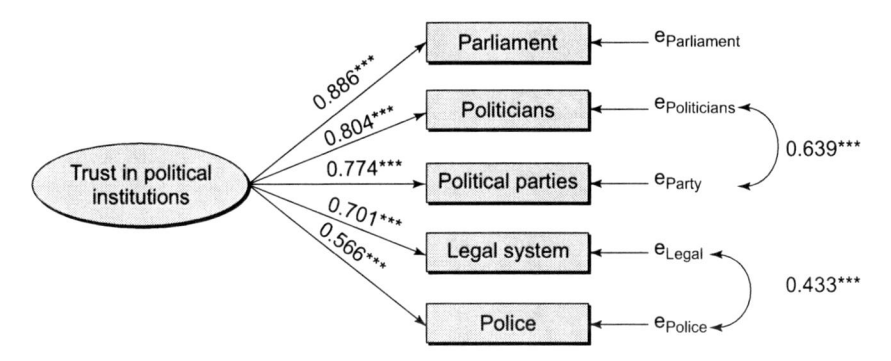

Figure 1, Appendix B: Solution Confirmatory Factor Analysis (2006)

Source: ESS 2006. 21 countries. *Notes:* standardised factor loadings resulting from a confirmatory factor analysis on the full sample. Fit indices: $\chi^2 = 178.842$; df = 3; p value = 0.000; RMSEA = 0.040; CFI = 0.999. n = 36,172.

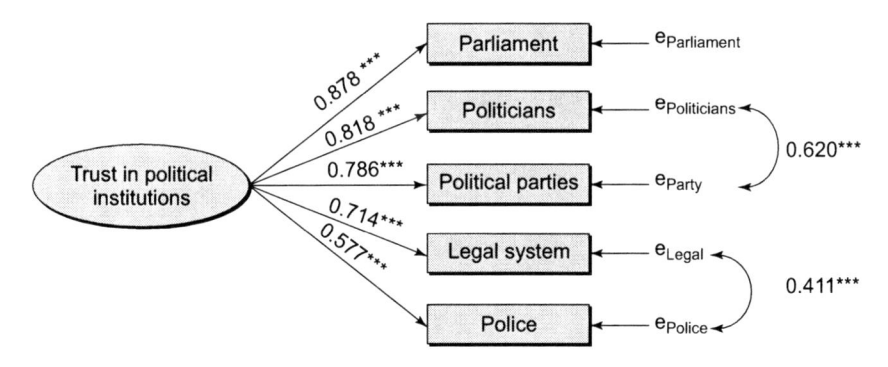

Figure 2, Appendix B: Solution Confirmatory Factor Analysis (2004)

Source: ESS 2004. 23 countries. *Notes:* standardised factor loadings resulting from a confirmatory factor analysis on the full sample. Fit indices: $\chi^2 = 172.497$; df = 3; p value = 0.000; RMSEA = 0.037; CFI = 0.999. n = 40,773.

Appendix C: Cross-Cultural Equivalence

Table 1, Appendix C: Testing for cross-cultural equivalence in trust in political institutions (2006)

Model specifications	χ^2	df	RMSEA	CFI	EPC	MI
Configural equivalence	298.196	63	0.047	0.998	–	–
Metric equivalence	1104.354	143	0.062	0.990	–	–
Free FI police	1025.595	142	0.060	0.991	-0.157	79.819
Free BG police	973.750	141	0.059	0.992	0.161	48.540
Free AT parliament	928.411	140	0.057	0.992	0.178	42.952
Free DK legal system	891.598	139	0.056	0.993	-0.133	37.950
Free DK police	846.406	138	0.055	0.993	-0.172	45.932
Free FI legal system	812.343	137	0.053	0.993	-0.117	34.975
Free HU police	778.245	136	0.052	0.994	0.128	32.118
Free CY police	739.314	135	0.051	0.994	0.156	35.580
Free SK police	708.907	134	0.050	0.994	0.112	29.543

Notes: Entries are the results of confirmatory factor analyses.
Source: ESS 2006. Twenty-one countries. N = 36,172.

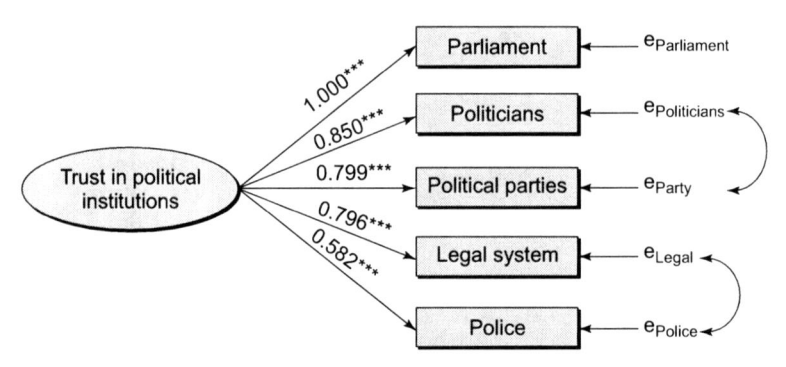

Figure 1, Appendix C: Solution Confirmatory Factor Analysis with Imposed Constraints (2006)

Source: ESS 2006. 21 countries. *Notes:* Factor loadings resulting from a confirmatory factor analysis. Fit indices: χ^2=708.907; df=134; RMSEA=0.050; CFI= 0.994; n=36,172.

Table 2. Appendix C: Testing for cross-cultural equivalence in trust in political institutions (2004)

Model specifications	χ2	df	RMSEA	CFI	EPC	MI
Configural equivalence	367.704	69	0.049	0.997	–	–
Metric equivalence	1162.237	157	0.060	0.991	–	–
Free FI police	1096.463	156	0.058	0.992	-0.155	66.786
Free CZ police	1045.063	155	0.057	0.992	0.103	48.788
Free CZ parliament	1000.479	154	0.056	0.993	-0.116	46.930
Free PT legal system	960.598	153	0.055	0.993	0.134	37.660
Free PT parliament	897.165	152	0.053	0.994	0.232	57.678
Free BE parliament	870.674	151	0.052	0.994	-0.142	27.529
Free HU legal system	845.578	150	0.051	0.994	0.100	23.852
Free AT parliament	823.814	149	0.051	0.994	0.115	20.858
Free DK police	802.367	148	0.050	0.994	-0.106	21.934

Notes: Entries are the results of confirmatory factor analyses.
Source: ESS 2004. Twenty-three countries. N = 40,773.

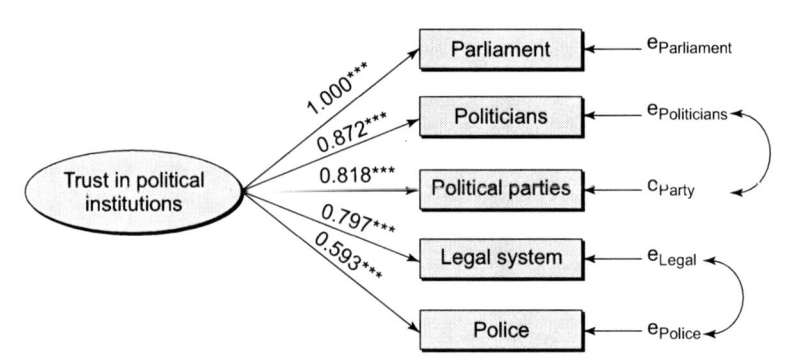

Figure 2, Appendix C: Solution Confirmatory Factor Analysis with Imposed Constraints (2004)

Source: ESS 2004. 23 countries. *Notes:* Factor loadings resulting from a confirmatory factor Fit indices: $\chi2$= 802.367; df=148; RMSEA= 0.050; CFI= 0.994; n=40,773

References

Aberbach, J. D. (1969) 'Alienation and political behavior', *American Political Science Review*, 63(1): 86–99.

Almond, G. and Verba, S. (1963) *The Civic Culture: Political attitudes and democracy in five nations*, Princeton: Princeton University Press.

Anderson, C., Blais, A., Bowler, S., Donovan, T. and Listhaug, O. (2005) *Losers' Consent: Elections and democratic legitimacy*, Oxford: Oxford University Press.

Bélanger, R. and Nadeau, R. (2005) 'Political trust and the vote in multiparty elections: The Canadian case', *European Journal of Political Research*, 44(1): 121–46.

Bovens, M. and Wille, A. (2008) 'Deciphering the Dutch drop: Ten explanations for decreasing political trust in the Netherlands', *International Review of Administrative Sciences*, 74(2): 283–305.

— (2011) 'Falling or fluctuating trust levels? The case of the Netherlands', in S. Zmerli and Marc Hooghe (eds) *Political Trust: Why context matters*, Colchester: ECPR Press.

Brown, T. A. (2006) *Confirmatory Factor Analysis for Applied Research*, New York: The Guilford Press.

Byrne, B. M., Shavelson, R. J., and Muthen, B. (1989) 'Testing for the equivalence of factor covariance and mean structures: The issue of partial measurement invariance', *Psychological Bulletin*, 105(3): 456–66.

Catterberg, G. and Moreno, A. (2006) 'The individual bases of political trust: Trends in new and established democracies', *International Journal of Public Opinion Research*, 18(1): 31–48.

Citrin, J. (1974) 'Comment: The political relevance of trust in government', *American Political Science Review*, 68(3): 973–88.

Crozier, M. J., Huntington, S. and Watanuki, J. (1975) *The Crisis of Democracy: Report on the governability of democracies to the trilateral commission*, New York: New York University Press.

Dalton, R. (2004) *Democratic Challenges, Democratic Choices. The erosion of political support in advanced industrial democracies*, Oxford: Oxford University Press.

Easton, D. (1965) *A Framework for Political Analysis*, Englewood Cliffs, N. J.: Prentice Hall.

European Social Survey Round 1 Data (2002) *Data File Edition 6.0*. Norway: Norwegian Social Science Data Services. Data Archive and distributor of ESS data. Online available http://ess.nsd.uib.no/ (accessed in December 2010).

— (2004) *Data File Edition 2.0*. Norway: Norwegian Social Science Data Services. Data Archive and distributor of ESS data. Online available http://ess.nsd.uib.no/ (accessed in December 2010).

European Social Survey Round 3 Data (2006) *Data File Edition 3.0*. Norway: Norwegian Social Science Data Services. Data Archive and distributor of

ESS data. Online available http://ess.nsd.uib.no/ (accessed in December 2010).
European Social Survey Round 4 Data (2008) *Data File Edition 3.0*. Norway: Norwegian Social Science Data Services. Data Archive and distributor of ESS data. Online available http://ess.nsd.uib.no/ (accessed in December 2010).
Fisher, J., van Heerde, J. and Tucker, A. (2010) 'Does one trust judgement fit all? Linking theory and empirics', *British Journal of Politics and International Relations*, 12(2): 161–88.
Gross, K., Brewer, P. R., and Aday, S. (2009) 'Confidence in government and emotional responses to terrorism after September 11, 2001', *American Politics Research*, 37(1): 107–28.
Hendriks, F. (2009) 'Contextualizing the Dutch drop in political trust: Connecting underlying factors', *International Review of Administrative Sciences*, 75(3): 473–91.
Hetherington, M. (2005) *Why Trust Matters*, Princeton: Princeton University Press.
Hetherington, M. J. and Nelson, M. (2003) 'Anatomy of a rally effect: George W. Bush and the war on terrorism', *PS: Political Science and Politics*, 36(1): 37–42.
Hibbing, J. R. and Theiss-Morse, E. (1995) *Stealth Democracy: Americans' beliefs about how government should work*, Cambridge: Cambridge University Press.
Holmberg, S. (1999) 'Down and down we go: Political trust in Sweden', in P. Norris (ed.) *Critical Citizens: Global support for democratic government*, Oxford: Oxford University Press.
Hooghe, M. (2011) 'Why there is basically only one form of political trust', *British Journal of Politics and International Relations*, 13(2): 269–75.
Hooghe, M. and Wilkenfeld, B. (2008) 'The stability of political attitudes and behaviors across adolescence and early adulthood: A comparison of survey data on adolescents and young adults in eight countries', *Journal of Youth and Adolescence*, 37(2): 155–67.
Hu, L. and Bentler, P. M. (1999) 'Cutoff criteria for fit indexes in covariance structure analysis: Conventional criteria versus new alternatives', *Structural Equation Modeling*, 6(1):1–55.
Inglehart, R. (1999) 'Postmodernization erodes respect for authority, but increases support for democracy', in P. Norris (ed.) *Critical Citizens: Global support for democratic government*, Oxford: Oxford University Press.
Jowell, R. and the Central Co-ordinating Team (2003) *European Social Survey 2002/2003: Technical report*, London: Centre for Comparative Social Surveys, City University.
— (2005) *European Social Survey 2004/2005: Technical report*, London: Centre for Comparative Social Surveys, City University.
— (2007) *European Social Survey 2006/2007: Technical report*, London: Centre for Comparative Social Surveys, City University.

— (2009) *European Social Survey 2008/2009: Technical report*, London: Centre for Comparative Social Surveys, City University.
Klingemann, H.-D. (1999) 'Mapping political support in the 1990s: A global analysis', in P. Norris (ed.) *Critical Citizens: Global support for democratic government*, Oxford: Oxford University Press.
Klingemann, H.-D. and Fuchs, D. (1995) *Citizens and the State*, Oxford: Oxford University Press.
Lipset, A. M. and Schneider, W. (1983) 'The decline of confidence in American institutions', *Political Science Quarterly*, 98(3): 379–402.
Lockerbie, B. (1993) 'Economic dissatisfaction and political alienation in Western Europe', *European Journal of Political Research*, 23(3): 281–93.
Macedo S. (ed.) (2005) *Democracy at Risk: How political choices undermine citizen participation, and what we can do about it: Towards a political science of citizenship*, Washington D.C.: Brooking Institution Press.
Magone, J. M. (2005) 'Portugal', *European Journal of Political Research*, 44(7–8): 1158–66.
Marien, S. and Hooghe, M. (2011) 'Does political trust matter? An empirical investigation into the relation between political trust and support for law compliance', *European Journal of Political Research*, 50(2): 267–91.
Mavrogordatos, G. T. (2008) 'Greece', *European Journal of Political Research*, 47(7–8): 990–7.
— (2009) 'Greece', *European Journal of Political Research*, 48(7–8): 968–72.
Miller, A. H. (1974) 'Rejoinder to 'Comment' by Jack Citrin: Political discontent or ritualism?', *American Political Science Review*, 68(3): 989–1001.
Norris, P. (ed.) (1999) *Critical Citizens: Global support for democratic government*, Oxford: Oxford University Press.
Nye, J., Zelikow, P. and King, D. (1997) *Why Americans Mistrust Government*, Cambridge: Harvard University Press.
Reeskens, T. and Hooghe, M. (2008) 'Cross-cultural measurement equivalence of generalized trust. Evidence from the European Social Survey (2002 and 2004)', *Social Indicators Research*, 85(3): 515–32.
Rothstein, B. and Stolle, D. (2008) 'The state and social capital: An institutional theory of generalized trust', *Comparative Politics*, 40(4): 441–67.
Tavits, M. (2005) 'The development of stable party support: Electoral dynamics in post-communist Europe', *American Journal of Political Science*, 49(2): 283–98.
van de Walle, S., van Roosbroeck, S. and Bouckaert, G. (2008) 'Trust in the public sector: Is there any evidence for a long-term decline?', *International Review of Administrative Sciences*, 74(1): 47–64.
Zmerli, S. and Newton, K. (2008) 'Social trust and attitudes toward democracy', *Public Opinion Quarterly*, 72(4): 706–24.

chapter three | falling or fluctuating trust levels? the case of the netherlands

Mark Bovens and Anchrit Wille

A sudden crisis of trust

At the turn of the century, levels of political trust in the Netherlands were at an all time high. In 1998, a full two-thirds of the population thought the government was functioning well, and a staggering 80 per cent was satisfied or very satisfied with the performance of the cabinet – percentages rivalling those of North Korea or Cuba. Suddenly, however, from 2002 onwards, public trust in government started to deteriorate. By 2004, only a third of the population still thought the government was functioning well and only 49 per cent was satisfied with the cabinet.

This abrupt and rapid decline in political trust was perceived with alarm. Many politicians, commentators and social scientists worried about the sudden loss of trust, as trust scores are often viewed as a litmus test of how well government is doing in the eyes of the citizens. Ever since Almond and Verba's (1963) *Civic Culture,* support for the democratic regime has been assumed to be an essential element in democratic politics. Dissatisfaction with the institutional arrangements is expected to affect their legitimacy and stability in the long run (Easton 1965). Disenchantment, distrust and cynicism—in one word dissatisfaction—are assumed to contribute to political alienation (Citrin 1974) and to undermine the very essence of democracy.

The Netherlands is not the only western democracy to experience such a sudden decline in political trust. Other western democracies, such as Belgium in the wake of the Dutroux affair and the White marches (see http://en.wikipedia.org/wiki/Marc_Dutroux) in the mid-1990s, or Germany after the fall of the wall and the reunification of West and East Germany, have also witnessed similar collapses in political trust within relatively short periods of time. Steep declines were also documented in Greece, Spain and Portugal in the 1990s (van de Walle *et al.* 2008: 54).

This chapter aims at shedding more light on the reasons for such extraordinary drops in trust levels by studying the case of the Netherlands. The Netherlands is an otherwise very stable and established democracy, and representative for similar Western European political systems. We will show that sudden declines are part of short-term trends in which trust orientations fluctuate. Abrupt losses of trust are short-run temporary dips, rather than part of long-run structural declines that are harmful to the working of government.

Looking at the current situation in the Netherlands, what do we see? Is political trust in the Netherlands withering away, or is it merely wavering? Has the abrupt loss in trust turned into a structural decline or was it a temporary dip? And how do the Dutch findings relate to international time series data on political trust in Europe? How is a sudden drop or decline to be explained? Building on the distinction between structural factors that explain long-term changes and shorter-term factors, we argue that structural changes in society, the media and government have created the conditions for an increased volatility in political trust. But first, we discuss various objects of political trust and how trust is measured.

What is political trust?

Although many theories assume that democracy cannot work without trust, there appears to be little consensus on how this should be defined and measured. Despite the important function that is attached to it in democratic politics, political trust remains a 'fuzzy' concept. It is one of those concepts that everybody has a sense of what it means, but of which no widely accepted definition has been given (Hardin 2000).

Trust in what?

It should be established that there are various *objects* of political trust. Should we see trust as generalised, as something not well specified (referring to a system or a principle)? Or must political trust necessarily refer to a particular person, such as a politician, the set of politicians, to an institution, such as the government, or an outcome, such as government policy?

For example, trust in *government,* where government is understood to refer to *public administration* or the *public sector*, should be distinguished from trust in the *cabinet* or the *national government*. The former – called *'overheid'* in Dutch – on the one hand, is the conglomerate of hundreds of public institutions, ranging from local councils, independent regulatory authorities and executive bodies, to government departments. The cabinet or the national government – *'regering'* in Dutch – on the other hand, is comprised of two or three coalition parties and a few dozen ministers and junior ministers. The perceptions citizens have of these two institutions need not coincide, or even be related – it is one thing to have little trust in the incumbent cabinet, but quite another to be dissatisfied with the performance of the public administration in general or with specific public services (van de Walle 2004).

Some surveys ask about trust in *parliament* or in *political parties*, which are very specific institutions within the political system. Others, such as the Dutch Parliamentary Election Studies (DPES) measure attitudes towards *politicians*, and in doing so, may or may not differentiate between members of parliament and members of the cabinet. Finally, there are surveys that focus more on a regime level, on trust in the *democracy*. The Commission's Eurobarometer, launched in the early 1970s, includes a question on the level of satisfaction with democracy – a question often drawn on as an indicator for measuring trust in government, although it is not clear whether this indicator measures support on a specific or on a regime level of the system (Canache *et al.* 2001; Karp and Bowler 2001; van de Walle *et al.* 2008).

In media reports about the decline of trust, these various institutions and actors are often lumped together. Low trust in the cabinet is sometimes equated with a decline of trust in government, in the sense of the whole public sector, or even with a decline in support for democracy. However, these are to be valued quite differently. Low trust figures for the cabinet can, in fact, be interpreted as a sign of a well-functioning democracy. They will be a matter of serious concern for the prime minister and his spin doctors, but need not disturb others beyond the inner circle of the current cabinet and the coalition members. However, low levels of satisfaction with democracy suggest a more systemic malaise and should be a major concern for all democratic-minded citizens. These differences in objects of trust are based on Easton's (1965) influential distinction between *diffuse support* (support for the system and the regime) and *specific support* (support for the incumbent authorities, i.e. the current political leaders and their policies). Easton believed that attitudes towards these objects have significantly different political consequences.[1]

Some trust measures have been faulted for their references to unclear objects (political leaders, institutions and regime) or performance (Citrin and Muste 1999; Levi and Stoker 2000; Cook and Gronke 2005). One of the problems is that, when asked in survey questions, these distinctions may have little meaning to many ordinary citizens, for whom politics is a remote world of little interest and who are not familiar with the subtle, but constitutionally very relevant distinctions between various political actors and institutions (Citrin and Muste 1999: 468). For example, less educated respondents in the Netherlands tend not to distinguish between Members of Parliament or the Cabinet.[2]

What is trust?

More complicated is the question of what the *meaning* is of 'trust' and how it can be measured. There are many competing and unclear definitions of political trust and there is little agreement on its precise meaning. Most researchers on trust have wrestled with this abundance of concepts and indicators (Citrin and Muste 1999; Levi and Stoker 2000). Much of the empirical work on political trust – usually based on survey results – does not proceed from any clear account of what is meant by political trust in the first place. 'Rather, trust is taken to be what is measured by one or more survey questions' (Nannestad 2008: 415).

Does political trust refer to the *faith* people have in their government (Citrin and Muste 1999)? Or does political trust mirror citizens' *evaluations* as to whether or not political authorities and institutions are performing in accordance with ex-

---

1. The conventional prediction is that a loss of support for the regime threatens its stability and diminishes the voluntary compliance of citizens with government policy, whereas the impact of support for authorities is confined to the domain of conventional electoral activity (Muller and Jukam 1977; Citrin and Muste 1999: 468).

2. Sociaal en Cultureel Planbureau, *Continu Onderzoek Burgerperspectieven*, Kwartaalbericht 2008/1: 25.

pectations held by the public (Miller and Listhaug 1999: 358; Hetherington 2005: 9)? Scholars like Uslaner (2002) see trust as norm-driven, as a moral worldview that develops during early socialisation. Trust is then deeply ingrained and difficult to change. Others, like Hardin (2000), depict trust as a rational (instrumental) concern, a set of interests existing between individuals that develop through life. Trust in this view is easily altered by new social or political conditions.

Empirical research on political trust relies for the most part on surveys. But few survey studies ask their respondents directly to indicate their levels of political trust. People are asked about their *confidence*, their *satisfaction*, their *opinions* and their *affective orientations* towards government or for an *instrumental evaluation* of these objects. This gap between the conceptual and the empirical realm makes it sometimes very difficult to theorise on the basis of these empirical results (Nannestad 2008). In the Netherlands, for example, the Social and Cultural Planning Office (SCP) asks respondents whether they think the government 'functions well' and whether they 'are satisfied' with the incumbent cabinet. In contrast, the Eurobarometer surveys explicitly ask respondents whether they 'tend to trust' specific institutions, such as the cabinet, parliament or political parties.

Political trust in the Netherlands: wavering or withering?

What is the state of play regarding political trust in the Low Countries? There seems to be a general belief that trust levels regarding all political institutions and actors are low and in a permanent state of decline (Hendriks 2006, 2009; Korsten and de Goede 2006). Media reports, invariably, are ominous. Many media reports tend to be biased, however – only downward fluctuations are reported, upward movements never make it to the headlines – or they are based on non-recurrent single measurements, markedly suggestive polls or selective reporting.

In order to gain more insight into questions of change in political trust, a time series analysis of longitudinal data is required. Decades of responses to the same survey questions are needed to provide a basis to assess variation across time. This is not easy, as not all studies always ask the same or similar (or equivalent) questions; or surveys have not included the same question over an extended period of time. Analysis of these trust trends over time is needed to answer the question of whether political trust is withering or merely wavering, but the choice of data is remarkably restricted (Hay 2007; Hetherington and Rudolph 2008; van de Walle *et al.* 2008). Using the sparse data available we will, nonetheless, attempt to trace the trends.

Every two years, usually in the fall, the Dutch Social and Cultural Planning Office (SCP) issues a major survey on social, political and cultural trends and attitudes in the Netherlands. The survey monitors, among other things, levels of satisfaction with the cabinet (*regering*) and the performance of the government (*overheid*). The results are provided in Figure 3.1. According to the data of the SCP, the evaluation of cabinet performance, and government in general, improved steadily in the 1990s. In 1998, 80 per cent of all respondents reported being satisfied or very satisfied with the cabinet and two-thirds of the respondents thought the

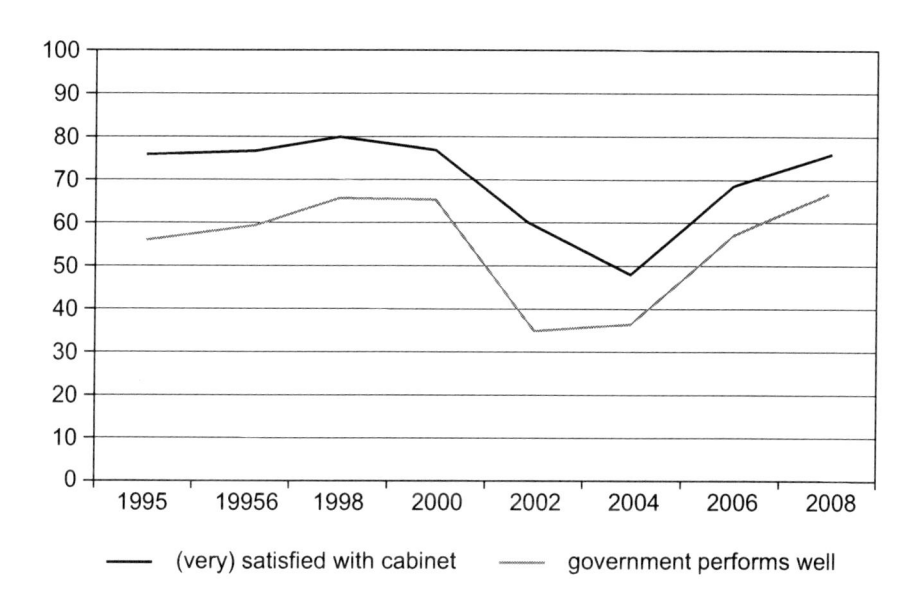

Figure 3.1: Satisfaction with cabinet and with government performance 1995–2008 (%)

Source: SCP 2009.

Dutch government was doing a good job. These numbers remained stable through the year 2000. However, by the end of 2002, the number of respondents who indicated that government was doing a good job had plummeted to less than a third of the population. This decline continued until 2004. Likewise, the number of respondents satisfied with the cabinet dropped to under 50 per cent in 2004. The swiftness and relentlessness with which public trust in government evaporated was especially striking. Yet in 2006, trust figures were on the rise again, as can be seen in Figure 3.1. According to the fall 2008 SCP survey, cabinet and government satisfaction ratings had returned to their 1995 levels.

These findings were corroborated by the *Belevingsmonitor Rijksoverheid*; a tri-monthly survey initiated in 2003 by the cabinet in response to the growing concern about the widely-publicised decreasing trust figures. This monitoring by the government clearly registered the ongoing decline in trust in the cabinet. At the time of the first survey, in early 2003, about half of the respondents still had trust in the cabinet. This soon fell to about a third, where it remained for several years.[3] In 2007, the cabinet, frustrated by its low marks, decided to discontinue the monitor. This proved to be premature as, by September 2006, the downward trend

---

3. The *Belevingsmonitor* figure does not exactly match the SCP figure – the SCP survey is conducted once every two years, whereas the monitor had four surveys each year – however, the trends are very comparable.

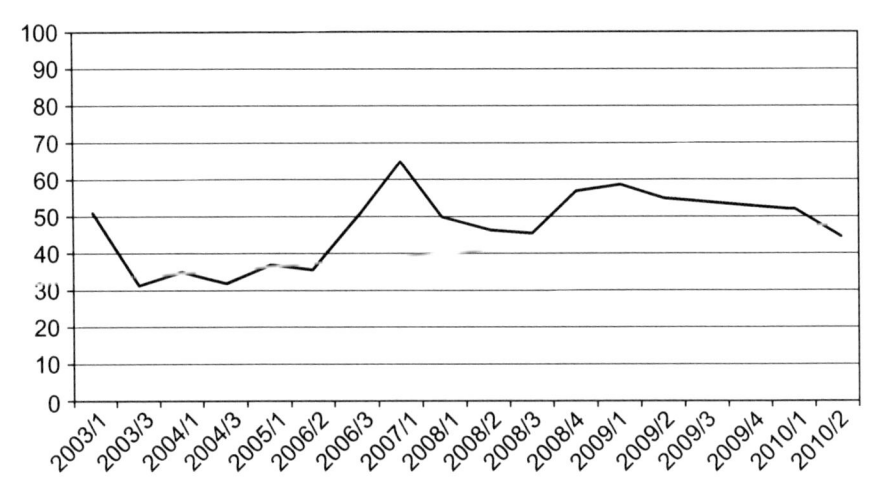

Figure 3.2: Trust in cabinet 2003–2010 (%)

Source: Belevingsmonitor Rijksoverheid and SCP, COB – from 2008/1.

had started to reverse as the monitor registered an upturn in trust in the cabinet. In March 2008, the SCP started its own quarterly survey, the *Continue Onderzoek Burgerperspectieven* (COB) as a successor to the *Belevingsmonitor*. The combined data from both surveys show how trust in the cabinet recovered after the steep decline at the beginning of the century (see Figure 3.2).

Another set of comparable, longitudinal data is provided by the Eurobarometer, which is conducted twice yearly in April and November. In most, but not all of these twice- yearly surveys, respondents are asked about their trust in a series of institutions.[4] The Eurobarometer data show a rather similar pattern of decline and recovery of trust in the major political institutions in the Netherlands, as can be seen from Figure 3.3.

Figure 3.3 shows how trust in cabinet ('national government') and parliament steeply declined, beginning in April 2002. Trust levels remained low throughout 2005. As with the other surveys, trust figures started to recover from early 2006. At the start of the new Balkenende-Bos cabinet, in April 2007, trust in the cabinet even peaked beyond the extraordinary high scores of the turn of the century. Trust figures then wavered again, as the financial crisis acutely manifested itself.

The Dutch Parliamentary Election Studies (DPES), conducted around each parliamentary election since 1977, measures the level of cynicism toward politicians and political parties. The Eurobarometer data show that political parties

---

4. The Eurobarometer's survey item is: 'I would like to ask you a question about how much trust you have in certain institutions. For each of the following institutions, please tell me if you tend to trust it or tend not to trust it.' We have listed the trust figures for the national parliament, the national government ('regering' in the Dutch survey), and the national political parties.

are trusted less than cabinet or parliament (see Figure 3.3). The DPES survey, in which respondents are asked whether they agree with a series of negative statements about politicians and political parties, allows us to investigate whether negative sentiment towards politics has grown (see Figure 3.4). Remarkably, no sharp increase in political cynicism can be discerned. At the elections of 2006, negative sentiment toward politicians and members of parliament was at roughly the same levels as in the 1970s and 1980s, or even lower. The only exception regarded the statement 'politicians promise more than they can deliver'. However, the number of respondents agreeing with this statement – arguably indicative of a politically mature attitude rather than one that is cynical – had already started to rise in the 1980s and 1990s.

Both the Eurobarometer and the DPES surveys also provide longitudinal data about attitudes towards democracy. Time series data indicating satisfaction with democracy in the Netherlands (drawn from the Eurobarometer) show similar patterns to those from the other institutions. Satisfaction with democracy reached an all time high of 90 per cent around the turn of the 2000. A steep decline followed

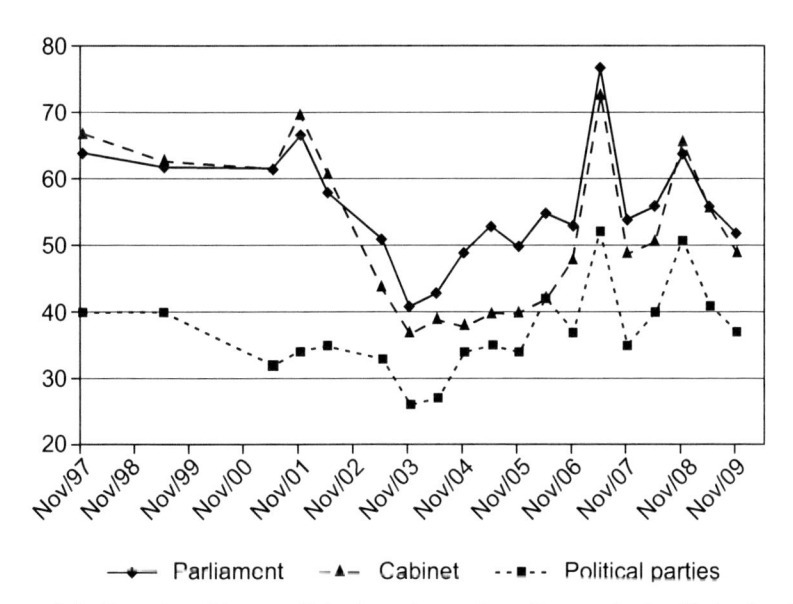

Figure 3.3: Trust in cabinet, political parties and parliament in the Netherlands 1997–2009

Source: Eurobarometer, April data are included. The item on trust in national institutions is not repeated in every single survey.

54 | political trust

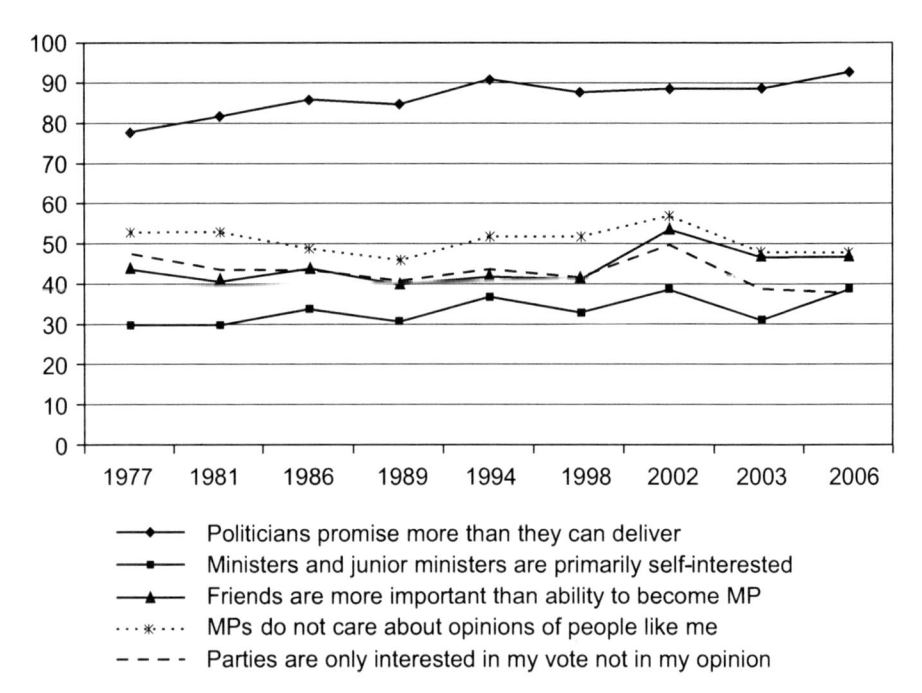

Figure 3.4: Agreement with negative statements about politicians and political parties in the period 1977–2006 (%)

Source: DPES 1977–2006.

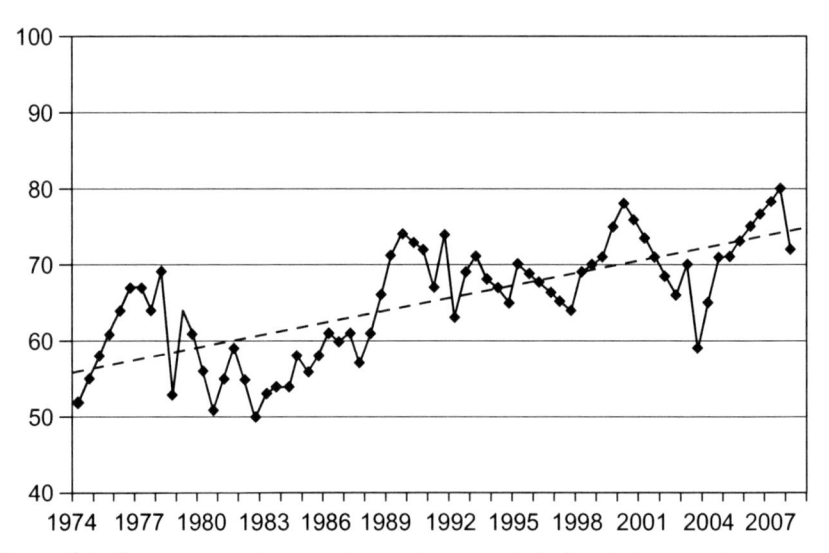

Figure 3.5: Percentage of respondents who are satisfied with the way democracy works in the Netherlands 1974–2009

Source: Eurobarometer

in the years 2002 and 2003, the lowest point of which, nonetheless, was still higher than the peaks of the 1980s. It was followed by a gradual recovery from 2004 onwards. In recent years, satisfaction with democracy has returned to the levels of the 1990s.[5] As can be observed from Figure 3.5, the overall trend tends to be positive. Over the past decades, an increasing number of respondents report satisfaction with the way democracy functions. On the basis of these longitudinal data, a number of observations can be made about the development of political trust in the Netherlands.

Trust is wavering but not withering

Despite the widely held view that trust in Dutch government and politics is in a long-term (and irreversible) decline, there is little actual evidence of this:

- After a strong dip at the start of the century, trust in the government had returned to the high levels of the 1990s by 2008. There is no evidence for a permanent decline.
- The strong dissatisfaction with the cabinet, that manifested itself between 2002 and 2004, was not structural. Satisfaction increased markedly in 2007, with levels overtaking even the high of the late 1990s. However, vigorous fluctuations are also seen.
- Trust in parliament follows a similar pattern – after a dip in 2003, this reverted to the level of the 1990s.
- Political parties tend to be trusted less than cabinet or parliament, but the fluctuations in trust levels tend to follow similar patterns.
- There are no indications that the cynicism about politicians has risen. Negative attitudes about politicians have remained stable in the past three decades.
- Satisfaction with democracy is very high. In 2008, around 80 per cent of the respondents were (very) satisfied with the way democracy functions in the Netherlands. Despite a strong dip around 2003, the long-term trend is positive.

Trust in Dutch political institutions is in flux, but not in decline.[6] The Netherlands is not exceptional in this respect. Trust levels have been moving both up and down since the mid-1970s in many other countries as well (Levi and Stoker 2000: 483; Hay 2007; van de Walle *et al.* 2008). In fact, most time series show that trust has been in flux since the early mid-1970s and early 1980s.

---

5. The DPES data show a similar pattern. Around the 1998 elections, 88 per cent of respondents were (very) satisfied with the way democracy functioned; in 2002 this was a mere 49 per cent and it rose to 71 per cent in 2003 and to 77 per cent with the 2006 elections.
6. Van der Brug and van Praag (2007) arrive at the same conclusion. Frank Hendriks (2006) considered the decline to be more structural in nature.

The Netherlands remains a high trust country

In the heat of the public debate, following the sharp decline of trust, it was suggested that the Netherlands has turned into a low trust country, on a par with countries like Belgium or France. There is no evidence to substantiate this view. Figure 3.6 compares the trust in cabinets in the Netherlands with that in those in the rest of the EU.

Figure 3.6 shows that, on average, all EU member states suffered from a decline in trust in their national government after the attacks of 11th September 2001 in the United States ('9/11') and recovered after 2006. However, although the dip was much deeper in the Netherlands, the trust figures in the Netherlands remained (far) above the EU average all throughout the dip.

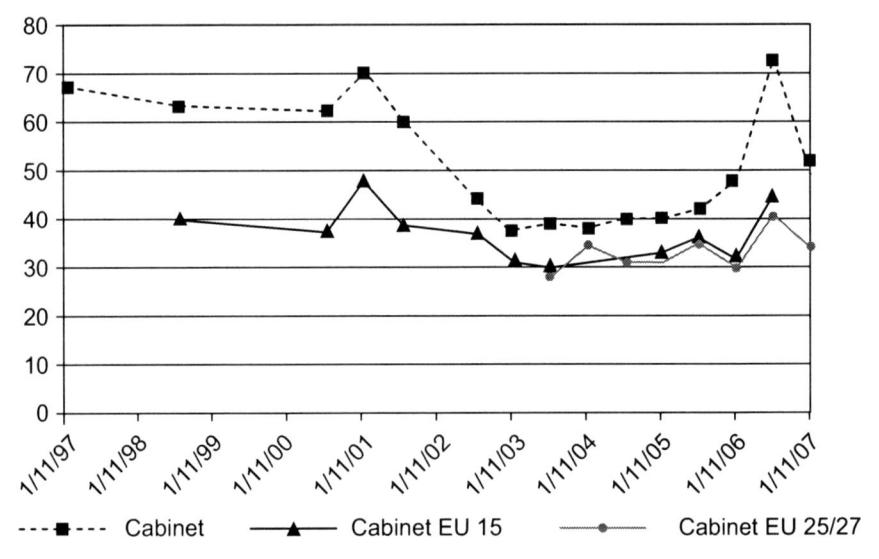

Figure 3.6: Trust in cabinets (national government) in the Netherlands compared with the other EU members 1997–2008

Source: Eurobarometer.

There are stark contrasts in levels of political trust among the EU member states. Salient results from the Eurobarometer are the persistently low satisfaction levels in Italy or Greece. The general trend in Denmark, Luxembourg, Ireland and the Netherlands, on the other hand, has been one of increasing levels of satisfaction with democracy, while other countries show dips and peaks, suggesting volatility (Norris 2009). Again, we see that the overall pattern in the EU is that of trendless fluctuations, rather than a steady erosion of trust (van de Walle *et al.* 2008; Norris 2009). There is no evidence that EU democracies have consistently experienced falling public satisfaction or that there are any steady trends across European democracies. Similar observations have been made about the United States (Levi and Stoker 2000; Hay 2007: 28; van de Walle *et al.* 2008).

Trust is generic and non-specific

Another observation is that the trust patterns analysed for various political institutions are remarkably alike, albeit at different levels. All political institutions in the Netherlands experienced an all-time high around the turn of 2000, a steep decline in 2002–2004 and a gradual, but volatile recovery from 2006 onwards. People seem to express a generic satisfaction or dissatisfaction with political institutions (Stimson 2004: 154). There is a very strong individual-level connection between how citizens evaluate the government or the performance of the cabinet and how they evaluate the parliament or the quality of democracy in the Netherlands, a finding that is demonstrated in comparable ways in other countries (Levi and Stoker 2000: 483; Cook and Gronke 2005). The rate and timing of the fluctuations of the different trust measures within a country are remarkably similar. These findings raise doubts about the possibility, theoretically or empirically, of distinguishing between different kinds of 'specific support'. People's trust in political institutions is of a general character: a high level of trust in one institution tends to extend to other institutions, as well (Christensen and Laegreid 2005).

This joint approval and disapproval of parliament/congress and government/cabinet indicates that the evaluations of legislative and executive branches are hard to pull apart and distinguish, because they are quite obviously measuring the same thing. As Stimson points out: 'What we are observing is generic approval and trust, a spirit that moves up and down over time and seems to respond to generalised satisfaction or dissatisfaction with the state of things' (Stimson 2004: 154).

Explaining the flux

How are we to understand the movements in political trust in the Netherlands, but also in other parts of the EU and elsewhere? Most common explanations on the decline in trust perceive this as *cross-national gradual erosion* of political support *over a relatively long term* within advanced industrial democracies (Norris 1999; Pharr and Putnam 2000; Dalton 2000; Dalton 2004: 81–3). Consequently, they tend to focus on long-term, often socio-demographic, explanatory variables, such as secularisation, generational replacement or the rise of post-materialism.

We have shown that trust in the Netherlands is in flux. Sudden dips – and consequent recoveries – in public trust cannot be explained by long-term demographic, social and political changes. To understand short-term fluctuations, we require an additional and more dynamic set of factors that is able to make sense of periods of increases and consequential decreases in political trust.

Fluctuations in trust can be understood as resulting from a combination of long-term changes and short-term performances. Building on the distinction between structural factors that explain long-term changes on the one hand, and shorter-term factors on the other, we argue that structural changes in society, the media and government, have created the conditions for political trust to become more volatile. The presence of specific short-term factors explains the dynamics in the movements of trust. Table 3.1 displays the factors that are relevant for understanding the fluctuations in political trust.

Table 3.1: Short- and long-term explanations for the flux in political trust

Structural changes that have made political trust more volatile:
– Changes in society and citizens
– Changes in government
– Changes in the media
Sources of short-term political trust fluctuations:
– Shifts in consumer confidence
– Shifts in political process
– (International) Crises

Long-term changes: conditions for volatility

One of the structural conditions that have made levels of trust in political institutions more unstable or variable is that citizens are better informed than in the past. Citizens know more about political leaders, what they do, and how they fail. People have become more attentive to public life and a growing body of evidence indicates that informed and interested people make decisions differently compared to those who are uninformed (Zaller 1992). Moreover, many citizens no longer associate themselves with political parties and are likely to change party allegiances from one election to another (Drummond 2006). Not only has voting behaviour become more volatile, public opinion, too, has become erratically moody.

Although there is a tendency in the literature to explain the changing trust levels by changes in what Hay (2007) has called *demand side factors* (rising expectations, more information, changed values), there are also a range of *supply-side factors* (changes in the 'substantive' content of the goods that governments and politics deliver to consumers/citizens) that have changed the relationship between government and citizens and can help to explain why trust has become more volatile.

Several governments have taken significant steps to respond to demands for better services, more responsive policy development and more accountable government structures. Reforms in government have created standards by which governments can be measured in terms of results and outcomes (Rosenvallon 2008). Also, at the political level, the idea has evolved that politicians can now be held accountable for their performance and for keeping their promises.

Globalisation and the explosion of the information age have dramatically changed the nature of governance around the world (Zussman 1997). The opening of national borders through globalisation has made it increasingly difficult for national governments to develop policies relating solely to the domestic market. Government's perceived ability – or inability – to respond effectively to persistent problems such as economic crises and climate change cause citizens to question government's ability to solve these problems effectively (Hay 2007). A trend towards more volatility in trust levels may well be a consequence of the newly emerging governance landscape.

Finally, *the role of the media* in the fickleness of political trust should not be underestimated. The media choose, select, and interpret what we see of our government and politicians. Live television has helped to turn a significant part of the political process into a public spectacle. The media approach is driven in large numbers by stories that portray conflict and controversy and journalists are often rewarded on the basis of these criteria (Zussman 1997: 250). These stories attract viewers, sell newspapers and impact heavily on the views of citizens, who follow the political process from a distance (Newton 2006).

In the age of TV and internet, political communication can become a critical part of trust building and trust loss. The rapid development of the internet has afforded governments and state-watch organisations the ability to provide more information on public services and to move their activities closer to citizens. Twitter, e-mail, internet, text messages, weblogs – these new information technologies have in fact contributed to many of the decentralising and democratising tendencies witnessed over the past few years. These media have opened up the access to information and made the way into traditionally closed government easier.

These structural changes may have created the conditions for rapid fluctuations in political trust to occur. We will discuss three short-term factors that help to explain the swift movements in public opinion.

Short-term performances: explaining the movements

Three sources appear to be important determinants for the fluctuations in political trust: consumer confidence, political processes and the upsurge of dramatic events or (international) crises. In the Netherlands, the temporal dip in political trust between 2002 and, approximately, 2006 calls for an explanation based on a combination of these three factors (Bovens and Wille 2008a, 2008b), which are also key in the EU and the US.

First and foremost, fluctuations in political trust over time are related strongly to movements in *consumer confidence* (van de Walle 2004; Tiemeijer 2006; van der Meer and Dekker 2009). For example, the rise and fall of support for the EU can be linked to the economy (Hix 2008). Hix calls this the 'fair-weather phenomenon' – citizens like government when the economy is booming and dislike government when the economy is declining – because they blame the government for the lack of success. A strong link between political trust and the economy also appears to exist in the US (Hetherington 2005; Hetherington and Rudolph 2008). Trust declined through the 1970s, a decade characterised by declining real income, high unemployment, and skyrocketing inflation. Trust then increased with the economic resurgence of the middle Reagan years, only to decline again in the early 1990s during a recession. During the long, uninterrupted economic recovery under Bill Clinton, trust in government rebounded, despite the scandals associated with the president.

Similarly, the rise and fall of trust in political institutions and democracy in the Netherlands is also strongly correlated to the patterns in citizen's perception of the state of the economy, as can be seen by comparing the patterns in reported satisfaction with democracy with the ups and downs in the reported levels of consumer confidence (see Figure 3.7).

These long-term trust figures display very similar fluctuations, with political trust following the pattern of economic trust with a delay of one or two years. The lowest levels of satisfaction with democracy were reported during the recession of the early 1980s, when consumer confidence was at its lowest in the past three decades. During the economic boom of the 1990s, satisfaction with democracy rose to an all-time high, but dropped abruptly after the internet bubble burst at the turn of 2000. When the economy recovered, from 2003 onwards, satisfaction rose steeply, until it dropped again after the financial crisis started to manifest itself from the fall of 2007 onwards.

Evidently, the bottom line is that when citizens are confident about their economic situation, their satisfaction with government increases. This also goes a long way towards explaining why all EU member states, on average, experienced similar patterns in decline and increase of trust in their national governments between 2001 and 2008 (see Figure 3.6). To a certain extent, they all suffered from an economic decline after the internet bubble evaporated at the turn of 2000. What remains to be explained is why the dip after 2001 was so much deeper in the Netherlands than elsewhere.

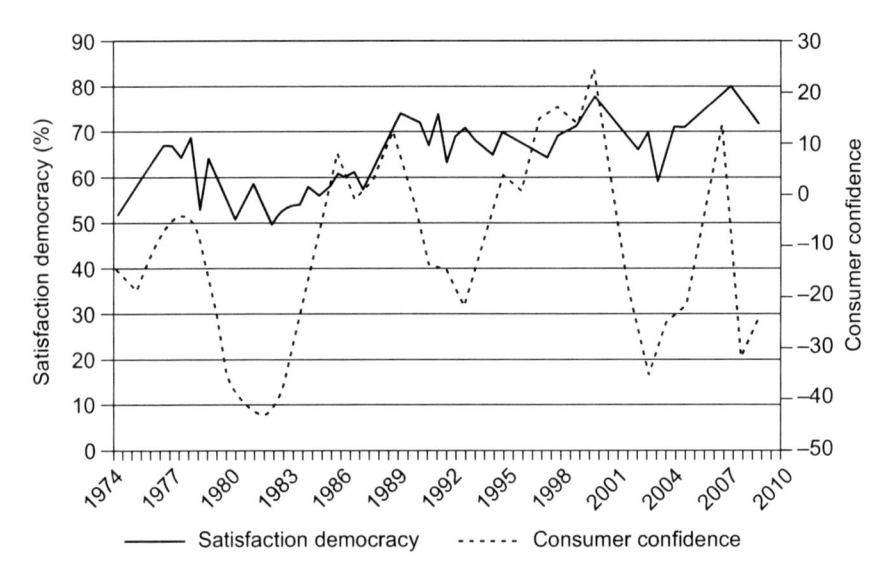

Figure 3.7: Satisfaction with the way democracy works in the Netherlands (%) and consumer confidence in the Netherlands 1974–2009

Source: Eurobarometer, CBS.

Another factor affecting the fluctuations in the trust-in-government levels is the perception of political processes and of political institutions. Citizens are often relatively satisfied with the performance of specific public services, yet express scepticism about the public sector when asked about its performance in general or in abstract terms (Bouckaert and van de Walle 2003). The opinion of citizens about government in general (i.e. public administration) tends to be determined by more general social or political sentiments (van de Walle 2004: 219–20). US citizens like democracy in theory, but are troubled by it in practice, disliking the sometimes bitter partisan disagreement inherent in the legislative process (Mutz and Reeves 2005). Congress is unpopular relative to the presidency and judiciary because its processes are so public (Hibbing and Theiss-Morse 1995). Congressional approval, a barometer of both performance- and process-related concerns, is a key determinant of political trust (Hetherington 1998).

The evaluation of political processes also determined popular support for the EU in the last decade. Citizens started to notice that the EU has become far more than simply an economic union (Hix 2008: 53–4); when EU meetings and decisions became more prominent on TV news and newspapers and politics in the EU became more publicly visible in the last decade, not surprisingly, then 'the anti-Europe bottle had been uncorked' (Franklin *et al.*1994).

In the Netherlands, public opinion on politics and the cabinet turned increasingly more negative in the fall of 2002. Dissatisfaction with the incumbent, short-lived, right-wing Balkenende cabinet and its policies partly explained why trust plummeted so steeply in the Netherlands, which served to fuel the Dutch dip (Bovens and Wille 2008b).

Finally, *(international) crises and dramatic events* are important for understanding the short-term dynamics of political trust. The emergence of (international) crises can affect trust in the short run. Sudden international crises, such as 9/11 or the banking crisis of October 2008, can rally the public around the flag and cause trust levels to *rise* temporarily (Hetherington and Rudolph 2008; Mueller 1970; Chanley 2002). 'During a crisis, people are more inclined to think collectively because only government can respond to the threat' (Hetherington and Rudolph 2008: 501). This explains the dramatic surge in trust in the fall of 2001 in the wake of 9/11 in the US and, to a lesser extent, in the Netherlands and the rest of the EU (see Figure 3.6).

Similarly, in November 2008, after Wouter Bos, the Dutch minister of Finance, bailed out a number of major Dutch banks and averted the collapse of the financial sector, trust in the Dutch cabinet showed a sudden peak, despite the declining confidence in the economy, as can be seen from Figure 3.3 and Figure 3.8. In the spring of 2009, the 'rally around the flag' was over, and political trust figures again followed the decline in consumer confidence.

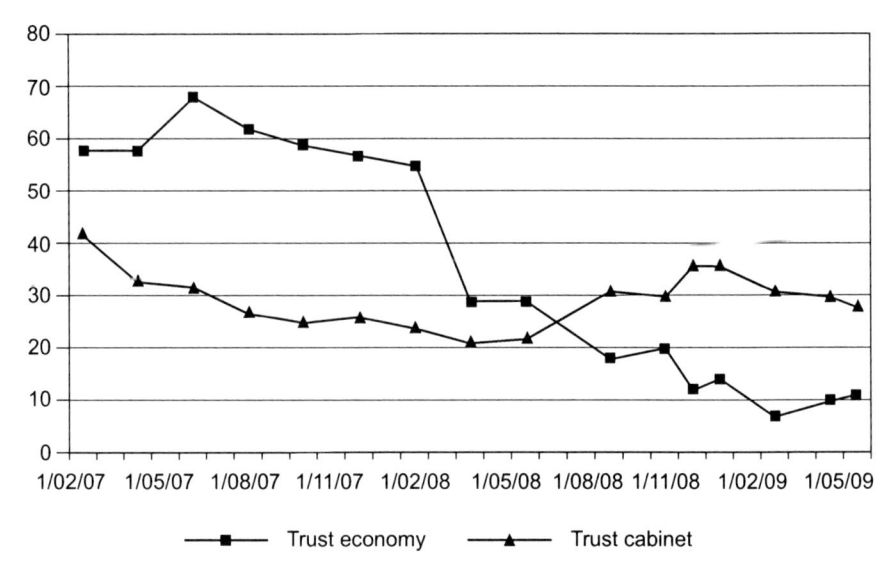

Figure 3.8: Confidence in the economy and trust in cabinet in the Netherlands February 2007–July 2009

Source: TNS NIPO/RTL Nieuws.

Dramatic events can also explain why trust *declines* spectacularly and suddenly. In the mid-1990s, in a period of economic austerity, trust in almost all political institutions in Belgium suddenly plummeted after the Dutroux affair and the subsequent White marches. Similarly, it can be argued that in the Netherlands, the assassination of the populist politician Fortuyn in May 2002 and the subsequent political turmoil can explain why trust levels decreased so sharply between late 2001 and late 2003, as compared to the rest of the EU.

The dynamics of trust: short-term fluctuations and long-term stability

In brief, political trust in the Netherlands has been wavering, but has not withered away. The trust figures have fluctuated for a number of political institutions, but there are no indications for a structural, long-term decline. Political opinion has become more volatile and this explains why political trust is in flux. The evolution of a more volatile form of trust is the result of a better educated, better informed cohort of politically-astute citizens that is more apt to use critical criteria when asked to evaluate government or political institutions. Citizens may well be more critical than they once were. But structural changes in the government (supply side) and the media have made it also likely that they have more to be critical about (Hay 2007: 49). The survey answers to the trust-in-government questions are above all affected by the assessment of contemporary political and economic circumstances (Cook and Gronke 2005: 799).

Political trust is generally perceived as the cement of democracy. The generally held view that the smooth functioning of political systems depends on trust has caused much concern about how much people trust government and why trust levels have dropped. But how worrisome are the current trends in government disenchantment and trust across a broad range of established democracies?

First, the *empirical evidence* supporting the idea that political trust and satisfaction with democracy has steadily eroded in liberal democracies is by no means clear-cut. Some of the claims that trust is now in decline and we are, therefore, worse off, are not supported by the data (Cook *et al.* 2005: 77; van de Walle *et al.* 2008).

Secondly, the role and function that is attached to political trust in the literature appears to be overrated. Political trust has been linked to a democratic culture since Almond and Verba's (1963) groundbreaking study *The Civic Culture*. But fifty years after this landmark, it is questionable whether high levels of trust in the national government are still indicative of a democratic culture. Polls in which trust in the cabinet or attitudes towards government are measured, are conducted on a weekly or sometimes even daily basis and have become a political factor. These polls are regarded more and more as sensitive barometers of public opinion that show the shift in opinions, not only in response to big and exciting events, but also in reaction to 'normal' politics (Stimson 2004: 21). Declining trust connotes a public that is not happy with the outcomes of government policy. Does this mean that a lack of trust, or fluctuating levels of trust, in government are bad for democracy?

Short-run fluctuations determine our day-to-day experiences, but the long-term trends are the ultimate determinants of the political conditions of democracies. As a result, short-run patterns of trust may vary considerably between years and these fluctuations describe the dynamics of trust; but to deduce a clear trend in the development of trust, we need a long-term perspective. If we perceive the short-term fluctuations in political trust as indicative for the political 'weather', the long-term trends in trust are those that determine the political climate. A change in the weather does not mean that we are experiencing a complete political 'climate change'. We may experience occasional spells of foul weather, but the climate, so far, has remained stable.

References

Almond, G. and Verba, S. (1963) *The Civic Culture: Political attitudes and democracy in five nations,* New Jersey: Princeton University Press.
Bovens, M. and Wille, A. (2008a) 'Politiek vertrouwen langs de meetlat', *Socialisme en Democratie,* 65(10): 32–43.
— (2008b) 'Deciphering the Dutch drop: Ten explanations for decreasing political trust in the Netherlands', *International Review of Administrative Sciences,* 74(2): 283–305.
Bouckaert, G. and van de Walle, S. (2003) 'Comparing measures of citizens trust and user satisfaction as indicators of "good governance": Difficulties in linking trust and satisfaction indicators', *International Review of Administrative Sciences,* 69(2): 329–43.
Canache, D., Mondak, J. and Seligson, M. (2001) 'Meaning and measurement in cross-national research on satisfaction with democracy', *Public Opinion Quarterly,* 65(4): 506–28.
Chanley, V. A. (2002) 'Trust in government in the aftermath of 9/11: Determinants and consequences', *Political Psychology,* 23(3): 469–83.
Christensen, T. and Laegreid, P. (2005) 'Trust in government: The relative importance of service satisfaction, political factors, and demography', *Public Performance & Management Review,* 28(4): 487–511.
Citrin, J. (1974) 'Comment: The political relevance of trust in government', *American Political Science Review,* 68(3): 973–88.
Citrin, J. and Muste, C. (1999) 'Trust in government', in J. Robinson, P. Shaver and L. Wrightsman (eds) *Measures of Political Attitudes,* 2, San Diego: Academic Press.
Cook, K. S., Hardin, R. and Levi, M. (2005) *Cooperation Without Trust?,* New York: Russell Sage Foundation.
Cook, T. and Gronke, P. (2005) 'The sceptical American: Revisiting the meanings of trust in government and confidence in institutions', *The Journal of Politics,* 67(3): 784–803.
Dalton, R. (2000) 'Value change and democracy', in S. J. Pharr and R. D. Putnam (eds) *Disaffected Democracies: What is troubling the trilateral countries?,* Princeton: Princeton University Press.
— (2004) *Democratic Challenges, Democratic Choices: The erosion of political support in advanced industrial democracies,* Oxford: Oxford University Press.
Drummond, A. J. (2006) 'Electoral volatility and party decline in Western democracies: 1970–1995', *Political Studies,* 54(3): 628–47.
Easton, D. (1965) *A System Analysis of Political Life,* New York: Wiley.
Franklin, M., Marsh, M. and McLaren, L. (1994) 'Uncorking the bottle: Popular opposition to European unification in the wake of Maastricht', *Journal of Common Market Studies,* 32(4): 455–72.
Hardin, R. (2000) 'The public trust', in S. J. Pharr and R. D. Putnam (eds) *Disaffected Democracies: What is troubling the trilateral countries?,*

Princeton: Princeton University Press.
Hay, C. (2007) *Why We Hate Politics*, Cambridge: Polity Press.
Hendriks, F. (2006) 'Waar kwam de argwaan vandaan?', *Bestuurskunde* 15(4): 65–77.
— (2009) 'Contextualizing the Dutch drop in political trust: Connecting underlying factors', International Review of Administrative Sciences, 75(3): 473–92.
Hetherington, M. J. (1998) 'The political relevance of political trust', *The American Political Science Review*, 92(4): 791–808.
— (2005) *Why Trust Matters: Declining political trust and the demise of American liberalism*, Princeton: Princeton University Press.
Hetherington, M. J. and Rudolph, T. J. (2008) 'Priming, performance, and the dynamics of political trust', *Journal of Politics*, 70(2): 498–512.
Hibbing, J. R. and Theiss-Morse, E. (1995) *Congress as Public Enemy*, Cambridge: Cambridge University Press.
Hix, S. (2008) *What's Wrong with the European Union and How to Fix It*, Cambridge: Polity Press.
Karp, J. and Bowler, S. (2001) 'Coalition government and satisfaction with democracy: An analysis of New Zealand's reaction to proportional representation', *European Journal of Political Research*, 40(5): 57–79.
Korsten, A. and de Goede, P. (eds) (2006) *Bouwen aan vertrouwen in het openbaar bestuur*, Den Haag: Elsevier.
Levi, M. and Stoker, L. (2000) 'Political trust and trustworthiness', *Annual Review of Political Science*, 3: 475–507.
Miller, W. E. and Listhaug, O. (1999) 'Political performance and institutional trust', in P. Norris (ed.) *Critical Citizens: Global support for democratic government*, Oxford: Oxford University Press.
Mueller, J. (1970) 'Presidential popularity from Truman to Johnson', *The American Political Science Review*, 64(1): 18–34.
Muller, E. and Jukam, T. (1977) 'Behavioral correlates of political support', *American Political Science Review*, 71(2): 1561–95.
Mutz, D. and Reeves, B. (2005) 'The new videomalaise: Effects of televised incivility on political trust', *American Political Science Review*, 99(1): 1–15.
Nannestad, P. (2008) 'What have we learned about generalized trust, if anything?', *Annual Review of Political Science*, 11: 413–36.
Newton, K. (2006) 'May the weak force be with you: The power of the mass media in modern politics', *European Journal of Political Research*, 45(2): 209–34.
Norris, P. (ed.) (1999) *Critical Citizens: Global support for democratic government*, Oxford: Oxford University Press.
— (2009) 'Trust in democracy', on Pippa Norris' Weblog. *The world of politics, politics of the world: Personal comments, rambles, and reflections.* Online. Available http://pippanorris.typepad.com/pippa_norris_weblog/2009/01/trust-in-democr.html (accessed 8 February 2009).

Pharr, S. J. and Putnam, R. D. (eds) (2000) *Disaffected Democracies: What's troubling the trilateral countries?*, Princeton: Princeton University Press.

Rosenvallon, P. (2008) *Counter-Democracy: Politics in an age of distrust*, Cambridge: Cambridge University Press.

Sociaal en Cultureel Planbureau (2002) *Sociaal en cultureel rapport 2002: De kwaliteit van de quartaire sector*, Den Haag: SCP.

— (2005) *De sociale staat van Nederland 2005*, Den Haag: SCP.

— (2007) *De sociale staat van Nederland 2007*, Den Haag: SCP.

— (2008) *Continu Onderzoek Burgerperspectieven, Kwartaalbericht 2008/1*, Den Haag: SCP.

Stimson, J. (2004) *Tides of Consent: How public opinion shapes American politics*, Cambridge: Cambridge University Press.

Tiemeijer, W. (2006) *Het geheim van de burger: Over staat en opinieonderzoek*, dissertatie, University of Tilburg.

Uslaner, E. M. (2002) *The Moral Foundations of Trust*, Cambridge: Cambridge University Press.

van de Walle, S. (2004) *Perceptions of Administrative Performance: The key to trust in governments?* PhD dissertation, K. U. Leuven.

van de Walle, S., van Roosbroek, S. and Bouckaert, G. (2008) 'Trust in the public sector: Is there any evidence for a long-term decline?', *International Review of Administrative Sciences*, 74(1): 47–64.

van der Brug, W. and van Praag, P. (2007) 'Erosion of support for political institutions in the Netherlands: Structural or temporarily? A research note', *Acta Politica*, 42(4): 443–58.

van der Meer, T. and Dekker, P. (2009) *Trustworthy states, trusting citizens? A multilevel study into objective and subjective determinants of political trust*, Paper presented at the 5th ECPR General Conference, Potsdam, 10–12 September 2009.

Zaller, J. R. (1992) *The Nature and Origins of Mass Opinion*, Cambridge: University Press.

Zussman, D. (1997) 'Do citizens trust their government?', *Canadian Public Administration*, 40(2): 234–54.

chapter four | winners, losers and three types of trust

Sonja Zmerli and Ken Newton

Introduction: Three types of trust and their interrelationship

According to Confucius, the three essential components of successful government are trust, food and weapons. Many since him have repeated, in one way or another, the general theme that trust is a crucial basis of social integration and of stable government. From Thomas Hobbes and John Locke, Adam Smith and de Tocqueville, John Stuart Mill, Georg Simmel, Ferdinand Toennies, Emile Durkheim and Max Weber, and all the way to current theories of social capital and civil society, writers have emphasised that modern social, economic and political relations are ultimately dependent upon the willingness of citizens to take the risk of trusting others (Misztal 1996). Modern research shows that trust is closely associated with things as diverse as economic growth, health, happiness, life satisfaction, longevity, educational achievement, democratic stability, and willingness to pay taxes. Trust seems to be, as Uslaner observes, 'the chicken soup of social life' (Uslaner 2002).

And yet trust is also a puzzle (Nannestad 2008). Its origins and nature remain controversial and unclear in spite of two decades of cross-national empirical research. For some time, the social capital claim that social and political trust are intimately related was questioned by surveys, which found little or no evidence of an association (Kaase 1999: 13; Orren 1997; Rothstein 2002: 320–1; Delhey and Newton 2003; Mishler and Rose 2005), although there was a difference between individual level and aggregate cross-national comparisons in this respect (Newton and Norris 2000). And while there was considerable survey evidence about general social trust and confidence in political and public institutions, there was little interest in particular social trust beyond Edward Banfield's case study of Montegrano (Banfield 1958) and some social psychology research on in-groups and out-groups. It was assumed by some that 'particular' (also known as 'thick' or 'specific' trust) was incompatible with 'general' ('thin') social trust, but there was little evidence and it did not produce robust results.

Recent survey research has started to clarify some of these issues. There is now good evidence that social and political trust are indeed associated at the individual level, as social capital theory predicts, when the two are measured carefully with batteries of questions (Glanville and Paxton 2007; Freitag 2003a, 2003b; Bäck and Kestilä 2009; Jagodzinski and Manabe 2004: 85–7; Zmerli and Newton 2008; Freitag and Bühlmann 2009). There is also strong evidence in the most recent World Values Survey of 2005–7 that particular trust is not only compatible with general social trust, but forms a platform or framework within which it can be developed (Newton and Zmerli 2011). Moreover, the World Values data has clear evidence that all three forms of trust – particular social trust, general social trust and political trust – are positively correlated with each other.

The associations between the three forms of trust are not simple, however. Most of those who express forms of general trust are also trusting of 'particular others', but the reverse is not necessarily true. An overwhelming majority of the population of democratic societies (more than 90 per cent) professes one form or another of particular trust, but less than half of them extend this to 'generalised others'. While almost all of those with high general trust scores are also high on particular trust, fewer than half (45 per cent) of those claiming strong particular trust also claim strong general trust. In other words, particular social trust seems to be a necessary but not sufficient cause of general social trust. Similarly, almost all of those with high political trust have high particular social trust, and a large proportion of the politically trusting are also generally trusting, but the reverse is not true. Most of those with strong particular trust do not have strong political trust. It seems from these results that particular social trust may form the foundation on which general trust can be developed, and that these two, in their turn, may form the basis on which political trust can be built.

These recent findings raise further questions for individual trust research: what sorts of people are able to combine particular social trust in those they know personally, or who are like them, with a more general form of trust in unknown or different others? In what sorts of circumstances are they likely to do this? What sorts of people are able to combine different forms of social trust with political trust and under what sorts of circumstances are they likely to do this? In this chapter, we try to provide some answers to these questions by examining the social, economic and political characteristics of different trust groups in the population of twenty-two democratic nations.

First, we outline the 'winner hypothesis', which suggests that the trusting in society are those who are successful in social, economic and political life. Secondly, we outline our data and methods, paying particular attention to the advantages of Mokken scale analysis, an analytical procedure enabling us to detect the latent features of twelve questionnaire items on trust and to identify hierarchical structures in response sets. We will examine how the three types of trust cluster in order to show that the same patterns repeat themselves both across nations and within them. The aim here is to show that our results are generally applicable to a wide range of democratic countries and to different social groups within them. Thirdly, we analyse the social, economic and political characteristics of different trust groups in society in order to establish the correlates of trust, with the aim of uncovering the individual origins of different forms of trust or, at least, the variables most closely associated with them. If the three forms of trust are indeed closely and positively associated, then we expect them to be correlated with a broadly similar set of independent variables. This will provide clues about why certain types of individuals combine different forms of trust and others do not. Finally, we discuss the broader implications of our findings for social integration and stability and for democratic development.

The winner hypothesis

In this chapter we examine three kinds of trust, two social and one political:

1. 'Particular' social trust (sometimes known as 'thick' or 'specific' trust) involves family and friends, neighbours and work colleagues because they are known to us personally. Some extend particular trust to unknown others who are like us in ethnic origin, socio-economic status, religion, language or culture (Uslaner 2000–1: 573; 2008: 102). In either case, particular trust is extended to those we know or are like us.
2. 'General' social trust, in contrast, is placed in unknown others, including those who are of a different ethnic origin, religion, class, language or culture. It is general in that it is not limited to a comparative narrow social circle.
3. 'Political' trust is either trust in particular politicians or trust in the main institutions of government and public life (the cabinet, parliament, police, legal system, the military, civil service, and political parties).

Why do some limit their trust to those they know personally or to those who are like them in terms of social and economic background, while others have a wider radius of trust that includes people of different religions and nationalities, people they do not know personally, and people who are not like them socially? And why do some people manage to combine different forms of social trust with political trust, while others do not?

There are some suggestions in the trust literature that help to answer these questions, as follows:

- It seems that those with the highest socio-economic status and incomes are the most trusting in society (Alesina and La Ferrara 2002; Newton and Delhey 2005), perhaps because the affluent can better afford to take the risks of trust compared with the poor, who can ill afford to lose money or property. Perhaps, as the 'rainmaker hypothesis' suggests (Newton and Norris 2000; Putnam *et al.* 2000: 26; van der Meer 2003) the better-off are more trusting because they are typically surrounded by trustworthy people who are, themselves, trusting.
- The most highly educated in society are generally the most trusting (Paxton 2007; Putnam 2000; Uslaner 2002: 1). This may be because the educated are better able to generalise and abstract their experience with known and similar others to unknown and dissimilar others, but it may also be that the better educated are usually of higher income, class, status, which, in their turn, are associated with trust.
- For the same sorts of reasons, unemployment is often associated with low trust (Brehm and Rahn 1997).
- So also is membership of minority groups that suffer from discrimination (Hero 2003; Patterson 1999: 190–1).

- Trust is usually associated with higher levels of subjective satisfaction, happiness, and health (Pelligra 2006; Kawachi *et al.* 1997; Inglehart 1999).
- From Tocqueville to modern theories of social capital, voluntary associations are seen as the great 'free schools' of civic education and reciprocity, teaching their members and especially their activists to co-operate and trust others (Putnam 1993: 171–6, 2000).
- Post-materialists are likely to claim comparatively high levels of trust because, being more affluent and less constrained by material concerns, they are able to focus more clearly on social values such as trust, co-operation, and respect for others irrespective of class, religion, nationality and ethnicity (Inglehart 1999; Inglehart and Welzel 2005).
- Trusting people tend to be optimists (Uslaner 2002), perhaps because life has given them plenty to be optimistic about.
- While political trust is often associated with the social and economic variables listed above, it is also associated with its own set of political variables, especially identification with the party in government and with political interest and knowledge (Newton 2001a).
- Trust in people may also be associated with the left–right scale insofar as leftist values are said to be based on a belief in the goodness of human nature, social equality and on the ability of individuals to co-operate in their common interest, while the ideologies of the political right are more likely to emphasise rational self-interest and competition rather than co-operation as the main motivating force behind human behaviour (Sullivan and Transue 1999; Bobbio 1997).

There may be a further link between social trust and political trust insofar as trust in the police and the courts is closely correlated with general social trust, probably because the law enforcement system is the social institution that is mainly responsible for maintaining the trustworthy behaviour of populations (Rothstein 1998; Rothstein and Stolle 2003). The better the system works, the more trustworthy citizens are and the more trust people are likely to express in each other.

The results of empirical research suggesting these correlates of trust tend to be fragmented, inconclusive, and patchy. They are rarely robust over time or across countries, and no single variable emerges as a consistently powerful predictor of trust. Nevertheless, the fragments seem to form a more general pattern in which social trust is most frequently expressed by the winners in society – those in dominant or majority groups, people of high class, status, income and education, the happy and satisfied, and individuals who benefit from better health and post-materialist security.

One might expect that those who have been treated kindly by life have a more trusting outlook, but apart from that there seem to be four general reasons why winners are trusting. These are, broadly, psychological, rational, sociological and institutional in nature.

Psychological: those that are trusting are optimistic and co-operative with a benevolent view of humanity. Rosenberg called the battery of questionnaire items he devised to measure trust and distrust 'the misanthropy scale' (Rosenberg 1956, 1957) and later work by Uslaner (Uslaner 1999: 138, 2002: 79–86; 2000–1: 571) argues that trust requires an optimistic view of life. The winners in society have much to be optimistic about. The losers have more to be cynical, pessimistic and distrusting about.

Rational: it is rational for winners to be trusting. It is often remarked that trust entails risk because the trusting put themselves at the mercy of the trustworthiness of others, who might betray the confidence placed in them. Winners in society may risk a lot in absolute terms if they lose their fortune, but they usually risk relatively less than losers. They can better afford to take risks and chances.

Sociological: winners in society may be trusting because they live their lives in a trustworthy environment. It is the underclass of slum dwellers, flophouse residents and street people who experience most of the crime, family problems, ill health, violence, drug addiction and discrimination in society. Those in penthouses and the green and pleasant suburbs are likely to meet with more courtesy, kindness, patience, helpfulness and understanding. If questionnaire items measuring general trust ('Generally speaking, would you say that most people can be trusted or that you can't be too careful in dealing with people?') are less about the psychological propensities of individuals and more about how they judge the trustworthiness of the society they live in, then winners may express greater trust simply because they live in more trustworthy environments.

Institutional: winners in society have more reason to place their trust in the institutions of society, especially in those that help them succeed and those that maintain law and order, protect property, and restrain citizens who might otherwise behave in an untrustworthy manner. Winners are better able to make their own use of social institutions because their money, status, power, education, life experience and social networks help them understand how organisations work, get them better access to people who matter, provide them with resources to defend their interests, and to plan strategies to get results.

Political trust also seems to be a characteristic of winners. It is most frequently expressed by those who win socially and also by those who win politically in that they identify with the party or parties in government. As a result they are more likely to trust both the particular government in power (the home team effect) and the system of government that produces it (Anderson and LoTempio 2002; Anderson *et al.* 2005). A variation on this theme is that political distrust (and possibly social distrust as well) is most frequently found among those with radical political views who form small minorities, possibly with paranoid tendencies. Their radical views consign them to the political fringe that rarely wins an election or a political struggle, and their lack of political success confirms their distrust of the political system (McClosky and Chong 1985). Political trust is also associated with political knowledge, interest and engagement and these are, in turn, associated with education, income, socio-economic status and life satisfaction.

In brief, the winner hypothesis suggests that the trusting in society are generally those who have come out on top in social, economic and political life. That is to say, particular social trust, general social trust and political trust is likely to be most expressed by the winners in society compared with the losers in society. Judging from recent work on the three kinds of trust (Newton and Zmerli 2011), the second hypothesis is that particular social trust is causally prior to general social trust, and that both particular and general social trust are causally prior to political trust.

Data and methods

Unlike any previous cross-national survey known to us, the latest World Values study of 2005–7 asks a set of six questions about social trust:

> I'd like to ask you how much you trust people from various groups. Could you tell me for each whether you trust people from this group completely, somewhat, not very much or not at all –
>
> Your family
> Your neighbourhood
> People you know personally
> People you meet for the first time
> People of another religion
> People of another nationality

The first three deal with forms of particular trust involving known others with whom respondents have close ties (family and those they know personally) or who live in their neighbourhood. The last three questions cover general trust in people who either are not known personally or who are not members of the same social group.

On the face of it, these six forms can also be distributed along a single radius of trust from the most particular to the most general. Trust in the family is the narrowest and most particular, followed by people known personally, and then by others in the neighbourhood. People of other religions and nationalities are more general, although the assumption is that something (perhaps quite a lot) may be known about them. People met for the first time, about whom nothing may be known, lie at the most general point on the radius and entail the highest degree of risk. In addition, the 2005–7 World Values survey also asks the standard, tried and tested trust question: 'Generally speaking, would you say that most people can be trusted or that you can't be too careful in dealing with people?' Previous work (Delhey *et al.* forthcoming; Newton and Zmerli, 2011) has established that the three general trust questions form a single scale that correlates strongly with the standard general trust question, but that the three item scales of social trust are probably a better measure.

The World Values survey asks the same questions about political trust in a set of six political and governmental institutions, as follows:

> I am going to name a number of organisations. For each one, could you tell me

how much confidence you have in them: is it a great deal of confidence, quite a lot of confidence, not very much confidence or none at all?

The organisations named are parliament, the government, political parties, the courts, the civil service, and the police. Altogether, therefore, we have three types of particular trust, three types of general trust and six measures of political trust – twelve measures of trust altogether.

Since this study is concerned with social and political trust, it selects from the World Values survey of 2005–7 a set of countries with the highest democratic scores in the Polity IV project. There is little sense in analysing survey responses to questions about political trust in non-democratic countries, where, apart from anything else, the absence of freedom of speech makes it difficult to give honest answers. What, for example, can we make of the finding that of seventy-seven nations covered in the World Values survey of 2000, trust in parliament is highest in Vietnam, China, Bangladesh, Tanzania, Uganda and Pakistan with scores of 76 to 98 per cent, compared with Ireland, Australia, the UK, Germany, Belgium, and USA, with scores of 31 to 38 per cent (Newton 2007: 347)?

Combining Polity IV democracy scores of 9 and 10 and the World Values data on trust produces a list of twenty-two democratic countries distributed across Europe, Asia, Africa, Oceania, and North and South America (see Appendix 1). Sampling and fieldwork methods in the World Values surveys of 2005–7 varied, but included face-to-face interviews and mailed questionnaires.[1] In the twenty-two selected democracies, 29,163 respondents participated in the survey. In this study, we wish to generalise as broadly as possible about the populations of modern democratic states and so, rather than conducting a country-by-country analysis, we pool the individual level data for the twenty-two nations in order to examine cross-national patterns of modern democracies.

To look for transnational patterns among the populations of democratic nations is not to deny national differences of significance and importance. It is simply to search for common patterns among individual citizens, irrespective of national variations. Our previous work (Newton and Zmerli 2011) has shown that there are indeed national differences as well as strong similarities among individuals with respect to social trust and political trust. This chapter is an attempt to push individual level analysis a step further in order to explore how and why different subgroups in society express different types of trust.

Mokken scale analysis

The first task is to establish whether there is an underlying, latent pattern to responses to the six social trust questions, or whether there are different and distinct forms of trust. To put it another way, do different forms of social trust lie on the same radius from particular to general or are they distinctive and unrelated? Mokken analysis is a scaling technique for dichotomous and polytomous items

---

1. See WVS 2005-7 codebook for further details.

that is similar to Gutmann scaling. Both techniques test for the existence of underlying, latent dimensions in a set of measures, but whereas Mokken scaling has a probabilistic basis, Gutmann scaling is deterministic. Mokken scales are also hierarchical in the sense that items in the scale can be ordered in terms of their positions in the hierarchy so that higher items will include lower items in such a way as to form a set of nested variables. This is a particularly useful method of scaling because it ranks items from the most to the least common and thereby allows us to explore which variables may be causally prior to others. In Mokken scale analysis, reproducibility is measured by Loevinger's coefficient Hi for each item i, and H for the entire scale. The calculation of Hi and H compares the probability of errors in ranking with the probability of such a ranking occurring among unrelated items. Hi and H values range from 0 to 1. H-scores of 0.3 to 0.39 indicate weak scales, scores of 0.4 to 0.49 are medium strength, and scores of 0.5 and more are strong. We select 0.4 as the cut-off point, H scores of less than 0.4 being rejected as too weak for our purposes (van Schuur 2003).

Results

Table 4.1 shows how the twelve forms of social and political trust are distributed in society. Uslaner (1999: 123) is right in claiming that everyone must trust someone and for most people this is trust in the family, which is virtually universal among the 22,770 individuals in the twenty-two democratic nations.[2] This means that the most particular form of trust that lies at the centre of the particular-general radius is also the most widespread. Other forms of social trust are then less widespread as they move out on the trust radius from people known personally and neighbours to people of different religions and nationality, and finally to those met for the first time. This means that the more specific the form of social trust, the more widespread it is likely to be, and vice versa, the more general it is, the less widespread it is likely to be. The logic of political trust is not the same but there is a difference between the civil and non-partisan institutions of police, courts and civil service, which are the most common forms of political trust, and the political ones of government, parliament and parties which are the least common.

To see if these twelve trust items scale, a Mokken analysis was run on the pooled individual data for all the selected twenty-two countries. As the results in Table 4.2 show these twelve trust items most usually produce two strong trust scales, one for social trust and the other for political trust, with H scores of 0.55 and 0.60 respectively. This is strong support for the conclusion that social and political trust represent separate dimensions of trust. There is one major exception to this general rule. Family trust does not reach the Hi = 0.3 level of significance necessary for Mokken scaling, so it is automatically dropped from all the calculations. This is because family trust is virtually universal (98 per cent) and cannot be used to measure a latent scale.

---

2. The case number is based on valid and weighted data.

Table 4.1: Distribution of social and political trust (in %)

	in %	N
Family members	97.5	22,770
People known personally	83.8	22,553
Neighbours	71.9	22,166
Other religion	53.1	20,602
Other nationality	50.2	20,206
People met for the first time	30.9	21,863
Police	63.2	22,497
Courts	50.9	22,126
Civil Service	40.3	21,569
Government	38.5	22,170
Parliament	34.0	21,924
Political parties	20.6	22,000

Notes: The newly-released WVS integrated data set presents equilibrated weights for the 2005 survey in which N = 1,000 or 1,500. All tables in this paper are based on equilibrated data in which N = 1,000. The percentages are based on respondents who score 3 or 4 on the trust rating scale.

Table 4.2: Mokken scale analysis, twelve trust items, pooled data (Hi and H scale coefficients)

	Social trust scale	Political trust scale	Mean	Mean
Family	0.25*	–	3.79	–
People known	0.50	–	3.07	–
Neighbours	0.47	–	2.83	–
Other religion	0.60	–	2.45	–
Other nationality	0.60	–	2.39	–
Unknown people	0.56	–	2.06	–
Police	–	0.53	–	2.66
Courts	–	0.60	–	2.50
Government	–	0.61	–	2.32
Civil service	–	0.57	–	2.31
Parliament	–	0.65	–	2.24
Political parties	–	0.62	–	2.00
H scale coefficient	0.55	0.60	–	–

Notes: * Hi for 'trust in family members' is too low and is, therefore, excluded from the social trust scale.

More important, the other five social trust measures are organised in hierarchical order from particular to general with trust in known others at the core. Trust in neighbours, in people of another religion, of another nationality and in people one meets for the first time are progressively less widely distributed in the general population and hence come lower down the hierarchical ordering. All six political trust items meet Mokken scaling requirements and all are, therefore, included in the analysis. The ordering of the items shows that trust in the police and courts are fundamental to the scale, followed, in order, by trust in government, the civil service, national parliament and political parties.

To check these results and to be sure that we have not forced questionnaire responses into a false pattern by pooling 22,000 individuals in twenty-two countries, the same Mokken scaling procedure was carried out on each country separately and also on sub-samples of the twenty-two-nation pooled data according to a set of thirteen objective and subjective independent variables that have often been found to be associated with trust.[3] For reasons of space, the figures are not presented here, but the analysis most generally produced the same two social and political trust scales found in the pooled data set of individuals. In a few cases, Mokken scaling uncovers a single social and political trust scale, but this occurs relatively rarely, and in no case does it produce more than two scales. Consequently, our results apply to the populations of all twenty-two countries and to subsets of the populations of every one of them.

Three conclusions follow from these findings:

1. The evidence clearly shows that social and political trust represent two distinct dimensions.
2. Particular and general social trust fall on a single continuum. They are not opposed or contradictory, and, moreover, their hierarchical ordering shows that general social trust most usually emerges only where there is particular trust; the former is a foundation for the latter.
3. Trust in family members is so widely spread throughout society that it is dropped from Mokken procedures because it does not meet their scaling criteria. Consequently, we concentrate on the remaining five particular and general social trust items, dropping family trust from the analysis that follows. Nevertheless, it is important to note that family trust is virtually universal in modern society and forms the basic framework or foundation for all other forms of social trust.

---

3. These are life satisfaction, education, class, income, employment status, voluntary association activity, gender, age, city size, materialism-postmaterialism, satisfaction with household income, happiness and church attendance.

From Particular to General Social Trust

Since particular and general social trust can be placed on a single continuum and are parts of a single syndrome of latent social trust variables, the question arises of how and why some people extend their particular trust to a more general level.

Table 4.3 suggests that the winner hypothesis is generally supported by the evidence. The table is built around a social trust count variable with a range of 0 to 5. Excluding trust in the family, it counts the number of times that respondents express trust or complete trust in each of the other five forms of social trust, and correlates their scores with the set of social, economic and political characteristics. High social trust is positively associated with feelings of happiness and life satisfaction, civic engagement, subjective health and social class, satisfaction with the financial situation of the household, educational attainment and income, and with post-materialism. Social trust is also positively correlated with political trust – easily the largest correlations in the column – and with interest in politics, which confirms previous results.

The winner hypothesis is also confirmed by the figures for political trust in Table 4.3. This is measured on a 0 to 6 scale covering all items of trust in civic and political institutions. Like social trust, political trust is positively associated with happiness and life satisfaction, civic engagement, subjective health and social class, education and income, and with satisfaction with the financial situation of the household. However, there is no significant correlation between postmaterialism and political trust. As we have now come to expect, it is also associated with general and particular social trust, as well as with interest in politics.

In almost all cases both social and political trust are usually associated with 'winner' characteristics, but before drawing this conclusion we can test the hypothesis in a different way that draws on a distinction between three types of trust and three types of trusters. The three types of trust are particular and general social trust and political trust. The three types of trusters are based on an empirical analysis of the main ways in which individuals combine different types of trust. Drawing on the results of Mokken scaling, it is possible to isolate three types of social trusters in the pooled individual data. The first type trusts only their family or (in the case of a tiny minority of thirty-one individuals or 0.1 per cent of the sample) nobody at all, and are called 'distrusters'. Distrusters make up only 9 per cent of the total sample and are of interest mainly as an extreme case of low trust rather than for their numbers. The second type consists of those who trust only the people they know, or their neighbours, and they are called 'particular trusters'. They make up one-third (32 per cent) of the pooled populations of the twenty-two democracies. The third type trusts people of another nationality or religion, or those they meet for the first time and are called 'general trusters' (58 per cent).[4]

---

4. Eagle-eyed readers may note an apparent discrepancy between the figures in Table 4.1 showing that particular trusters outnumber general trusters, and figures here showing the reverse. The explanation is that Table 4.1 shows the distribution of social trust while these figures here refer to the distribution of the types of trusters.

Table 4.3: Nonparametric correlations (Kendall's tau b) between social trust (count variable 0–5), political trust (count variable 0–6) and socio-economic and attitudinal items

	Social trust scale	Political trust scale
Sex	-.010	-.002
Age	.073***	.044***
Highest educational level attained	.126***	.060***
Feeling of happiness	.149***	.127***
Subjective state of health	.128***	.119***
Life satisfaction	.107***	.113***
Satisfaction with the financial situation of household	.122***	.135***
Subjective social class	.144***	.121***
Income	.106***	.097***
Political trust index	.249***	–
Left–right placement	-.030***	.033***
Interest in politics	.167***	.160***
Particular trust count variable (0–2)	–	.230***
General trust count variable (0–3)	–	.234***
Membership of voluntary associations	.151***	.113***
Inglehart index	.106***	.008

Notes: *** p< 0.001

Although the three types of trusters are not only the empirical types found in democratic nations, they do constitute the main types and they account for a large percentage of the total population. Table 4.4 shows that social distrusters are most generally on the loser end of social, economic and political life, while general trusters are most generally found among the winners. As hypothesised, the measures of winning in society correlate negatively and significantly with distrust and particular trust, but positively and significantly with general trust.

Finally, we are concerned with a more systematic and multivariate analysis of the interrelationship between social and political trust and its correlates. Our strategy mainly builds on previous multilevel analysis evidence which unambiguously shows that particular, general and political trust are strongly and positively related with each other, and that contextual factors affect general and political trust more than particular social trust (Newton and Zmerli 2011). A likely explanation is that particular trust is based on first-hand experiences with family, friends and neighbours, while political trust and general trust in (relatively) unknown others is more strongly influenced by the environment of trustworthiness and the institutions that preserve it. The positive impact of both types of social trust on political trust is also in line with the Mokken scaling evidence since the latter reveals a single continuum running from the particular to the general. However, these findings are not sufficiently informative as to the relevance of different types of trusters. Are exclusively particular trusters inclined to trust politically as much as general trusters, or do they restrict their willingness to trust to the narrow, private sphere of people they know personally?

Table 4.4: Nonparametric correlations (Kendall's tau b) between three types of trusters (0–1) and socio-economic and attitudinal items

	Distrusters	Particular trusters	General trusters
Sex	.009	−.006	−.002
Age	−.038***	−.030***	.050***
Highest educational level attained	−.090***	−.090***	.138***
Feeling of happiness	−.118***	−.070***	.141***
Subjective state of health	−.107***	−.053***	.117***
Life satisfaction	.075***	−.048***	.092***
Satisfaction with the financial situation of household	−.080***	−.055***	.104***
Subjective social class	−.098***	−.064***	.124****
Income	−.093***	−.046***	.095***
Left–right placement	.029***	.000	−.018**
Interest in politics	−.114***	−.079***	.148***
Political trust index	−.189***	−.098***	.211***
Membership of voluntary associations	−.096***	−.113***	.166***
Inglehart index	−.064***	−.072***	.108***

Notes: ** p< 0.05, *** p< 0.001

We follow up these questions by running linear and logistic regression analysis. An index of political trust is used as dependent variable in the linear regression model, but in contrast to our previous analysis of types of social trust in Table 4.4, we use count variables of particular and of general trust as predictors of political trust in Table 4.5. In addition, we avoid multicolinearity among the winner and loser indicators by building two 'winner in life' indices, the first combining happiness, health and life satisfaction (attitudes towards life) and the second combining education and income (socio-economic resources – see Appendix 2). As control variables in these regressions, we use gender, age, voluntary association activity, political interest and church attendance.

The results in Table 4.5 show that political trust is significantly and positively associated with both the winner indices as well as political interest, life satisfaction, materialist values and voluntary association membership and regular church attendance. However, the coefficients for particular and general social trust are the strongest in the regression, showing once again the strong three-cornered association between the types of trust.

Table 4.5: Linear regression, political trust index with particular and general social trust (count variables) as predictors

	b	Std. error	Beta
Constant	1.29	.03	–
Sex	.02	.01	.02*
Age	.00	.00	.01
Attitudes towards life index	.07	.01	.09***
Socio-economic resources index	.02	.01	.02**
Particular trust (count variable 0–2)	.15	.01	.16***
General trust (count variable 0–3)	.08	.00	.16***
Membership of voluntary associations	.04	.01	.06***
Political interest	.09	.01	.14***
Inglehart index	-.05	.00	-.08***
Church attendance	.02	.00	.05***
Adjusted R² in %		14.1	
N		18,743	

Notes: * $p < 0.05$, ** $p < 0.01$, *** $p < 0.001$

However, this picture changes when we replace the count variables of particular and general social trust by our three trust types (see Table 4.6). In this second linear regression model, the group of general trusters serves as our reference category and distrusters and particular trusters are included as predictors. As the results show, both trust types strongly and *negatively* affect political trust compared to general trusters. It seems that only where particular trust combines with general trust can we expect positive correlates with political trust.

We now reverse our dependent and independent variables by inspecting the impact of political trust on the two types of social trust. For this analysis we use our index of political trust as an independent variable alongside the same predictors used in Tables 4.5 and 4.6. To extend the winner hypothesis a little further, we also include employment status, using the full and part-time employed as the reference category and the unemployed and other employment status groups as predictors. Table 4.7 presents the findings for particular trusters. As the rather weak Nagelkerke's R^2 suggests, we must be careful not to overestimate the results even though they are consistent with our previous results. Most notably, being politically trustful significantly *decreases* the odds of being an exclusively particular truster. The same is true for voluntary activity, which reduces the likelihood of trusting only one's personal social network. The other predictors are also consistent with the results presented in Table 4.4. Particular trusters are more likely to be found among men, materialists, the young, and those dissatisfied with their life, and among those with fewer socio-economic resources and low political interest. Attending mass regularly, however, increases the liklihood of belonging to this limited trust type.

Table 4.6: Linear regression, political trust index with three types of trusters as predictors

	b	Std. error	Beta
Constant	1.65	.03	–
Sex	.02	.01	.02*
Age	.00	.00	.03***
Attitudes towards life index	.08	.01	.11***
Socio-economic resources index	.02	.01	.02**
Distrusters[a]	-.45	.02	-.20***
Particular trusters	-.19	.01	-.14***
Membership of voluntary associations	.04	.01	.06***
Political interest	.10	.01	.15***
Inglehart index	-.05	.00	-.08***
Church attendance	.01	.00	.05***
Adjusted R^2 in %		12.1	
N		18,724	

Notes: [a] reference category general trusters. * $p < 0.05$, ** $p < 0.01$, *** $p < 0.001$

The results for general trusters in Table 4.7 are the mirror image of those for particular trusters. In their case, Nagelkerke's R^2 indicates a better goodness of fit and all but two variables improve the chances of being a general truster. High political trust and civic engagement stand out in this regard, but being on the sunny side of life also encourages general trust, as does being a woman, interest in politics, and postmaterialism. The self-employed, housewives and regular churchgoers are less likely to trust in general.

Finally, we extend the analysis to recent suggestions and evidence suggesting that the police and the justice system are particularly important promoters of general social trust (Rothstein 1998; Rothstein and Stolle 2003) because they are the primary public institutions responsible for maintaining the trustworthiness of their populations (Newton 2001b: 234). For this purpose, we construct two indices of political trust instead of one and use them as predictors in the same logistic regression models. The first index measures trust in the police and courts, and the second deals with trust in parliament, government, civil service and political parties. The figures in Table 4.8 confirm the positive importance of public institutions for general social trust, suggesting an important top-down influence on levels of social trust, but they do not suggest that the police and the courts are particularly significant – civil and political institutions play an equally significant role in this respect.

Table 4.7: Logistic regressions, particular trusters and general trusters

	Particular trusters			General trusters		
	b	Std. error	Exp(B)	b	Std. error	Exp(B)
Constant	1.49	.12	4.46***	-3.49	.13	.03***
Sex	-.08	.04	.93*	.14	.03	1.15***
Age	-.01	.00	.99***	.01	.00	1.01***
Attitudes towards life index	-.07	.02	.96***	.22	.02	1.25***
Socio-economic resources index	-.12	.02	.89***	.14	.02	1.15***
Membership of voluntary associations	-.21	.02	.81***	.28	.02	1.33***
Political trust index	-.34	.03	.71***	.67	.03	1.96***
Political interest	-.06	.02	.95**	.11	.02	1.12***
Inglehart index	-.13	.02	.88***	.15	.02	1.12***
Church attendance	.02	.01	1.02**	-.07	.01	.94***
Unemployed[a]	.00	.07	1.00	.09	.07	1.09
Self employed	-.11	.06	.89	-.12	.06	.88*
Pensioner	-.03	.06	.97	.04	.06	1.04
Housewife	.06	.06	1.06	-.40	.06	.67***
Student	.00	.07	1.00	.08	.07	1.08
Other	-.23	.12	.80	.31	.12	1.36*
Nagelkerke's R^2 in %		5.1			14.8	
N		23,107			22,908	

Notes: [a] reference category fully or part-time employed. * $p < 0.05$, ** $p < 0.01$, *** $p < 0.001$

Table 4.8: Logistic regressions, particular trusters and general trusters with two types of political trust as predictors

	Particular trusters			General trusters		
	b	Std. error	Exp(B)	b	Std. error	Exp(B)
Constant	1.42	.12	4.13***	-3.41	.12	.03***
Sex	-.09	.04	.92*	.14	.04	1.15***
Age	-.01	.00	.99***	.01	.00	1.01***
Attitudes towards life index	-.07	.02	.93***	.22	.02	1.24***
Socio-economic resources index	-.12	.02	.88***	.14	.02	1.15***
Membership of voluntary associations	-.21	.02	.81***	.29	.02	1.33***
Trust in civil institutions	-.05	.03	.96	.29	.03	1.34***
Trust in political institutions	-.27	.03	.77***	.33	.03	1.39***
Political interest	-.05	.02	.95**	.12	.02	1.12***
Inglehart index	-.12	.02	.88***	.15	.02	1.16***
Church attendance	.03	.01	1.03**	-.06	.01	.94***
Unemployed[a]	.00	.07	1.00	.09	.07	1.09
Self-employed	-.09	.06	.91	-.14	.06	.87*
Pensioner	-.03	.06	.97	.04	.06	1.04
Housewife	.08	.06	1.08	-.41	.06	.67***
Student	.01	.07	1.01	.08	.07	1.08
Other	-.22	.12	.80	.30	.12	1.35*
Nagelkerke's R^2 in %		5.0			14.3	
N		22,880			22,696	

Notes. [a] reference category fully or part-time employed. * $p < 0.05$, ** $p < 0.01$, *** $p < 0.001$

Conclusion

In recent years, two puzzles about trust have been solved. First, there is now good evidence that general social trust and political trust are closely and positively associated at both the aggregate cross-national and at the individual level: those that are socially trusting are, indeed, also politically trusting. Secondly, fresh evidence about particular social trust shows that it is not incompatible with general social trust, and, moreover, that particular social trust seems to be a foundation for the development of general social trust. Consequently, there is not only a close and positive association between particular and general social trust, but also between these two and political trust.

However, the associations are not simple and direct, but asymmetrical and complex. An overwhelming majority of the population of democratic societies claim high particular trust and virtually all of those who are high on general social trust are also high on particular social trust, but the reverse is not true. Only slightly more than half of particular trusters are also general trusters. There is a similarly uneven and partial overlap between social and political trust; virtually all political trusters are high on particular and general social trust, but only a minority of those high on particular and general social trust are also politically trusting. It would seem that particular trust is the foundation on which general social trust and political trust are based, but building on the foundations does not inevitably or even generally occur. Particular trust is a necessary but not sufficient cause of general trust; and both particular and general trust are a necessary but not sufficient cause of political trust. This raises the more general question of what sorts of people in what sorts of circumstances express trust in other people and in political institutions, and why?

The main hypothesis developed in this chapter is that the winners in society are likely to be trusting for a set of reasons concerning their psychological make-up, their trustworthy social environment, the risks they face, and their relationship with the main social and political institutions of society. By 'winners' we mean those with money, socio-economic status and education, those who are happy and satisfied with their life and claim to be in good health, and those who are on the winning side of party competition for political power or who view the political system as giving them a chance of being on the winning side. This chapter tests the winner hypothesis against survey data for some 22,000 individual citizens in twenty-two democratic countries covered by the World Values survey of 2005–7.

Perhaps the first thing to note is that there are strong international patterns of social trust among the citizens in these countries. This is not to deny that there are national variations that may well be both interesting and important, but the pooled individual data for all twenty-two nations also shows that different kinds of trust are combined in broadly similar ways in all the populations. Mokken scale analysis clearly demonstrates that trust forms two hierarchical scales, one social and one political, in the pooled populations of all these countries, in each country separately and in a large number of sub-groups within them. The main purpose of this chapter is to concentrate on trying to explain these common cross-national patterns among individual citizens, rather than focussing on national variations.

The winner hypothesis is consistently supported by the evidence. All three types of trust – particular and general social trust and political trust – are closely associated with variables measuring different aspects of winning and losing. And all of the three main types of trusters in society – distrusters, particular trusters and general trusters – are similarly closely associated with winning and losing variables. Trust of different kinds is most strongly found among the rich, happy, satisfied, healthy, educated, and high socio-economic status groups in society. We cannot show that political trust is characteristic of the political winners in each national system because party ID and the winning parties cannot be matched in the WV survey, but it is clear that political trust levels are also highest among the social and economic winners in society.

We should be careful not to over-interpret these results. With 22,000 observations even small coefficients are statistically significant, but the explained variance in our regression models is usually quite small, as it usually is with individual level data. It is clear that winning and losing is part of the explanation of trust, but by no means the only explanation. Nevertheless, the evidence suggests some more general conclusions:

1. All the correlation and regression analysis in this chapter shows either that the three different forms of trust are positively and significantly associated with each other (see Tables 4.2 to 4.5) or that political trust is most usually found among individuals who combine particular and general social trust (see Tables 4.6 and 4.7). This, in turn, confirms the main claim of the social capital theory that social and political trust are interdependent.

2. The results (see Table 4.8) also support the idea that trust in institutions matters for trust in individuals. This is further evidence that trust can be generated by top-down processes in which institutions reinforce trustworthy behaviour. It also suggests that the origins of the rainmaker effect may lie in institutions that reinforce trustworthiness, which, in turn, helps to create a culture of trust.

3. The results presented here help to integrate the findings of individual level and cross-national comparative work insofar as both now show that trust levels of countries and of individuals alike are associated with the winning characteristics of wealth and its associated variables. It is beginning to look as though there is much more unity and convergence in trust studies than appeared to be the case a decade or so ago. It does not mean that we should now start looking for a 'theory of everything' to do with trust, but it does show that trust is less of a puzzle than it seemed.

These findings, in turn, open up a set of related questions about the connections between different forms of trust and the structural characteristics of modern societies, most notably their wealth, income equality, democratic performance, the public services they provide, the quality of their political and civil institutions, and the heterogeneous nature of their populations. These characteristics are often linked together. Wealthy societies are generally democratic and egalitarian, they often have good public services and high quality civil and political institutions and they are usually the countries with comparatively high particular and general social trust scores and the highest levels of trust in political institutions. It is too early to draw clear and firm conclusions, but it is beginning to look as if there is a syndrome of social and political characteristics associated with social and political trust, and as if these may be similar at both country and individual levels.

The finding that the three types of trust are normally positively associated also has theoretical and practical implications for the heterogeneous nature of modern societies. Some studies find that societies that are mixed in terms of ethnic, religious, linguistic, national and cultural sub-groups suffer from low levels of trust, but others argue that this is not always or necessarily the case (Glaeser *et al.* 2000; Helliwell 1996; Knack and Keefer 1997; Putnam 2007; Alesina and La Ferarra 2000; Hero 1998, 2003; Costa and Kahn 2003). If, as some argue, in-group trust is incompatible with out-group trust and that there is a natural tendency to trust the people we know and are like us (Alesina and La Ferarra 2000; Banfield 1958; Uslaner 2000-1: 573), then heterogeneous societies are always likely to suffer from low trust. But if, as we find, in-group trust is not incompatible with out-group trust (see also Bahry *et al.* 2005), then heterogeneity and low trust are not necessarily connected. They may be in some circumstances, but it is not an automatic association. And if, as we find, large proportions of the democratic populations of the world are able to combine high levels of particular trust with high levels of general and political trust, there is no reason in principle why heterogeneous societies should not maintain comparatively high levels of particular, general and political trust. It may depend on the extent to which the immigrants and the minorities in society are also losers. We can speculate that the larger the loser percentage in the population, the lower trust levels are likely to be. But it is not only about immigrants, it is also about the growing share of those who perceive themselves as the losers in society that can threaten social cohesion. Support for this suggestion is found in the research showing that the greater the income inequality of a country the lower its general trust level is likely to be (Delhey and Newton 2005).

The practical lesson that might be drawn from our results concerns the difference between multicultural integration and monocultural assimilation of immigrants as government policies designed to handle the problems of heterogeneity (see Heath 1997; also Kymlicka 1998; Gutmann 1994: 5; Rudolph 2006; Harles 1997). Broadly speaking, assimilation is based on the idea that social stability and peace requires a common culture, a consensus about values and identification with a single nation state. Immigrant groups are expected to change in order to fit into their host societies. Integration is a broader, looser, and more inclusive form of citizenship that permits greater cultural diversity with multiple identities and loyalties. The idea that particular and general social trust can reinforce each other fits well with theories of integration because strong ethnic and national identities are not incompatible with strong general trust in others in the wider society.

Finally, in showing how political trust is associated with different forms of social trust and their social and economic correlates, the results of this analysis help to further explicate the social basis of politics. It demonstrates the close connection between social conditions and politics – and at the same time, suggests ways in which political institutions may affect the nature of interpersonal relations and political attitudes.

Appendix 1

Countries included in the analyses, WVS 2005–7, unweighted N

	Unweighted N
Australia	1,404
Bulgaria	990
Chile	998
Cyprus	1,049
Finland	1,014
France	1,001
Germany	2,061
Great Britain	1,037
India	1,807
Italy	1,007
Mexico	1,550
The Netherlands	1,047
New Zealand	924
Peru	1,490
Poland	983
Romania	1,755
Slovenia	1,013
South Africa	2,974
Spain	1,189
Sweden	1,003
Switzerland	1,240
USA	1,211

Appendix 2

Variables	Coding
Particular social trust: Trust in family, neighbourhood, people one knows personally	1 do not trust at all to 4 trust completely
General social trust: Trust in people one meets for the first time, other religion, other nationality	1 do not trust at all to 4 trust completely
Particular social trust count variable: count 3 and 4 of trust in people known personally and neighbours	0 to 2
General social trust count variable: count 3 and 4 of trust in people of another religion, another nationality or people one meets for the first time	0 to 3
Distruster: exclusively trust in family members (3 or 4) or no trust at all	0 no, 1 yes
Particular truster: exclusively trust in people known personally or in neighbours (3 or 4; trust in family members not excluded)	0 no, 1 yes
General truster: trust in people of another religion or another nationality or people one meets for the first time (3 or 4; trust in family members, people known personally and neighbours not excluded)	0 no, 1 yes
Trust in institutions: Parliament, government, political parties, courts, civil service, police	1 do not trust at all to 4 trust completely
Political trust index: responses to all political trust items are summed and divided by the number of valid responses	1 do not trust at all to 4 trust completely
Interest in politics	1 no interest to 4 very interested
Sex	0 male, 1 female
Age in years	
Highest educational level	1 no formal education to 9 university-level
Membership of ten different types of voluntary associations	0 no member, 1 passive member, 2 active member
Feeling of happiness	1 not at all happy to 4 very happy

Variables	Coding
Subjective state of health	1 poor to 4 very good
Life satisfaction	1 dissatisfied to 10 satisfied
Subjective social class	1 lower, 2 working, 3 lower middle, 4 upper middle, 5 upper class
Employment status: full time employee or part time employee (combined), self employed, retired/pensioned, housewife or not otherwise employed, student, unemployed, other	0 no, 1 yes, separately for each employment status category
Scale of incomes	1 lower step to 10 upper step
Satisfaction with financial situation of the household	1 dissatisfied to 10 satisfied
Left–right placement	1 left to 10 right
Church attendance	1 never to 7 more than once a week
Inglehart index: First and second preference with regard to maintaining order in the nation, give people more say, fighting rising prices, protecting freedom of speech	1 materialist to 4 postmaterialist
Attitudes towards life index: count variable happiness (3 or 4), state of health (3 or 4), life satisfaction (6 to 10)	0 to 3
Socio-economic resources index: count variable education (7 to 9), scale of incomes (6 to 10)	0 to 2

References

Alesina, A. and La Ferrara, E. (2002) 'Who trusts others?', *Journal of Public Economics*, 85(2): 207–34.

— (2000) 'Participation in heterogeneous communities', *The Quarterly Journal of Economics*, 115(3): 847–904.

Anderson, C. J. and LoTempio, A. J. (2002) 'Winning, losing and political trust in America', *British Journal of Political Science*, 32(2): 335–51.

Anderson, C. J., Blais, A., Bowler, S., Donovan T. and Listhaug, O. (2005) *Losers' Consent: Elections and Democratic Legitimacy*, Oxford: Oxford University Press.

Bäck, M. and Kestilä, E. (2009) 'Social capital and political trust in Finland: An individual-level assessment', *Scandinavian Political Studies*, 32(2): 171–94.

Bahry, D., Kosolapov, M., Kozyreva, P. and Wilson, R. K. (2005) 'Ethnicity and trust: Evidence from Russia', *American Political Science Review*, 99(4): 521–32.

Banfield, E. (1958) *The Moral Basis of a Backward Society*, New York: The Free Press.

Bobbio, N. (1997) *Left and Right: The significance of a political distinction* (translated by Allan Cameron), Chicago: University of Chicago Press.

Brehm, J. and Rahn, W. (1997) 'Individual-level evidence for the causes and consequences of social capital', *American Journal of Political Science*, 41(3): 999–1023.

Costa, D. L. and Kahn, M. E. (2003) 'Civic engagement and community heterogeneity: An economist's perspective', *Perspectives on Politics*, 1(1): 103–11.

Delhey, J. and Newton, K. (2003) 'Who trusts? *'The origins of social trust in seven societies'*, *European Societies*, 5(2): 93–137.

Delhey, J., Newton, K. and Welzel, C. (forthcoming), 'How general is trust in 'most people'? Solving the radius of trust problem', *American Sociological Review*.

Freitag, M. (2003a) 'Social capital in (dis)similar democracies: The development of generalized trust in Japan and Switzerland', *Comparative Political Studies*, 36(8): 936–66.

— (2003b) 'Beyond Tocqueville: The origins of social capital in Switzerland', *European Sociological Review*, 19(2): 217–32.

Freitag, M. and Bühlmann, M. (2009) 'Crafting trust: The role of political institutions in a comparative perspective', *Comparative Political Studies*, 42(12): 1537–66.

Glaeser, E. L., Laibson, D. I., Scheinkman, J. A. and Soutter, C. L. (2000) 'Measuring trust', *The Quarterly Journal of Economics*, 115(3): 811–46.

Glanville J. L. and Paxton, P. (2007) 'How do we learn trust? A confirmatory tetrad analysis of the sources of generalized trust', *Social Psychology Quarterly*, 70(3): 230–42.

Gutmann, A. (1994) 'Introduction', in A. Gutmann (ed.) *Multiculturalism: Examining the politics of recognition*, Princeton: Princeton University Press.

Harles, J. C. (1997) 'Integration before assimilation: Immigration, multiculturalism and the Canadian polity', *Canadian Journal of Political Science*, 30(4): 711–36.

Heath, J. (1997) 'Immigration, multiculturalism and the social contract', *Canadian Journal of Law and Jurisprudence*, 10(2): 343–61.

Helliwell. J. F. (1996) 'Do borders matter for social capital? Economic growth and civil culture in US states and Canadian provinces', *NBER Working Paper No. Q5863*.

Hero, R. E. (1998) *Faces of Inequality: Social diversity in American politics*, Oxford: Oxford University Press.

— (2003) 'Social capital and racial inequality in America': *Perspectives on Politics*, 1(1): 113–22.

Inglehart, R. (1999) 'Trust, well-being and democracy', in M. E. Warren (ed.) *Democracy and Trust*, Cambridge: Cambridge University Press.

Inglehart, R. and Welzel, C. (2005) *Modernization, Cultural Change and Democracy: The human development sequence*, New York: Cambridge University Press.

Jagodzinski W. and Manabe, K. (2004) 'How to measure interpersonal trust? A comparison of two different measures', *ZA-Information*, No. 55: 85–97.

Kaase, M. (1999) 'Interpersonal trust, political trust and non-institutionalised political participation in Western Europe', *West European Politics*, 22(3): 1–23.

Kawachi, I., Kennedy, B. P., Lochner, K. and Prothrow-Stith, D. (1997) 'Social capital, income inequality, and mortality', *American Journal of Public Health*, 87(9): 1491–98.

Knack, S. and Keefer, P. (1997) 'Does social capital have an economic payoff? A cross-country investigation', *Quarterly Journal of Economics*, 65(4): 1251–88.

Kymlicka, W. (1998) *Finding our Way: Rethinking ethnocultural relations in Canada*, Toronto: Oxford University Press.

McClosky, H. and Chong, D. (1985) 'Similarities and differences between left-wing and right-wing radicals', *British Journal of Political Science*, 15(3): 329–63.

Mishler, W. and Rose, R. (2005) 'What are the consequences of political trust: A test of cultural and institutional theories in Russia', *Comparative Political Studies*, 38(9): 1050–78.

Misztal, B., (1996) *Trust in Modern Societies*, Oxford: Blackwell.

Nannestad, P. (2008) 'What have we learned about generalized trust if anything?', *Annual Review of Political Science*, 11: 413–36.

Newton, K. (2001a) 'Social trust and political disaffection: Social capital and democracy', *Paper prepared for the EURESCO Conference on Social Capital: Interdisciplinary Perspectives*, Exeter, 15–20 September 2001.

— (2001b) 'Social capital and democracy', in B. Edwards, M. J. Foley and M. Diani (eds) *Beyond Tocqueville: Civil Society and the Social Capital Debate in Comparative Perspective*, Hanover, NH: Tufts University Press.

— (2007) 'Social and political trust', in R. J. Dalton and H.-D. Klingemann (eds) *The Oxford Handbook of Political Behaviour*, Oxford: Oxford University Press.

Newton, K. and Delhey, J. (2005) 'Predicting cross-national levels of social trust: Global pattern or Nordic exceptionalism?', *European Sociological Review*, 21(4): 311–27.

Newton, K. and Norris, P. (2000) 'Confidence in public institutions: Faith, culture, or performance?', S. J. Pharr and R. D. Putnam (eds) *Disaffected Democracies: What's troubling the trilateral countries?*, Princeton: Princeton University Press.

Newton, K. and Zmerli, S. (2011) 'Three forms of trust and their association', *European Political Science Review*, 3(2): 169-200.

Orren, G. (1997) 'Fall from grace: The public's loss of faith in government', in J. S. Nye, P. D. Zelikow and D. C. King (eds) *Why People Don't Trust Government*, Cambridge: Harvard University Press.

Patterson, O. (1999) 'Liberty against the democratic state: On the historical and contemporary sources of American distrust', in M. E. Warren (ed.) *Democracy and Trust*, Cambridge: Cambridge University Press.

Paxton, P. (2007) 'Association memberships and generalized trust: A multilevel model across 31 countries', *Social Forces*, 86(1): 47–76.

Pelligra, V. (2006) 'The not-so-fragile fragility of goodness: The responsive quality of fiduciary relationships', in L. Bruni and P. L. Porta (eds) *Handbook on the Economics of Happiness*, Cheltenham: Edward Elgar.

Putnam, R. D. (1993) *Making Democracy Work: Civic traditions in modern Italy*. Princeton: Princeton University Press.

— (2000) *Bowling Alone: The collapse and revival of American community*, New York: Simon and Schuster.

— (2007) 'E pluribus unum: Diversity and community in the twenty-first century – The 2006 Johan Skytte Prize', *Scandinavian Political Studies*, 30(2): 137–74.

Putnam, R. D., Pharr, S. J., Dalton, R. J. (2000) 'Introduction: What's troubling the trilateral democracies', in S. J. Pharr and R. D. Putnam (eds) *Disaffected Democracies: What's troubling the trilateral countries?*, Princeton: Princeton University Press.

Rosenberg, M. (1956) 'Misanthropy and political ideology', *American Sociological Review*, 21(6): 690–95.

— (1957) 'Misanthropy and attitudes toward international affairs', *The Journal of Conflict Resolution*, 1(4): 340–5.

Rothstein, B. (1998) *Just Institutions Matter: The moral and political logic of the universal welfare state*, Cambridge: Cambridge University Press.

— (2002) 'Sweden: Social capital in the social democratic state: The Swedish model and civil society', in R. D. Putnam (ed.) *Democracies in*

Flux. Political Culture as a Condition for Democracy, Oxford: Oxford University Press.
Rothstein B. and Stolle, D. (2003) 'Social capital, impartiality, and the welfare state: An institutional approach', in M. Hooghe and D. Stolle (eds) *Generating Social Capital: Civil society and institutions in comparative perspective*, Basingstoke: Palgrave.
Rudolph, J. (2006) *Politics and Ethnicity: A comparative study*, Basingstoke: Palgrave Macmillan.
Sullivan, J. L. and Transue, J. E. (1999) 'The psychological underpinnings of democracy: A selective review of research on political tolerance, interpersonal trust, and social capital', *Annual Review of Psychology*, 50: 625–50.
Uslaner E. M. (1999) 'Democracy and social capital', in M. E. Warren (ed.) *Democracy and Trust*, Cambridge: Cambridge University Press.
— (2000–1) 'Producing and consuming trust', *Political Science Quarterly*, 115(4): 569–90.
— (2002) *The Moral Foundations of Trust*, Cambridge: Cambridge University Press.
— (2008) 'Trust as a moral value', in D. Castiglione, J. W. van Deth and G. Wolleb (eds) *Handbook of Social Capital*, Oxford: Oxford University Press.
van der Meer, J. (2003) 'Rain or fog? An empirical examination of social capital's rainmaker effects', in M. Hooghe and D. Stolle (eds) *Generating Social Capital: Civil society and institutions in comparative perspective,* Basingstoke: Palgrave.
van Schuur, W. H. (2003) 'Mokken scale analysis: Between the Gutmann scale and parametric item response theory', *Political Analysis*, 11(2): 139–63.
Zmerli, S. and Newton, K. (2008) 'Social trust and attitudes towards democracy', *Public Opinion Quarterly*, 72(4): 706–24.

chapter five | trustworthy states, trusting citizens? a multilevel study into objective and subjective determinants of political trust

Tom van der Meer and Paul Dekker

Introduction

It is widely known that countries strongly differ in the extent to which their citizens trust politics. Political trust tends to be high in the Nordic countries and the Netherlands, and rather low in Central and Eastern Europe (Fuchs *et al.* 1995; Listhaug and Wiberg 1995; Catterberg and Moreno 2006; Dogan 2005; Denters *et al.* 2007; van der Meer 2010). High levels of political trust are considered to be beneficial to society as a whole, but not unambiguously so. Trust in the political system is crucial to warrant the legitimacy of the system: political trust functions as the glue that keeps the system together and as the oil that lubricates the policy machine. However, to keep a democracy in good shape we also need critical and questioning mistrust (Lenard 2008). Some suspicious distrust towards incumbent officeholders can even be positive as it may motivate people to engage in politics (Hibbing and Theiss-Morse 2002).

Because of these supposed benefits and problems related to political trust, scholars and politicians are eager to understand the causes of the large cross-national differences. Facing this challenge, scholars have theoretically raised and/or empirically tested many explanations (Bovens and Wille 2008; van der Meer 2010). Most studies on political trust predominantly focus on the characteristics of respondents who trust or distrust (i.e. their resources and values) or on the characteristics of the political institutions that are trusted (e.g. their performance). These characteristics, however, can only offer a limited explanation for differences across countries. A more interesting approach is to look not only at the *subject* of political trust (the one who trusts) or the *object* of political trust (that which is trusted), but simultaneously at both. In such an approach, political trust is considered to be a relational characteristic rather than a personality characteristic of the subject or an institutional characteristic of the object.

The scholarly quest to explain cross-national differences in political trust faces two challenges. First, we need to assess which characteristics (composition, functioning and outcomes) of the object of political trust matter. In other words, which characteristics are relevant determinants of political trust? Secondly, when we find significant 'objective' determinants of political trust, we need to assess how they are linked to citizens' attitudes, their perceptions and evaluations. What are the 'subjective' mechanisms by which to explain the effects of characteristics of the object of political trust on levels of trust?

To date, scholars have focused more extensively on the former question than on the latter. We get ever more empirical knowledge as to which objective – for individual citizens: contextual – characteristics explain the large country level differences in political trust. However, the mechanisms that should link objective characteristics to individual level attitudes have been assumed theoretically rather than tested empirically. The aim of this chapter is therefore twofold. First, it aims at re-testing traditional models as to which contextual characteristics explain political trust. Specifically, this chapter replicates the model of van der Meer (2010) on a similar but more specific data set. The second aim is to extend our knowledge on the macro-micro mechanisms that link contexts to citizens' levels of political trust. To have an effect on political trust, the objective state characteristics should be intermediated by citizens' subjective evaluations of political institutions and politicians. Objective state characteristics are therefore linked to subjective evaluations of political institutions and politicians. Moving from the *objective incentives* for trust at the macro-level, we should now attempt to understand the mechanisms of political trust at the micro-level through citizens' *subjective perceptions* of the political system in different aspects. This brings us to two research questions:

1. To what extent do country level characteristics explain political trust, taking individual characteristics into account?
2. To what extent do citizens' evaluations of politicians and politics explain the relationship between country level characteristics and political trust?

In answering these questions, we hope to make several contributions to the scientific knowledge of political trust. Theoretically, we relate existing hypotheses to a single theoretical frame that conceptualises political trust as a more or less rational evaluation of citizen-state relationships, depending on four aspects: competence, care, accountability, and reliability. Moreover, we explicate which mechanisms supposedly explain how state characteristics relate to these four aspects of trust. Empirically, this study replicates the empirical test of a range of competing hypotheses on the effects of various state institutions simultaneously, and thereby functions as a robustness check of previous studies, specifically of van der Meer (2010). More importantly, this study extends empirical knowledge on institutional effects, as it tests which mechanisms explain the macro-micro linkage between state institutions and individual citizens' levels of political trust.

Theory: Political trust as a relational concept

Trust is an ambiguous concept. People may trust different institutions for different reasons. This chapter assumes that people do not simply trust or distrust, solely because of their personality or their social trust. Although social standing and trust in various political institutions are systematically related (Zmerli *et al.* 2007), correlations are so weak that there is no 'syndrome of trust' (Uslaner 2002). Rather, trust is a subjective evaluation of a specific relationship: 'A trusts B to do X' (Hardin 2000). The relational aspects of trust are often forgotten in survey-based political research, but are common in social-psychological and institutional approaches.[1] Kasperson *et al.* (1992) argue that trust is a rational evaluation of social situations along four aspects. A person who trusts (the subject) thinks that the object of trust is *competent, intrinsically committed* (caring), *extrinsically committed* (accountable because of encapsulated interest) and *predictable*.

'Competence' suggests that the subject of trust thinks the object of trust has the ability to perform according to expectations or in the subject's interest. 'Commitment' implies that the subject thinks the object will act in the best interests of the subject for either of two reasons. According to the first, the object would have an intrinsic need to act in line with the subject's interests, e.g. because they care for each other or share the same goals. Kasperson *et al.* (1992) label this aspect 'care'. The second reason for commitment lies in the subject's ability to enforce the object's actions, if only through the threat to punish untrustworthy behaviour by denying future support. When the object of trust can be held accountable, the subject binds the object to his or her interests: the interests of the subject become encapsulated self-interests of the object (Hardin 2000). The fourth aspect of trust is reliability or predictability: the extent to which the object's past behaviour is consistent.

Even though the four aspects of trust of Kasperson *et al.* (1992) were developed to investigate trust between persons, state institutions also differ in the extent to which they meet these four demands. For that purpose, we specify the wide category of political trust to a specific aspect for which cross-national data is available, namely trust in parliament.[2] Parliaments may be judged to be competent when the policy output is successful socially, economically and/or politically. They may be considered to be inherently committed (caring) when they represent a larger share of the electorate. Parliamentary behaviour may be enforced when citizens are able to dismiss politicians that do not function well. And parliaments may be more predictable to the extent that parliamentarians are true to their word, party coalitions fulfil their terms and the system as a whole is well-established.

Indeed, in a recent survey, Dutch citizens refer to these four aspects of political trust when they explain their opinion on politics (van der Meer 2009). Some focus on the competence of government ('[Prime Minister] Balkenende is capable, so is [Minister] Bos'; 'the government reacts far too late and far too timidly on what happens in society'), others on care ('government and parliament do their best'; 'politicians do not govern with their hearts, but with their wallets'). Similarly, some citizens mention accountability ('we have a democratically elected govern-

---

1. See contributions in the Russell Sage Foundation series on trust, for instance in Braithwaite and Levi (2000) and Cook *et al.* (2009).
2. In this chapter we focus on parliament and not on government, because trust in government will be more affected by partisan sympathies, which are difficult to handle in a comparative study with more than twenty countries.

ment that is checked by parliament: citizens' wishes and demands are thus taken into account'; 'they do not listen to the people: the Big Whigs in The Hague do exactly what they want with our money'). Finally, a few comments reflect the reliability of government ('the current government is rather stable and does not deal with difficult issues in too much of a rush'; 'emotion politics').

We distinguish between objective (external) criteria of competence, commitment and reliability, and the subjective evaluations thereof by citizens to understand which objective and subjective criteria are most important to develop political trust. In this chapter, we focus first on the objective criteria (characteristics of the state) and then continue with subjective evaluations of politics and politicians (characteristics of the citizens). The inclusion of these subjective evaluations serves two goals. First, they are useful to test macro-micro mechanisms: they allow us to assess whether the relationship between objective, external state characteristics and political trust is intermediated by subjective evaluations. Second, they can shed more light onto the relative importance of each of the four aspects of trust at the individual level.

Hypotheses

From the four aspects of trust relationships proposed in the previous section, we deduce several hypotheses (see below) as to how state characteristics affect citizens' likelihood to trust parliament. The hypotheses all build on the ideas that trust is relational and that to have an effect on political trust, the objective state characteristics should be intermediated by citizens' *subjective* evaluations of political institutions and politicians. State characteristics may contribute to (perceptions of) competence, care, commitment and reliability. Each hypothesis is formulated in two parts. The first part (i.e. 'a') states the contextual effects we expect to find. The second part of each hypothesis (i.e. 'b') describes the mechanism through which a supposed contextual characteristic should affect political trust.

Theoretically, the most likely system level influence on citizens' distrust in their political system is the level of corruption (Della Porta 2000). Corruption represents the opposite of all four aspects of trust. First, widespread corruption in politics and society seriously undermines the efficiency and effectiveness of parliamentary rule. Moreover, corruption points to parliament's incompetence in dealing with that problem. Second, corruption implies the absence of moral scruples: by their actions, corrupt governments and parliaments[3] show they do not inherently care for their citizens. Third, corruption thrives on (institutional) limitations for citizens to hold public officials accountable. Forth, corrupt societies are unreliable, in the sense that citizens do not know which policy outcomes to expect. All in all, corruption appears to be the antithesis to a trust relationship on all four aspects. Moreover, there is evidence for a negative dynamic between corruption and trust, 'a vicious circle wherein corruption breeds a climate of distrust that in turn feeds corruption' (Morris and Klesner 2010: 21).

---

3. In fact, the distinction between government and parliament is less evident: in corrupt societies both institutions are dominated or held hostage by a conglomerate of corrupt elites.

Hypothesis H1a: The lower is a country's level of corruption, the more its citizens are likely to trust parliament.

Hypothesis H1b: The negative contextual effect of corruption is explained by subjective evaluations of competence (performance), care, commitment and reliability.

In line with the *competence* aspect of trust, several scholars have studied the relationship between countries' performances and political trust. The performance of the political system is often judged by economic success (McAllister 1999; Miller and Listhaug 1999; Keele 2007). Supposedly, trust in parliament is higher when a country's economic performance is better, regardless of citizens' own income level.[4] Cross-national studies have emphasised different aspects of economic performance, such as the level of economic development (McAllister 1999), economic growth and unemployment rates (Miller and Listhaug 1999).[5] Evidently, the national political system is not solely responsible for the economic performance of a country. Nevertheless, in the public perception this need not matter. Citizens' trust in politics and consumers' trust in the economy follow rather similar trend lines (Keele 2007). Bovens and Wille (2008) suggest that economic performance is the most likely explanation for what they considered the Dutch drop in political trust between 2002 and 2006. In our earlier research (van der Meer 2010), we found no evidence for cross-national or longitudinal effects of economic performance on trust in parliament, but we give the idea of an economic effect another chance.

Hypothesis H2a: The higher is a country's levels of economic development, the more its citizens are likely to trust parliament.

Hypothesis H2b: The positive contextual effect of economic development is explained by subjective evaluations of competence (performance).

The big divide as regards electoral systems is between proportional and majoritarian representation. Majoritarian systems translate citizens' political preferences unequally into parliamentary seats with a bias towards bigger parties and a loss of many (minority) votes (Banducci *et al.* 1999). Because political power is bundled in a small number of political parties (that generally need not form coalitions to reach majority governments), political responsibilities are appointed more clearly

---

4. It is crucial to distinguish between individual and contextual effects of economic well-being. At the individual level, citizens that have high income (or an increase in income) may be more satisfied and therefore trust parliament more. At the contextual level, citizens trust parliament more when the country as a whole performs well, regardless of their own income (even if they should experience a relative or an absolute decline in their household income).

5. An alternative measure, which focuses more strictly on government performance, is the size of the budgetary deficit (cf. Miller and Listhaug 1999). However, in some situations, e.g. economic crises, having a budgetary deficit might in fact be the trustworthy thing to do. Deficits thus do not equal governmental failure. Similarly, we did not include unemployment rates, as the measures are not cross-nationally equivalent due to differing social laws and definitions.

than in proportional (multiparty, coalition) systems (Thomassen and Aarts 2005). It is easier to hold politicians accountable in majority systems (Powell 2000) and for that reason they can be expected to generate higher levels of trust than proportional systems.[6] However, the opposite was found in earlier research conducted by the co-author of this chapter (van der Meer 2010). Proportional representation might have other trust benefits than accountability. Proportional systems allow citizens 'access to the power structures of society' (Gabriel and Walter-Rogg 2008) by translating the preferences of as many citizens as possible to parliament (Norris 1999; Magalhaes 2006). The more parliament mirrors the electorate, the more it intrinsically cares for the citizens, at least in the perception of these citizens (Banducci *et al.* 1999). From the care perspective, parliament would be trusted more in proportional systems than in majoritarian systems. Because of our earlier findings, this is what we want to test.

> Hypothesis H3a: In proportional electoral systems, citizens will have more trust in parliament than in majoritarian electoral systems.
>
> Hypothesis H3b: The positive contextual effect of proportional electoral systems is explained by subjective evaluations of care.

Citizens need to be familiar with democratic traditions in order to trust the political system (McAllister 1999). A neutral political system is an important precondition to trust parliament. In authoritarian and totalitarian regimes, state power is hardly limited, while policy makers are more likely to abuse their discretionary powers. Consequently, citizens will not feel safe under such regimes. Even after a democratic transition, it takes time for trust to develop (Rose and Mishler in this volume; cf. Rose 1994, Dimitrova-Grajzi and Simon 2010). Trust may even drop slightly in newly-established democracies after the so-called 'honeymoon effect' wears off (Catterberg and Moreno 2006). All in all, we therefore expect that trust in parliament is lower in newly-established democracies than in longstanding democracies. Trust in parliament should be especially low in former communist countries, where individual political rights had been curtailed the most.

> Hypothesis H4a: In longstanding democracies, citizens will have more trust in parliament than in newly-established democracies (former authoritarian or totalitarian regimes).
>
> Hypothesis H4b: The positive effect of democratic rule is explained by subjective evaluations of care, commitment and reliability.

---

6. In a majoritarian system, parliamentary preferences also appear to be more representative of the preferences of the general population (Anderson and Guillory 1997). Moreover, district systems enable citizens to throw the rascals out. Because citizens are more likely to experience that their vote matters, they are more likely to trust parliament (Ulbig 2008; cf. Magalhaes 2006).

Method and data

The research questions and hypotheses call for multilevel modelling (Snijders and Bosker 1999), as they combine individual and state characteristics.[7] We study two levels of analysis simultaneously: the individual level (level 1) and the country level (level 2). To estimate country level effects, the data set needs to contain a large number of countries. To estimate whether individual level characteristics might explain these country level effects, the data set needs to include questions that are related to evaluations of competence, care, commitment, and reliability. These demands are best – but not ideally – met by the first wave (2002/3) of the European Social Survey (ESS), from which we therefore derive the individual level data. The ESS has a mean response rate of over 70 per cent. Data collection was based on strict cross-national procedures of sampling, questioning, and coding.

Twenty-two countries participated in the first wave of the ESS. One of them (Israel) is left out of the analysis because it differs too much on several individual and contextual determinants. This results in a rather similar design. The German sample is split into the former West Germany and the former East Germany, to test the effects of former regime type and of economic development. This leaves twenty-two societies, with a total of 36,740 respondents of eighteen years and older. To a large extent, these countries share general cultural and political characteristics as they are all European liberal democracies, dominantly Christian and members of the European Union (or about to be in a few years).

Dependent variable

Trust in parliament is assessed through the question to what extent citizens trust their national parliament (Lower House). It ranges from 0 (no trust at all) to 10 (complete trust).

Country level determinants

Lacking a cross-national measure of actual *corruption*, the level of perceived corruption was measured through the Corruption Perceptions Index (CPI) 2002, issued by Transparency International. The CPI is based on expert multiple surveys per country and (after our recoding) ranges from 0 (no corruption) to 10 (highly corrupt). GDP/Capita PPP (the national income per head of the population corrected for differences in price levels) measures *economic development*. We use

---

7. Two alternatives to multilevel modelling should not be applied. Aggregating individual level characteristics to the country level (cf. Delhey and Newton 2005) is statistically correct but ignores individual level variance and possible composition effects. Alternatively, disaggregating contextual characteristics to the individual level (cf. Miller and Listhaug 1999) is an incorrect procedure, as it decreases the standard errors (S.E.) of the effects. In this analysis we would assign characteristics of twenty-two countries (i.e. large S.E.) to tens of thousands of individuals (i.e., small S.E.). Consequently, disaggregated analyses run a very high risk of falsely concluding that country level characteristics are significant.

the measure provided by the World Bank, which is strongly correlated (>.99) to kindred measures of Eurostat, the OECD and the IMF. The dichotomous distinction between proportional and disproportional *electoral systems* is derived from the Quality of the Government data set (Teorell *et al.* 2007).[8] Finally, we classify countries based on their *former regime type* (i.e. the regime type in 1970, one generation before). We distinguish between democratic, authoritarian and totalitarian (communist) regimes.[9] The list of countries and their characteristics is presented in Appendix 1.

Intermediary variables

Previous studies have established that most of the above-mentioned contextual characteristics are significant determinants of trust in parliament. However, the theoretical underpinning of these effects remains somewhat unclear. Therefore, intermediary variables should be included to assess *why* we find these contextual effects: models with intermediary effects can shed light on the mechanics of how contextual institutions are related to individual attitudes, whenever they explain away the original effects statistically.

To assess whether contextual effects are explained by citizens' subjective assessments of the four aspects of trust, we need to include intermediary variables that capture these aspects. Although the ESS is the best available data set, the subjective assessments do not match the theoretical design optimally. Perceptions of *competence* (or rather: evaluations of the performance of state institutions) are measured by three variables: citizens' satisfaction with the economy, with the education system, and with the health care system. Perceptions of *care* are measured by two variables: (1) to what extent the respondent thinks that politicians care what people like him/her think; and (2) to what extent the respondent thinks that politicians are interested in people's opinions rather than in their votes.

Perceptions of *commitment* (accountability) and *reliability* are not really included in the data set, as standard questions are lacking in the ESS. We do include two variables of intrinsic efficacy, which is the attitude that one has the personal abilities to take part in politics (and by implication might even hold politicians accountable). These variables cover some aspects of commitment and reliability: (1) the extent to which politics seems too complicated to understand; and (2) the extent to which the respondent can take an active role in a group with political aims.

---

8. The effect of proportional systems was tested for robustness by a second measure of proportionality, namely the Gallagher index of proportionality, which assesses the ratio between vote shares and seat shares. It shows that the effect was robust, although the major distinction remains between those countries that are strictly proportional by institutional design and those that are not.

9. Because all former authoritarian countries in the data set underwent a democratic transition in the 1970s and all former communist countries in the late 1980s and early 1990s, we cannot distinguish between effects of the former regime type and the effect of the time since regime change. There is simply insufficient variation in time between the former communist countries, as there is insufficient variation between the former authoritarian countries.

Individual level control variables

The models control for several background characteristics: level of education, net household income,[10] citizenship, age (modelled as a potentially non-linear effect), gender, religiosity and denomination, urbanisation, and household composition.

Results

Analysis of variance

Many of these individual and contextual characteristics go hand in hand. The long-standing democracies of North-western Europe have the highest levels of economic development, the highest levels of education, and suffer the least from corruption. Bivariate analyses would not offer conclusive answers as to which of these related determinants truly explain trust in parliament. Therefore, we employ multivariate, multilevel analyses, using the ML-WIN 2.10 package (Goldstein 1995).

The same three contextual level effects are significant as in van der Meer (2010). First, we established a baseline two-level model of trust in parliament (i.e. with no determinants) and subsequently a model with only individual level determinants of trust in parliament. Respondents with missing values on any variable (except for income, see footnote 10) were left out of the analyses; subsequent models are all based on the same set of respondents. Next, we included government determinants stepwise, based on their influence on the chi-square distributed -2LogLikelihood (-2LL) to minimise the risk of Type 1 and Type 2 errors (cf. Tolsma *et al.* 2009).[11] Non-significant determinants were left out of the model for reasons of parsimony. As the dependent variable has eleven categories and is normally distributed, we employ linear multilevel regression analysis with the 'maximum likelihood' estimation procedure.

The variance estimates in Model 1 (see Table 5.1) describe that most of the difference in trust (91 per cent) is situated at the individual level. Differences between citizens matter more than those between countries, which tends to be a given in cross-national survey research where the dependent variable is measured at the individual level (Steenbergen and Jones 2002). Nevertheless, differences between countries account for 9 per cent of all variance, which is a lot. Because cross-national survey-based public opinion research often involves more than 1,000 respondents per country while the number of countries tends to be limited to a few dozen, 5 per cent of contextual variance is already quite substantial (Rahn and Rudolph 2005).

---

10. Nearly a third of the respondents refused to report their income. To cope with the large non-response on this variable, we assigned average scores to the missing values and included an extra variable that categorises them as 'missing'.

11. When we include all characteristics simultaneously, most effects are not significant at the .05 level (although several would be significant at the .10 level). Only the effect of corruption is significant in all models.

In a second step, we include individual level determinants. Although these determinants are not the primary interest of this study, they are necessary to take composition effects into account. Model 3 (Table 5.1) shows, for instance, that trust in parliament is higher when citizens are Protestant. Consequently, countries tend to have a higher level of trust in parliament when a larger share of their inhabitants are Protestant. This difference in composition may explain part of the country level differences. Indeed, there are composition effects. Most of the individual characteristics in Model 2 are significant. They explain about 17 per cent of the variance between countries. Nevertheless, a large and significant level of variance remains at the contextual level.

Contextual effects

Model 3 (Table 5.1) includes government characteristics as determinants of trust in parliament. This model mainly confirms the robustness of the findings of van der Meer (2010), which were based on a larger data set both in the number of countries and in the number of respondents.

The same three contextual level effects are significant as in van der Meer (2010). First, trust in parliament is lower in countries where corruption is more widespread (b= -0.17). This supports hypothesis H1a. Secondly, there is no significant effect of the level of economic development on trust in parliament. In other words, there is no additional effect of the average (i.e. gross domestic) income beyond the individual effect of household income. If we excluded the individual effect of household income, a significant contextual effect would have been found. This suggests that it is highly relevant in cross-national studies on the relationship between economic performance and political trust to take individual level income into account. Overall, hypothesis H2a is refuted: trust in parliament does not depend on actual economic performance. Thirdly, care aspects are more important than accountability aspects. Hypothesis H3a stated that trust in parliament should be higher in countries with a proportional electoral system, because citizens are better represented there. Model 3 (see Table 5.1) shows support for this hypothesis (b= 0.53). Fourthly, trust in parliament is lower in former communist countries than in longstanding democracies (b= -0.61): the legacy of the totalitarian regime apparently lingers on in a culture of widespread political distrust in Central and Eastern Europe (at least in 2002/3, at the time of the first wave of ESS). This supports hypothesis H4a. Additional cross-level analyses show that the negative effect of a recent communist regime is not weaker for the young than for the old. The negative effect of communist rule on political trust thus endures even after more than a decade since its downfall.

Table 5.1: Determinants of trust in parliament (OLS multilevel, random intercept models)

	Model 1	Model 2	Model 3
Individual determinants (L1)			
Level of education		.21***	.21***
Income		.08***	.08***
Income (missing values)		-.22***	-.21***
Age		-.01	-.01
Age squared (/100)		.02***	.02***
Urbanisation		.04***	.04***
Gender female		-.26***	-.26***
Household size		.01	.01
Children living at home		-.04	-.04
Denomination (none)			
Roman Catholic		.18***	.18***
Protestant		.32***	.32***
Orthodox		-.19	-.15
Jewish		-.56	-.56
Muslim		.42***	.42***
Other		-.17*	-.17*
Frequency of church attendance		.12***	.12***
Citizenship		-.29***	-.29***
Contextual determinants (L2)			
Corruption			-.17*
Economic development (GDP/cap. PPP)			
Electoral system: proportional			.53*
Regime (longstanding democracy)			
Former authoritarian			.02
Former communist			-.61*
Variance at level 1 (individuals)	5.35	5.09	5.09
Total explained variance at level 1		5%	5%
Variance at level 2 (countries)	.53	.44	.18
Total explained variance at level 2		17%	65%

Notes: Significance: *** p<.001-level (one-tailed), * p<.05-level (one-tailed); non-significant contextual effects were left out.

Table 5.2: Bivariate correlations of intermediary factors with contextual determinants and with trust in parliament (pooled data set, OLS)

	Politicians interested in opinions	Politicians care	Politics not too complicated	Could take active role	Satisfaction economy	Satisfaction education system	Satisfaction health care
Contextual determinants (X)							
Corruption	-.26	-.27	-.09	-.08	-.36	-.21	-.27
Years of democratic rule	.16	.21	.05	.07	.26	.17	.26
Electoral system: PR	ns	-.01	.03	.04	ns	.04	ns
Economic development	.24	.26	.08	.10	.36	.20	.25
Dependent variable (Y)							
Trust in parliament	.40	.41	.15	.16	.42	.29	.30

Notes: All effects are significant at p<.001 (2-tailed) except three, indicated as 'ns'. Intermediary variables have been standardised by the pooled data set.

Intermediary effects

We now arrive at our second research question: to what extent do evaluations of politicians and politics explain the relationship between country level characteristics and trust in parliament? To study whether these political evaluations do indeed function as intermediary variables (Z) and explain the relationship between the contextual factors (X) and trust in parliament (Y), we first assess how they are bivariately related to both X and Y (see Table 5.2).

The correlations in Table 5.2 suggest that corruption is consistently harmful to care, internal efficacy and satisfaction, while democratic rule and economic development stimulate all three. Having a proportional electoral system stimulates efficacy, but does not stimulate perceptions of care. The electoral system is unrelated to the evaluation of the national economy and of health care. Additional analyses show that the measures of care and satisfaction with the economy are most strongly related to the contextual determinants.

With regards to the dependent variable, all measures of care, efficacy and satisfaction are positively related to trust in parliament. Again, the strongest effects are found for satisfaction with the economy and the two care measures. These three factors are therefore most likely to function as intermediary variables in the model.

Yet, although it provides insight in the possibility of intermediary effects, it is hardly a crucial test. The correlations are strictly bivariate, and – more importantly – Table 5.2 does not show whether these correlations would explain away the original relationships between X and Y. Therefore, turning to Table 5.3, we carefully build up the model stepwise in an attempt to pull effects apart as much as possible. Model 4 includes the three perceptions of performance, whereas Model 5 includes the other subjective attitudes towards politicians and politics. Finally, Model 6 includes all intermediary variables simultaneously.

All effects in Table 5.3 are in line with those in Table 5.2. Initially, we focus on Model 6. Of the seven factors of intermediary determinants, satisfaction with the economy is the strongest determinant of political trust, followed by the two care aspects.[12] Efficacy is least important. Moreover, the inclusion of these seven factors reduces the formerly significant effects of corruption and communist rule to non-significance. The effect of the PR system is also reduced, but not as strongly and uniformly as the other variables. Overall, Model 6 supports the general proposition of this chapter that the contextual effects are to a large extent explained by intermediary factors.

However, Model 6 in Table 5.3 also contains a surprising result regarding the effect of authoritarianism: although it was non-significant in Model 3 (see Table 5.1), it unexpectedly turns to a sizeable and significant positive effect once subjective attitudes towards politics and politicians are included. In other words, trust levels are higher in these countries than would be expected based on the way their

---

12. The tables display (unstandardised) b-coefficients. After standardising the variables, the beta-coefficients report which variables have the strongest effect on the dependent variable – as reported above.

citizens evaluate their system's output and their politicians. This must imply that citizens in former authoritarian regimes (Greece, Spain and Portugal) evaluate their output and their politicians far more negatively than citizens in traditional democracies – even more so than we would expect from the political characteristics of these regimes. All in all, we might consider this a statistical artefact, but one with intriguing implications for the study on subjective attitudes towards politics and politicians in former authoritarian regimes. Or was it the wisdom of the crowds of 2002/3, who sensed problems that were not yet visible in the objective (economic) indicators of their time, but only became manifest in the financial crisis of 2008?

Model 6 shows that contextual characteristics are to a large extent explained by some combination of subjective evaluations of performance (competence), care, commitment, and reliability. However, we want to pull the specific causal relations further apart. Is the effect of a proportional electoral system indeed mainly explained by care and commitment, rather than competence? Is the effect of democratic rule indeed mainly explained by reliability and efficacy, rather than competence? And what does best explain the effect of corruption?

Unfortunately, it is very difficult to further specify the causal relationships. A comparison of Models 4 and 5 (see Table 5.3) to Model 3 (see Table 5.1) implies that the contextual effect of corruption is somewhat better explained by evaluations of institutional performance than by evaluations of care, commitment and efficacy. This implies that corruption mainly leads citizens to have a low evaluation of the performance of state institutions, which in turn leads them to trust parliament less. Nevertheless, evaluations of care, commitment and efficacy also decrease the original contextual effect of corruption. This supports in most general terms hypothesis H1b.

According to hypothesis H3b, a positive effect of proportionality should be explained by measures of intrinsic care. However, a comparison of Model 3 (Table 5.1) to Models 4 and 5 (Table 5.3) illustrates that this is not the case. The positive effect of proportionality is diminished by evaluations of institutional performance and not at all by opinions on politicians' levels of caring. In other words, trust is higher in proportional systems, not because citizens tend to think more favourably about the intrinsic good nature of their politicians, but because they think the regime performs better. Hypothesis H3b should therefore be rejected.

Finally, hypothesis H4b argued that the effect of former regime type on current levels of trust in parliament should be explained by citizens' high uncertainty about the care, commitment and reliability of their politicians. However, when we look at Models 4 and 5 we find no support for this hypothesis. The effect of former regime type is mainly reduced by – again – perceptions of institutional performance. Citizens of former communist countries trust their parliaments less because they think less favourably about institutional performance. We should therefore reject hypothesis H4b.

In summary, the analyses confirm that the contextual effects are explained by evaluations of politics and politicians. However, only for hypothesis H1b do we find confirmation about the specific mechanisms that explain each contextual effect separately.

Table 5.3: Explaining contextual effects on political trust (OLS, random slope model)

	Model 4	Model 5	Model 6
Intermediary determinants (L1)			
Politicians interested in opinions rather than votes	–	.49***	.37***
Politicians care about what people like me think	–	.56***	.45***
Politics is not too complicated to understand	–	.10***	.08***
I could take an active role in a political group	–	.04***	.07***
Satisfaction with the economy	.31***	–	.24***
Satisfaction with the education system	.12***	–	.10***
Satisfaction with health care	.13***	–	.10***
Contextual determinants (L2)			
Corruption	-.02	-.09†	.01
Electoral system: proportional	.25	.54	.38
Regime (longstanding democracy)			
▪ former authoritarian	.45	.41†	.68*
▪ former communist	-.30	-.40†	-.19
Variance at level 2 (countries)	.148	.103	.100

Notes: Significance: *** $p<.001$-level (one-tailed), * $p<.05$-level (one-tailed), † $p<.10$-level (one-tailed). The effects are controlled for education, income, urbanisation, gender, household size and composition, denomination, church attendance and citizenship (not displayed in Table 5.3).

Conclusion

This chapter built on previous cross-national studies, which found effects of a range of contextual factors on the levels of political trust. Implicitly or explicitly most of these studies made claims about the mechanisms through which these contextual factors would influence citizens' levels of political trust. In this study, we re-tested to what extent contextual factors explain levels of trust in one political institution, namely parliament, and tested to what extent these relationships may be explained by the theoretically expected mechanisms. For that purpose we considered trust as an evaluation of the state-citizen relationship rather than a personality or country characteristic, emphasising characteristics of the one who trusts, that which is trusted, as well as their interplay. Theoretically, four aspects of the object may motivate subjects to trust: competence, intrinsic commitment (caring), extrinsic commitment (accountability) and reliability.

This chapter raised two research questions. The first research question concerned the relationship between contextual characteristics and trust in parliament. Theoretically, we linked the four aspects of trust relations to contextual characteristics. Empirically, we tested their effects in multilevel models and found that these models explain country level differences very well (overall, the models explain over 65 per cent of all variance between countries). Three contextual effects are significant. First, corruption has a consistent, negative effect on trust in parliament, which may be explained by all four aspects. Second, trust in parliament is higher in proportional electoral systems. This implies that intrinsic commitment may be more important to political trust than extrinsic commitment. Third, trust in parliament is lower in former communist countries. We find no differences between various age groups. Therefore, the effect of communist rule does not appear to be a remnant of old socialisation effects. Rather, the negative effect of communist rule probably points to the current regime, which in the early 2000s still faces the pressures and uncertainties of a new and somewhat unconsolidated democracy.

The second research question of this chapter focused on the mechanisms through which state characteristics affect political trust. We showed that satisfaction (especially with the national economy) and the perception that politicians care stimulate political trust. Internal efficacy is far less relevant. Moreover, these aspects do indeed explain the relationships between state characteristics and political trust. In other words, objective system characteristics affect the various subjective perceptions of the system, which in turn influence political trust.

Yet, while this study was rather successful in explaining cross-national differences in political trust and why some state characteristics affect political trust, it failed to find empirical support for the theoretically-hypothesised pathways through which these effects should go. Only the effect of corruption was explained by the theoretically-expected mechanisms. However, this may have more to do with the various mechanisms allowed in hypothesis 1b. By contrast, as we had not found a contextual effect of economic development, there was no need to test the theoretical mechanism. However, surprisingly, subjective perceptions of economic performance are the strongest determinant of trust, even though the actual performance is not even significantly related to it. The positive effect of proportionality is not explained by (perceived) care relationships, but by evaluations of institutional performance. The negative effect of former communist regimes is not explained by the theoretically most likely pathways either: the effect does not run through care, commitment or reliability aspects but through evaluations of institutional performance.

The disappointing results for the intermediary effects raise various questions. How can we explain the significant effects of state institutions on trust in parliament, if the mechanisms through which we would expect them to run theoretically do not hold? What does this imply? Should we dispense with the general idea of citizens who evaluate politics and politicians rationally and instead opt for political trust as a more non-descript reflection of media images? Or should we conclude that even the detailed cross-national data sets of the last decade are still too crude to do the path analyses that are required to separate theoretical plausible mechanisms empirically?

We suggest three ways to continue the search for the mechanisms between the trustworthiness of politics and the trust put in politics by the citizens. First, cross-national survey data should be expanded with alternative indicators to check more causal pieces in the area of individual perceptions and evaluations. One evident innovation should be the inclusion of more specific subjective perceptions of accountability and reliability than those available in ESS. Simultaneously, it is advisable to focus on more political institutions. We analysed trust in parliament both because this was available in ESS, and because there are good theoretical reasons to do so (parliament is the core institution of representative democracy; trust in parliament is probably less parochially biased than trust in government). However, government is probably perceived more often as the performing political institution, to which criteria of competence and commitment apply more concretely.

Second, the causal mechanisms explicated in this chapter may not be restricted to processes in the heads of individual citizens. Media have an important intermediary role between circumstances and their appreciations by individuals. How these media cover issues of corruption, how they evaluate the economic contributions and burdens of politics, how they pay attention to parliamentary debates or how they report about coalition formations – all that might truly explain under which circumstances objective criteria matter. There is no evident direct link between the 'characteristics of the political objects' and the individual citizen; most citizens obtain such political information primarily through the media. Future studies of these mechanisms should therefore attempt to include collective, public and mediated processes.

The third way to continue the search for the mechanisms – and possibly most interesting avenue of research – is the use of more qualitative research techniques to investigate the causal and narrative links that citizens themselves describe between their (lack of) political trust and the assumed facts of politics. Qualitative research may shed light on the norms by which citizens judge political institutions. For instance, Steenvoorden *et al.* (2009) found that trusters and distrusters do not so much disagree about politics, but rather emphasise different aspects of politics.

Those who trust politicians emphasise their good intentions and their expertise, while those who distrust politicians lament their lack of responsiveness and lack of decisiveness.

Appendix 1

Countries, objective characteristics, and average levels of trust in parliament

	Corruption Perceptions Index	Economic development	Electoral system	Gallagher index of proportionality	Regime type (1970)	Trust in parliament (country average)
Austria	2.2	24816.2	PR	1.33	democratic	5.1
Belgium	2.9	24468.1	PR	2.99	democratic	5.0
Czech Republic	6.3	6953.8	PR	5.73	communist	3.6
Denmark	0.5	32959.4	PR	1.58	democratic	6.2
Finland	0.3	24576.4	PR	3.24	democratic	5.8
France	3.7	23196.5	Majoritarian	21.95	democratic	4.5
Germany (East)	2.7	17440.2	PR	4.61	communist	3.9
Germany (West)	2.7	25896.6	PR	4.61	democratic	4.6
Great Britain	1.3	25566.3	Majoritarian	17.76	democratic	4.6
Greece	5.8	12021.2	PR	6.78	authoritarian	4.8
Hungary	5.1	5916.3	PR	8.20	communist	5.0
Ireland	3.1	30209.9	PR	6.62	democratic	4.4
Italy	4.8	20398.9	PR	10.22	democratic	4.8
Luxembourg	1.0	46754.2	PR	3.22	democratic	5.6
The Netherlands	1.0	25889.6	PR	0.88	democratic	5.2
Norway	1.5	39805.0	PR	3.22	democratic	5.7
Poland	6.0	4670.0	PR	6.33	communist	3.4
Portugal	3.7	11564.0	PR	4.64	authoritarian	4.3
Slovenia	4.0	11083.1	PR	1.51	communist	4.1
Spain	2.9	16593.3	PR	6.10	authoritarian	4.8
Sweden	0.7	25463.8	PR	1.52	democratic	5.9
Switzerland	1.5	36838.4	PR	3.17	democratic	5.7

Note: The reported average level of trust in parliament is calculated on the respondents with non-missing values.

References

Anderson, C. J. and Guillory, C. A. (1997) 'Political institutions and satisfaction with democracy: A cross-national analysis of consensus and majoritarian systems', *American Political Science Review*, 91(1): 66–81.

Banducci, S. A., Donovan, T. and Karp, J. A. (1999) 'Proportional representation and attitudes about politics: Evidence from New Zealand', *Electoral Studies*, 18(4): 533–55.

Bovens, M. and Wille, A. (2008) 'Deciphering the Dutch drop: Ten explanations for decreasing political trust in the Netherlands', *International Review of Administrative Sciences*, 74(2): 283–305.

Braithwaite, V. and Levi, M. (eds) (2000) *Trust and Governance*, New York: Russell Sage Foundation.

Catterberg, G. and Moreno, A. (2006) 'The individual bases of political trust: Trends in new and established democracies', *International Journal of Public Opinion Research*, 18(1) 31-48.

Cook, K. S., Levi, M. and Hardin, R. (eds) (2009) *Whom Can We Trust?*, New York: Russell Sage Foundation.

Delhey, J. and Newton, K. (2005) 'Predicting cross-national levels of social trust: Global pattern or Nordic exceptionalism?', *European Sociological Review*, 21(4): 311–27.

Della Porta, D. (2000) 'Social capital, beliefs in government and political corruption', in S. J. Pharr and R. D. Putnam (eds) *Disaffected Democracies: What's troubling the trilateral countries?*, Princeton: Princeton University Press.

Denters, B., Gabriel, O. W. and Torcal, M. (2007) 'Political confidence in representative democracies: Socio-cultural vs. political explanations', in J. W. van Deth, J. R. Montero and A. Westholm (eds) *Citizenship and Involvement in European Democracies: A comparative analysis*, London: Routledge.

Dimitrova-Grajzi, V. and Simon, E. (2010) 'Political trust and historical legacy: The effect of varieties of socialism', *East European Politics & Societies*, 22(2): 206–28.

Dogan, M. (2005) 'Erosion of confidence in thirty European democracies', *Comparative Sociology*, 4(1–2): 11–53.

Fuchs, D., Guidorosso, G., and Svensson, P. (1995) 'Support for the democratic system', in D. Fuchs and H.-D. Klingemann (eds) *Citizens and the State*, Oxford: Oxford University Press.

Gabriel, O. W. and Walter-Rogg, M. (2008) 'Social capital and political trust', in H. Meulemann (ed.) *Social Capital in Europe: Similarity of countries and diversity of people?*, Leiden: Brill Academic.

Goldstein, H. (1995) *Multilevel Statistical Models*, London: Edward Arnold.

Hardin, R. (2000) 'Do we want trust in government', in M. E. Warren (ed.) *Democracy and Trust*, Cambridge: Cambridge University Press.

Hibbing, J. R. and Theiss-Morse, E. (2002) *Stealth Democracy: Americans' beliefs*

about how government should work, Cambridge: Cambridge University Press.
Kasperson, R., Golding, D. and Tuler, S. (1992) 'Social distrust as a factor in siting hazardous facilities and communicating risks', *Journal of Social Issues*, 48(4): 161–87.
Keele, L. (2007) 'Social capital and the dynamics of trust in government', *American Journal of Political Science*, 51(2): 241–54.
Lenard, P. T. (2008) 'Trust your compatriots, but count your change: The roles of trust, mistrust and distrust in democracy', *Political Studies*, 36(2): 312–32.
Listhaug, O. and Wiberg, M. (1995) 'Confidence in political and private institutions', in D. Fuchs and H.-D. Klingemann (eds) *Citizens and the State*, Oxford: Oxford University Press.
McAllister, I. (1999) 'The economic performance of governments', in P. Norris (ed.) *Critical Citizens: Global support for democratic government*, Oxford: Oxford University Press.
Magalhaes, P. (2006) 'Confidence in parliaments: Performance, representation and accountability', in M. Torcal and J. R. Montero (eds) *Political Disaffection in Contemporary Democracies: Social capital, institutions and politics*, London: Routledge.
Miller, A. and Listhaug, O. (1999) 'Political performance and institutional trust', in P. Norris (ed.) *Critical Citizens: Global support for democratic government*, Oxford: Oxford University Press.
Morris, S. D. and Klesner, J. L. (2010) 'Corruption and trust: Theoretical considerations and evidence from Mexico', *Comparative Political Studies*, 43(10): 1258–85.
Norris, P. (1999) 'Institutional explanations for political support', in P. Norris (ed.) *Critical Citizens: Global support for democratic government*, Oxford: Oxford University Press.
Powell, G. B. (2000) *Elections as Instruments of Democracy: Majoritarian and proportional visions,* New Haven: Yale University Press.
Rahn, W. M. and Rudolph, T. J. (2005) 'A tale of political trust in American cities', *Public Opinion Quarterly*, 69(4): 530–60.
Rose, R. (1994) 'Postcommunism and the problem of trust', *Journal of Democracy*, 5(3): 18–30.
Rose, R. and Mishler, W. (2011) 'Political trust and distrust in post-authoritarian contexts', in S. Zmerli and M. Hooghe (eds) *Political Trust: Why context matters*, Colchester: ECPR Press.
Snijders, T. and Bosker, R. (1999) *Multilevel Analysis: An Introduction to basic and advanced multilevel modelling,* London: Sage.
Steenbergen, M. R. and Jones, B. S. (2002) 'Modeling multilevel data structures', *American Journal of Political Science*, 46(1): 694–713.
Steenvoorden, E., van der Meer, T. W. G. and Dekker, P. (2009) *Continu Onderzoek Burgerperspectieven 2009|3*, Den Haag: Netherlands Institute for Social Research | SCP.

Teorell, J., Holmberg, S. and Rothstein, B. (2007) *The Quality of Government Dataset, Version 1 July 07*, Göteborg: The Quality of Government Institute of Göteborg University. Online. Available: http//www.qog.pol.gu.se.

Thomassen, J. J. and Aarts, K. (2005) *Electoral institutions and satisfaction with democracy*, Paper presented at the Annual Meeting of the American Political Science Association, Washington DC, 31st August–3rd September 2005.

Tolsma, J., van der Meer, T. W. G. and Gesthuizen, M. (2009) 'The impact of neighborhood and municipality characteristics on social cohesion in the Netherlands', *Acta Politica*, 44(3): 286–313.

Ulbig, S. G. (2008) 'Voice is not enough: The importance of influence in political trust and policy assessments', *Public Opinion Quarterly*, 72(3): 523–39.

Uslaner, E. M. (2002) *The Moral Foundations of Trust*, Cambridge: Cambridge University Press.

van der Meer, T. W. G. (2009) 'Politiek vertrouwen internationaal verklaard.', in P. Dekker, T. W. G. van der Meer, P. Schyns and E. Steenvoorden (eds) *Crisis in aantocht?* Den Haag: Netherlands Institute for Social Research | SCP.

— (2010) 'In what we trust? A multi-level study into trust in parliament as an evaluation of state characteristics', *International Review of Administrative Sciences*, 76(3): 517–36.

Zmerli, S., Newton, K. and Montero, J. R. (2007) 'Trust in people, confidence in political institutions, and satisfaction with democracy', in J. W. van Deth, J. R. Montero and A. Westholm (eds) *Citizenship and Involvement in European Democracies: A comparative analysis,* London: Routledge.

chapter six | political trust and distrust in post-authoritarian contexts

Richard Rose and William Mishler[1]

Introduction

Political trust and its complement, distrust, are universal characteristics of every political system. However, the level of trust or distrust varies with the context. There are differences *between* societies in the aggregate level of trust. There are also differences *within* every society between some citizens who tend to trust political institutions and those who do not. Trust and distrust can vary across time, especially when a post-authoritarian regime is established. While, initially, citizens will only have had experience of its communist predecessor, with the passage of time people will learn to evaluate the new regime for what it is, whether it is a democracy or one type of authoritarian rule is substituted for another.

One set of theories emphasises the importance of national context and cross-national variations in political culture (e.g. Eckstein 1966; Inglehart 1997) or in the performance of political institutions (Dalton 2004). A second set of theories emphasises the importance of differences between individuals in their socialisation experiences and in the political and economic attitudes they use to evaluate political institutions. Studies of trust that rely on cross-sectional data cannot take time into account. Yet insofar as the durability and performance of a regime varies, this too may affect trust in political institutions. This chapter tests theories that offer explanations for the variability of political trust in different national, temporal and social structural contexts. We do so by analysing sixty-seven New Europe Barometer surveys collected in fourteen countries of Central and Eastern Europe and the former Soviet Union between 1993 and 2004.

Theories about the sources of trust

Theories about the causes of trust differ in whether they emphasise the influence of macro-level characteristics of a society as a whole, which tend to be common to all its citizens, or micro-level characteristics of individuals, which differ within a given society. In principle, the two approaches are complementary: both macro- and micro-level influences can affect the extent to which individuals trust or distrust the political institutions of their particular society (for a broader discussion, see Mishler and Rose 2001: 31 *et seq.*).

---

[1]. Part of a research project on Testing the Durability of Regime Support: Term Limits in Putin's Russia, funded by the British Economic & Social Research Council, RES-062-23-0341.

Macro-context matters

A generalised predisposition to trust or distrust is postulated in *cultural theories* that stress the development and maintenance of values and belief from one generation or even one century to another. Trust not only favourably disposes citizens to specific political institutions but is also expected to generate diffuse support (Easton 1965). In a democratic political system, a civic culture with a high level of trust is deemed vital for 'making democracy work' (Putnam 1993; Almond and Verba 1963; Dahl 1971). Some area specialists explained the compliance of Soviet subjects with their communist regime as a consequence of the authoritarian character of traditional Russian culture which encouraged submissive attitudes, such as trust in the Tsar (Keenan 1986; Jowitt 1993; Eckstein *et al.* 1998). Theories of holistic national cultures differing in their values and beliefs leads to the following:

> Hypothesis H1 (national culture): Trust in political institutions tends to be homogeneous within a country but variable between countries according to their political culture.

One set of cultural theories explains trust in political institutions as exogenous to the political system; it is expected to reflect norms arising from an individual's face-to-face relations with significant others. Interpersonal trust is expected to make political institutions work because, as Putnam describes it, it 'spills over' into cooperation with people in local civic associations and then, 'spills up' to create a nationwide network of trusted institutions necessary for representative democracy (cf. Almond and Verba 1963; Putnam 1993; Inglehart 1997: 188 *et seq.*; for criticisms, see e.g. Levi 1996; Jackman and Miller 1996; Foley and Edwards 1999). To paraphrase Jimmy Carter, a country can expect a government as good as its people. However, if the culture transmits values of 'amoral familism' such as Banfield (1958) described in southern Italy, then the result will be a government as bad as its people, a point Putnam emphasises in contrasting southern and northern Italy.

Informal networks used by citizens to insulate them from an intrusive government can create what Max Weber (1968) described as the 'inner morality' of trust in those you know, as against the 'outer morality' of distrusting all who are not close friends or family. Many scholars of Russian history have emphasised that the totalitarian aspirations of communist regimes created an 'hour glass' society in which distrust of other people and macro-institutions of society caused people to seek to insulate themselves from the authority of the regime (cf. Pipes 1974; Hedlund 1999: part II; Rose 1995; Shlapentokh 2001).

Theories of political culture emphasise the stability of popular attitudes, including trust, from one generation to the next. In consolidated democracies, institutions are expected to be stable in terms of their respect for the rights of citizens and the respect that public officials show to the rule of law. However, theories that stress economic performance as important for trust predict short-term fluctuations in trust due to the ups and downs of the business cycle.

In a new regime, *time matters* because at its launch many citizens are likely to be uncertain about whether to trust unknown institutions. To the extent that the regime it replaces was distrusted – and Central and East European citizens had many grounds to distrust communist regimes – a post-authoritarian regime, even if defective in some respects, can initially benefit by comparison with the evils of its predecessor (Churchill 1947). Although institutions can be formally abolished quickly, it is not possible to dismiss all public officials trained in the communist practice of dealing with ordinary subjects. To produce a significant turnover in the personnel of public agencies takes time, both to recruit and train replacements. Thus, the more distant in time the communist regime is, the more trust post-communist institutions should have – and it is now two decades since the fall of the Berlin Wall.

Hypothesis H2 (passage of time): The extent of trust or distrust in political institutions tends to vary across time within a country.

Whereas cultural theories treat trust in political institutions as having exogenous causes, institutional theories hypothesise that political trust is endogenous. It is the expected utility of the performance of political institutions. In other words, trust is a consequence rather than a cause of institutional performance (Dasgupta 1988; Coleman 1990). Theories of *institutional performance* emphasise that political trust and distrust are rational responses by individuals to the performance of institutions, which will vary across context and across time (March 1988; North 1990). In other words, institutions that can deliver whatever are deemed to be 'good' goods will be more trusted than those that do not work as they ought to work. Empirical analysis of aggregate indicators of regime performance finds that there is wide variation in the capacity of governments to act effectively (Fortin 2010).

Hypothesis H3 (institutional performance): The extent of trust or distrust in political institutions tends to vary between countries with their political and economic performance.

Performance is often judged in terms of the capacity of political institutions to be effective in managing the economy (Przeworski *et al.* 1996; Duch and Stevenson 2008). Political institutions in post-communist regimes faced a unique challenge to their economic effectiveness, the need to create institutions of a market economy in order to fill the void created by the collapse of the political system that had maintained their command non-market economy (Kornai 1992). While many determinants of economic effectiveness are beyond the reach of national governments, the performance of political institutions is the distinctive responsibility of governors. This is above all true for adherence to the rule of law by public officials, including elected representatives. Officials whose actions are not bound by the rule of law are untrustworthy in the sense of being unpredictable rather than rule-bound Weberian bureaucrats. Insofar as they predictably violate laws, for example, by being corrupt, the institutionalisation of corrupt norms about how the system works can encourage popular distrust (cf. Mishler and Rose 2007).

In post-authoritarian regimes, the political performance of institutions is of special importance, inasmuch as citizens can assess it by comparison with a predecessor regime. In countries where communist regimes had repressed individuals and the rule of law was systematically violated, citizens are likely to value institutions that succeed in reducing corruption, removing restrictions on individual liberty and providing increased freedoms (cf. Rose 2009: Ch. 10; Diamond 1999: 7). The more new institutions perform consistently with democratic expectations, the more they are likely to be considered trustworthy.

Individual differences matter

Macro-level theories postulate aggregate characteristics of context determine how individuals evaluate their political institutions. However, they make little allowance for variations in trust among individuals within societies. By contrast, microlevel theories focus on differences between individuals that cause political trust to vary significantly within a society.

Socialisation theories predict that trust is a consequence of a lifetime of learning from interaction with significant others (Eckstein 1966). Children learn to trust or distrust other people by experiencing how they are treated by others. Initially, the 'others' are parents and immediate family and school friends. In turn, these affect life chances in the world of work. While socialisation is a generic process, within a society the socialisation of individuals varies by gender, generational cohort, parental circumstances, education and adult employment. In turn, these differences are predicted to influence their evaluation of the political system.

Hypothesis H4 (socialisation): The extent of trust or distrust in political institutions varies with differences in individual socialisation experiences.

A change of regime creates a structural discontinuity in political socialisation, because institutions that have been the object of individual learning are replaced by new institutions with new political values. This is especially important in postcommunist societies, since there was a treble transformation affecting the economy and social relations as well as the polity (Rose 2009). When there is a regime change, an individual's political trust is affected not only by their early learning, but also by re-learning experiences in reaction to a new regime.

The *attitudes* of individuals, however formed, provide criteria that citizens use to evaluate government. A small number of basic norms concern how the political system functions, while many relate to preferences about what the government ought to do (Easton 1965). In order for a political system to function efficiently and effectively, virtually everyone in a society ought to accept the basic norms that constitute the 'rules of the political game'. However, insofar as politics is about the articulation of conflicting opinions about what government ought to do (Easton 1965; Dahl 1971), then citizens ought to disagree about the trustworthiness of their political institutions. It is an open empirical question whether a consensus about political trust is necessary for the maintenance of a regime or whether disagreement about the trustworthiness of government is part of political life in a democracy and, in a muted form, in an undemocratic system.

Aggregate evidence of national economic performance does not have a uniform effect on a country's citizens. How people evaluate the performance of their government reflects their perceptions and norms. Individuals can differ about the economic performance of government according to whether they personally benefit. They can also differ by whether they give greater priority to the choice posed by the Keynesian and monetarist paradigms: fighting inflation or unemployment. Whereas macro-level assessments of political corruption assign a single rating to government, public opinion surveys show that individuals differ in their views of how corrupt or honest their government tends to be. Similar differences can be found in evaluations of the fairness of government and its responsiveness to citizens or their preference for an authoritarian – as against a democratic – system of government.

> Hypothesis H5 (political and economic evaluations): The extent of trust or distrust in political institutions tends to vary with individual evaluations of institutional performance.

In new regimes, influences on individual trust can change over time either as a consequence of changes in national context or as a function of individual learning. The impact of economic perceptions on trust may decline in the face of sustained macro-economic growth as citizens begin to take prosperity for granted. Conversely, citizens may learn to accept persisting national corruption as inevitable with the consequence being that perceptions of corruption have diminishing effects on political trust over time. Together, changes in individuals and in context can create cross-level influences on trust.

> Hypothesis H6 (cross-level effects): Individual influences on political trust vary between national and temporal contexts.

While theories differ in the emphasis given to different causes of political trust or distrust, they can be complementary rather than in conflict. This is most likely to be the case as regards hypotheses H2, H5 and H6, since the extent to which people judge the performance of their political system as trustworthy is likely to be influenced, at least in part, by the extent to which its macro-level institutions are honest, democratic and effective. Hypothesis 3, which stresses the importance of macro-level change over time, is complemented by the socialisation hypothesis H4, which emphasises how individual attitudes can adapt by re-learning. The chief conflict is between these hypotheses and the hypothesis that national culture is of primary importance, for the former predict that trust in political institutions will vary between individuals within a society, whereas the latter stresses that public opinion will be homogeneous within a country, while differing between trustful and distrusting cultures.

The distribution of trust and distrust

The political institutions of communist regimes were founded on distrust. Subjects were not trusted to decide for themselves what to think about political institutions. The party line was laid down in Moscow and repeated by national parties in Central and Eastern Europe. It was then amplified by party members in control of the media, and repeated in face to face indoctrination at places of work and in schools. The state security system maintained continuing surveillance of the population and recruited, sometimes under duress, informers who were expected to report anything said that indicated distrust of the party line. At election time, voters were not trusted to mark their ballots in secret but to show openly their nominal support for official candidates.

While communist regimes are no more, their legacy has not disappeared, inasmuch as the median Central or East European adult was socialised for the first half of their life in a communist system and in post-Soviet states there has been a change from one type of 'unfree' or partly-free regime to another. Post-communist regimes are thus specially suited to testing why trust varies because there are a priori theoretical grounds for expecting divisions between trusting and distrusting citizens within societies; between them; and across time.

Empirical testing of hypotheses requires both aggregate measures of institutional performance and survey data about trust, socialisation and perceptions of economic and political performance. The New Europe Barometer (NEB) series of surveys by the Centre for the Study of Public Policy is uniquely suited to this purpose. The NEB surveys analysed here cover fourteen different countries. Ten have had their democratic credentials validated by becoming members of the European Union (Bulgaria, the Czech Republic, Slovakia, Hungary, Poland, Romania, Slovenia, Estonia, Latvia and Lithuania); three are post-Soviet countries (Russia, Belarus and Ukraine); and Croatia is a Yugoslav successor state that has moved from being a military dictatorship to a candidate for EU membership. Equally important, the NEB makes it possible to test what can account for stability or change, because the same questions about trust have been asked in each country in five different years between 1993 and 2004. In each survey, a stratified nationwide sampling frame was used to locate approximately 1,000 randomly selected respondents for face-to-face interviews in their home. All surveys were conducted by established professional institutes with trained interviewing staffs. In all, the NEB constitutes a data base of sixty-seven surveys with individual-level data about political institutions and much else for 78,289 people (for sample details and the questionnaire, see Appendices A and B and go to http://www.abdn.ac.uk/cspp/catalog13_0.shtml). To measure trust in institutions, the NEB asks:

> There are many different institutions in this country, for example the government, courts, police, civil servants. Please show me on this seven-point scale, where one represents great distrust and seven represents great trust, how much is your personal trust in each of the following institutions –

An important theoretical advantage of the NEB question is that the degree of trust in institutions is asked without reference to personalities in charge or to institutional outputs. By contrast, questions used in the Eurobarometer and elsewhere often ask about confidence in the people running government and whether institutions are doing what is right (Dalton 2008: 241*et seq.*), thus biasing responses in favour of performance-oriented theories of trust. In addition, our use of a seven-point scale provides both an arithmetic and a psychological mid-point for people who neither trust nor distrust an institution. This is absent in a four-point or a ten-point scale.

Responses on the seven-point scale can be grouped into three categories: trustful – points 5 to 7; sceptical – the mid-point on the scale, 4; and distrustful – points 1 to 3. For each institution public opinion is divided between all three categories (see Table 6.1). More than half of respondents are actively distrustful of parliament and political parties, and the mean score for the police and courts is also negative. Across all fourteen countries,[2] the mean level of trust varies substantially between political institutions. It is relatively highest for the army – just above the neutral point of 4.0. A fifth of respondents are sceptical about each institution. From a dynamic perspective, sceptical citizens are especially important because they have not yet committed themselves to a positive or negative view of an institution. They are thus open to changing their views in the light of more experience (Mishler and Rose 1997).

Table 6.1: Trust in political institutions

	Trustful	**Sceptical**	**Distrustful**	**Mean 7-pt scale**
		(% in category)		
Army	48	20	32	4.3
Courts	31	21	49	3.6
Police	31	20	49	3.6
Parliament	21	19	60	3.1
Political parties	13	18	69	2.8

Source: Centre for the Study of Public Policy New Europe Barometer; 67 surveys in fourteen countries, 1993–2004. Total number of weighted interviews, 67,000. For details, see Appendix A. *Q. Please show me on this 7-point scale, where 1 represents great distrust and 7 represents great trust, how much you trust each of the following institutions.* (Trusting: Codes 5–7 on 7 point scale; Sceptical, 4; Distrustful, 1–3)

---

2. To test the effects of both national context and individual differences, we pooled the survey data from the fourteen countries in a single multinational file in which each country is weighted equally as having 1,000 cases.

To test the extent to which political trust reflects a generalised disposition toward institutions, a factor analysis was undertaken of the individual replies with regard to the five political institutions. Notwithstanding major institutional differences between 'input' institutions, such as parties and parliament, and institutions concerned with producing authoritative outputs, such as the army, courts and police, a single principal component accounts for 53.1 per cent of the total variance in attitudes. The loadings for each indicator are high: 0.79 for the courts, 0.78 for police, 0.75 for parliament, 0.69 for parties and 0.63 for the army. This justifies the creation of a single scale, which is the mean score on the seven-point scale of individual trust in five political institutions.[3]

The NEB questionnaire follows up questions about trust in political institutions by asking: 'How much do you trust most people you meet?' And then: 'How much trust do you have in most people in society?' Whereas Putnam's theory of social capital implies a more or less one-to-one correspondence between an individual's trust in face-to-face contacts, in fellow citizens and in national institutions, Fukuyama's (1995) theory of trust postulates that the radius of trust differs between these objects. It is expected to be greatest for people you know, less for aggregates of people, and less still for institutions covering the whole of society. Fukuyama also emphasises that there are cross-cultural variations in the radius of trust within Europe with significant effects on economic enterprises and, by implication, political institutions.

The NEB evidence strongly supports Fukuyama's theory of the radius of trust. A total of 69 per cent of individuals trust most people they know, while trust in most people in the country falls to 44 per cent. Trust in political institutions is lower still; only one in four trusts at least three out of five institutions. The population of NEB societies thus divides into the following groups:

- those who trust most people they know;
- those who trust most people in society whether they know them personally or not; and
- a limited minority who also extend interpersonal trust to trust in political institutions.

However, contrary to Fukuyama's generalisation about cross-national variations in the radius of trust, it differs little across CEE and post-Soviet countries. In every country except Bulgaria, an absolute majority trusts most people they know.

Consistent with Putnam's idea that social trust 'spills over and up' into trust for political institutions, there is a relatively strong and properly signed zero-order correlation ($r = .31$) between interpersonal and institutional trust across NEB countries. However, previous research applying two-stage least squares and structural equation models to NEB and NRB data (Mishler and Rose 2001, 2005) shows that there is little or no causal connection between social and political trust. To the lim-

---

3. Separate analyses of the structure of institutional trust in each of the fourteen countries produces very similar results. The best fitting model is one-dimensional in every case.

ited extent that the two are causally connected, the impact of political trust appears much stronger on social trust than vice versa. Based on this evidence, social trust is not included in the subsequent multilevel model of institutional trust. Doing so would artificially inflate the variance explained by the model and would also risk rendering spurious or undermining other relationships in the data.

Contextual and Individual Influences

The effect of space and time

Theories of political culture lead to the holistic prediction of hypothesis H1 that, whether the level of political trust is high or low, it will be relatively homogeneous within a given country. However, hypothesis H1 is not supported, because there is substantially more variation in trust *within* each country than across countries. This is shown in Figure 6.1 by the wide variation of opinion around national means. One-third or more of respondents are at least one full point outside the mean level of trust and in Croatia the standard deviation in trust is as high as 1.4. Given such disagreement within society, we should not generalise about trustful and distrustful political cultures.

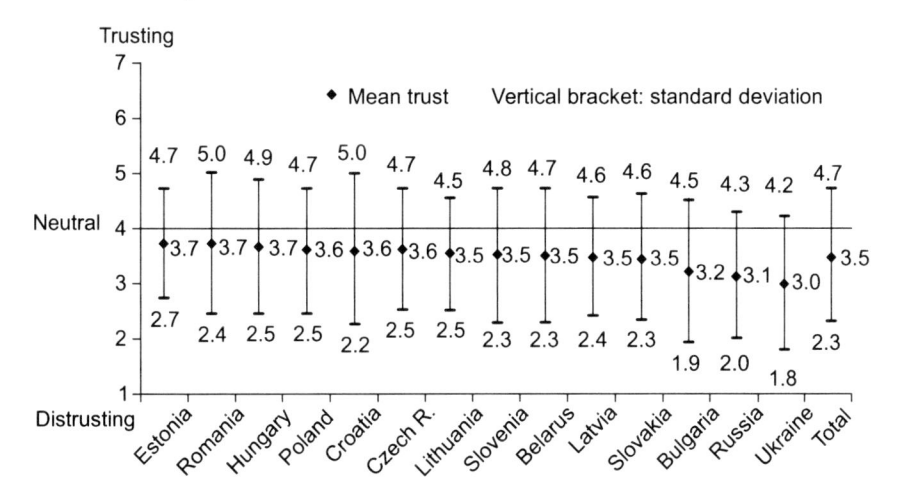

Figure 6.1: Variations in trust within and across nations

Source: As in Table 6.1.

Cross-national comparison offers some support for hypothesis 2: with the passage of time there is some change in the mean level of national trust. However, there is no consistent pattern of change, but rather a lot of fluctuations up and down (Figure 6.2). When the means of trust in 1993 and 2004 are compared, the data more often show a fall rather than an increase in trust, but the fluctuations are such that no general pattern emerges to support a theory of a common downward trend in trust. In five countries, the national mean is down by less than one-third

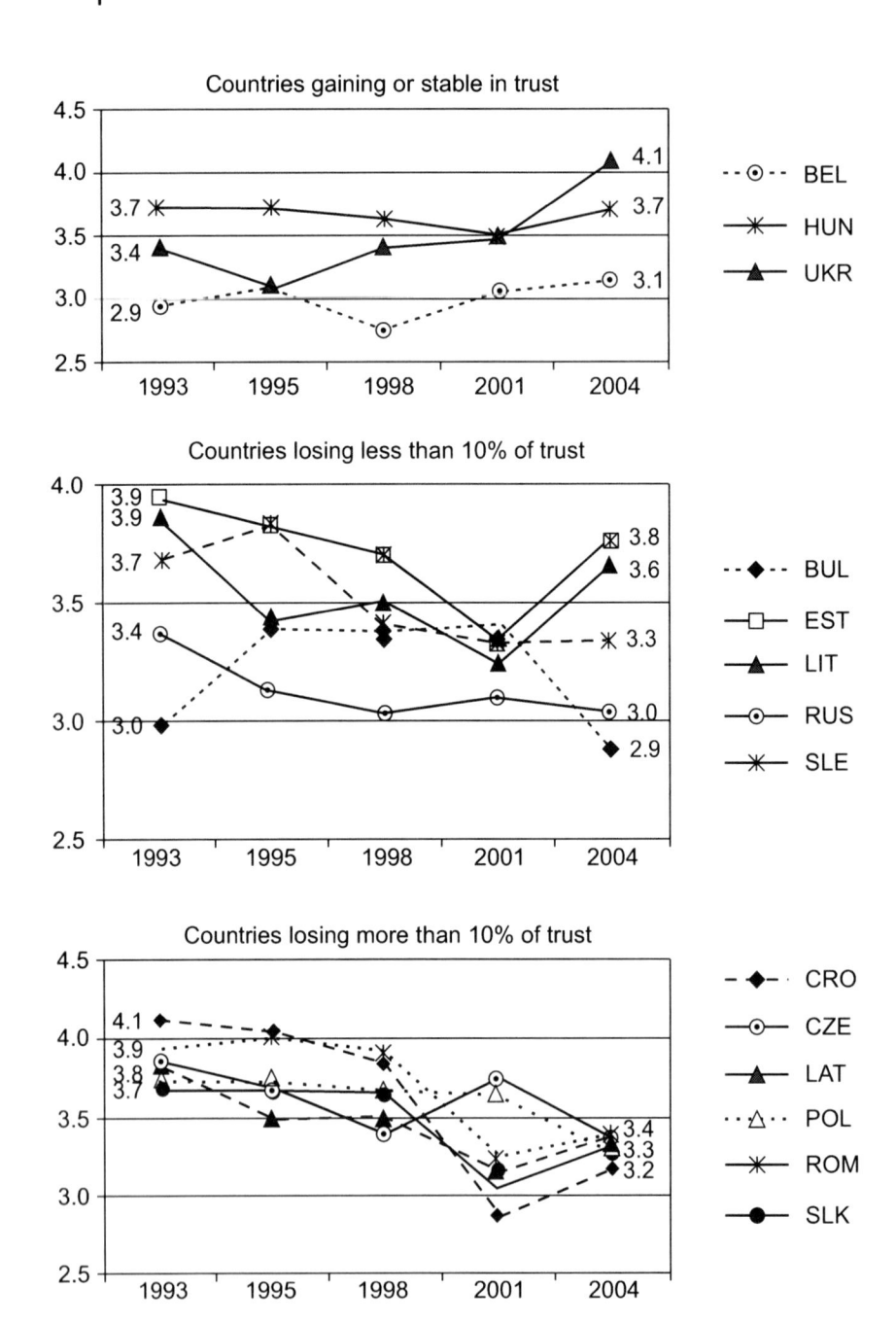

Figure 6.2: Trends in political trust 1993–2004
Source: As in Table 6.1.

of a point on the seven-point scale. In five countries, the decline is no more than half a point, and in Croatia, where the mean level of trust has fallen most, it has not done so by as much as a full point. Moreover, in three countries, the mean level of trust has risen since 1993. In every country, the change in the mean level of national trust is much less than the variation around the mean at any given point in time (see Figures 6.1 and 6.2). Thus, mean scores are insufficient to understand variations in trust.

Combining contextual and individual differences

Since political trust is a consequence of the interaction between individuals and institutions, the fullest understanding of its determinants requires combining the influence of contextual measures, survey data about individuals and their possible interaction. Multilevel Modelling (MLM) provides an appropriate statistical method to take both contextual and individual influences into account. It corrects the standard errors associated with aggregate-level time series variables and assesses cross-level interactions (Steenbergen and Jones 2002; Raudenbush and Bryk 2002). In constructing the multilevel model, the choice of aggregate contextual variables is constrained by two related considerations. Given fourteen countries and a maximum of five time periods for each country, the analysis has sixty-seven 'country-year' aggregate level units, e.g. Poland 1993, Poland 1995, Russia 1993, Russia 1994, and so forth. Second, many potentially interesting aggregate level variables are highly correlated. In combination, the relatively small number of aggregate-level cases and the high aggregate-level correlations severely limited the number of macro-level variables that could be included in the analysis. The selection of contextual variables for inclusion was a trial and error process in which theoretically meaningful variables were added and deleted one at a time until the 'best fitting' model was achieved.

At the individual level, the NEB questionnaire offers data about a great variety of experiences and attitudes, many common to individuals in established democracies. It also has measures that take into account the re-learning experiences arising from being socialised into a communist regime and adapting to a post-communist system. However, the structure of the multilevel model severely constrains the number of individual variables that can be estimated. To identify those most important in determining how much or how little individuals trust their political institutions, a preliminary OLS regression was undertaken, with many indicators of socialisation experiences and political and economic attitudes. The results have been used to screen out measures that have no substantial influence on trust and thus focus attention on those that have the greatest effects.[4]

The importance of considering both individual and contextual influences on political trust is confirmed by the Hierarchical linear modelling (HLM) analysis. Individual characteristics account for 12.6 per cent of the variance among individuals and contextual influences for 35.0 per cent of the variance across countries

---

4. A full list of these variables and results is available from the authors.

and time (see Table 6.2). The model finds significant support for the influence of performance, socialisation and time on trust (hypotheses H3 through H6) but, after controlling for all other effects, the degree of trust in political institutions is not the same.

The tendency for citizens in post-communist regimes to distrust political institutions makes negative as well as positive measures of *political performance* important. Corruption is an important measure of political performance (Lambsdorff 2007). Transparency International's (TI) Perception of Corruption Index consistently reports a wide variation in corruption between national political systems (http://www.transparency.org). Half of NEB countries have a rating that is as high, or higher, than such established European Union member countries as Greece and Italy, while post-Soviet countries, such as Russia and Ukraine, are much lower than both new and old EU member states. Similarly, the NEB question that asks what proportion of public officials are corrupt in a country, consistently finds that 73 per cent view most or almost all of their national officials as corrupt as against 27 per cent crediting the bulk of officials with being honest. Both measures record the perception of corruption, but differ in that NEB surveys show how perceptions of corruption differ between individuals within a country whereas Transparency International provides an aggregate score for the political system as a whole.

Consistent with theoretical expectations, the more a government is perceived as corrupt, the less its political institutions tend to be trusted and both individual and aggregate measures of corruption are significant. While NEB surveys find that the popular perception of corruption has tended to remain constant over time, its effect on trust has grown increasingly negative as indicated by the significant cross-level interaction with time (b coefficient, -0.015). There is no significant cross-level interaction between the aggregate TI measure of corruption and the NEB measure. This means that the effect on trust of individual perceptions of corruption is much the same cross-nationally.

The extent to which citizens enjoy freedom from the state shows whether the performance of government respects democratic norms (Berlin 1958). Freedom House (http://www.freedomhouse.org) annually rates the overall performance of national governments in respecting the liberties of its citizens. There is substantial variation between NEB countries in the extent to which they are rated as free, partly free or, like Belarus, 'unfree'. The New Europe Barometer asks individuals whether they feel freer under their current political system than under the communist regime. Consistently, a great majority of people see themselves as freer now than before. It is a commentary on the repressive nature of the communist regime that individuals not only feel themselves freer in democratic contexts, but also in countries that Freedom House does not rate as free such as Russia, Belarus and Ukraine.

Individuals who subjectively feel freer now are significantly more likely to trust their political institutions. Context also has a significant influence on political trust and it does so in contrasting ways (see Table 6.2). Although there is evidence that aggregate trust can correlate with a country's democratic status (McAllister and White 2009: 196), when a host of individual and aggregate influences are

Table 6.2: Combining contextual and individual influences on trust. Multilevel model of institutional trust: restricted maximum likelihood estimates with robust standard errors

	Coefficient	S.E.	P
LEVEL II			
Year	-0.04	0.01	0.001
Annual inflation	-0.00	0.00	0.001
Freedom House	-0.10	0.03	0.01
TI Corruption Index	0.07	0.03	0.01
Cumulative economic growth	0.00	0.00	0.05
Proportional representation	0.12	0.06	0.05
District magnitude	-0.00	0.00	0.05
LEVEL I			
Perception of corruption	-0.27	0.04	0.001
x Year	-0.01	0.01	0.10
Feels freer now	0.08	0.02	0.001
x Year	-0.01	0.00	0.05
x Freedom House	0.02	0.01	0.05
Favours authoritarian alternatives	-0.03	0.01	0.001
Can influence political process	0.09	0.01	0.001
x Year	0.01	0.00	0.001
x Freedom House	0.02	0.00	0.001
Government treats people fairly	0.17	0.01	0.001
Favours national economic system	0.04	0.00	0.001
x Year	0.00	0.00	0.10
Household economic situation favourable	0.14	0.01	0.001
Education	-0.06	0.01	0.001
Age	0.00	0.00	0.001
Female	0.06	0.01	0.001
Level I reduction in variance: 12.6% Level II reduction: 35.0%			

Note: Given the substantially different number of cases at the aggregate (n = 67) and individual (n = 67,000) levels, probability levels of .001 are appropriate for attributing significance to Level I relationships whereas probability levels of .05 and even .10 are appropriate for attributing significance to Level II and cross-level relationships.

taken into account, as in our MLM analysis, the net effect is that political trust tends to be depressed in countries that Freedom House classifies as 'freer'. However, this result is qualified by a positive interaction between individuals feeling freer and the performance of their institutions having a high Freedom House rating. However, the effect of this interaction tends to diminish with the passage of time (b: −0.008), as the memory of the old regime fades and citizens begin to take new freedoms for granted.

The expansion of freedom and introduction of democratic institutions after the fall of the Berlin Wall was contemporaneous with the costs of transforming non-market into market economies. Political economy and rational choice theories warned that the economic costs of transformation could undermine new institutions by encouraging support for authoritarian institutions for which there were ample historical examples. In the event, these fears were much exaggerated. NEB surveys found a majority rejected establishing a dictatorship, a return to communist rule or the army ruling. A composite indicator of support for authoritarian alternatives shows that this group is less inclined to trust its current political institutions. However, their number is limited and further discounted by the fact that even among those who would prefer a different regime from their current distrusted government, there is little expectation of another change in regime happening.

In every NEB country, the introduction of competitive elections has provided the institutional means for citizens to exert a measure of influence on government. However, NEB respondents differ in their views on the performance of these institutions. A majority think they have no greater influence on government than under their old regime – and this is so across the whole range of NEB countries. If an individual believes that people like themselves now have some influence on what government does, it significantly increases their trust in political institutions. Moreover, the effect is also stronger in contexts in which Freedom House assesses a regime as conducting free and fair elections and the positive effect is increasing from year to year. The impact, however, of individual political efficacy is limited by the fact that across the region it is not high.

The electoral institutions that give citizens their chief means of exerting political influence are uniform within a national context, but vary across national boundaries. In some NEB countries proportional representation is the exclusive means used to elect Members of Parliament, while others have a mixed system, combining proportional representation and electing MPs from single-member districts (Rose and Munro 2009). The link between a citizen and representatives as well as the proportionality of a system varies with the district magnitude, i.e. the number of MPs elected from a constituency. As proponents of proportional representation claim, its performance does promote a greater sense of political trust. However, this positive effect is somewhat offset by the fact that PR requires districts with a greater magnitude than single-member districts and this has a negative effect on political trust (see Table 6.2).

Communist regimes boasted that they were welfare states, but they were missing an important ingredient of Bismarckian and Scandinavian welfare states, that of administering programmes in accord with the rule of law (Flora and Alber

1981). Even though all citizens were formally entitled to many benefits, in the absence of a rule-bound bureaucracy, whether or how they received social services depended on how they were treated by public officials. If treated fairly, then they would receive their entitlements. If treated unfairly, then corruption or other forms of negative social capital had to be invoked to overcome the refusal of benefits. While communist regimes have disappeared, many of the officials trained under the old regime remain in place and the extent of perceived corruption indicates their legacy still affects official behaviour.

The response to a New Europe Barometer question as to whether people such as themselves are treated equally and fairly shows a division of opinion within every society; the mean indicates that there is a little more fairness than before. Insofar as individuals do see public officials as treating people like themselves fairly, they are more likely to trust political institutions (see Table 6.2). The absence of any cross-level effect of national context or time shows that individual assessments of fairness are independent of the extent to which their political system is democratic or corrupt.

Political economy theories emphasise that *economic performance* is what counts and at the aggregate level there are many macro-economic indicators. Moreover, the distribution and perception of economic conditions vary between individuals within every society. Kinder and Kiewiet (1979) have found that the political effect of evaluations of the national economy, for which the government is responsible, and an individual's personal situation, for which people hold themselves responsible, has a political effect (on post-communist economies, see Rose, Mishler and Munro 2011: Ch. 6).

The way in which citizens evaluate the performance of the system that replaced the non-market command economy has a substantial effect on political trust (see Table 6.2). The more positive people are about the new economic system, the more they tend to trust the political institutions responsible for it. In addition, the b coefficient for its cross-level interaction with the passage of time has increased by .0009 each year. Although this appears small, over a dozen years of NEB surveys the cumulative effect is substantial. Moreover, popular evaluation of the economy has become increasingly positive. In 1993, when the shock of transformation was harshly felt, only 31 per cent of NEB respondents were positive about the system. By 2004, the percentage of positive across the region had risen to 56 per cent.

Subjective evaluations of economic performance, which vary between individuals within a society, are substantially more important for political trust than is aggregate gross domestic product (GDP), which is expressed as a single notional estimate of the state of the national economy.[5] To take into account the cumulative

---

5. Gross domestic product (GDP) is a construct created by summarising a large and heterogeneous mass of data about activity in the official economy according to Standard National Accounting procedures designed for market economies as they were in 'best practice' economies more than three decades ago. In post-Communist societies, GDP has been specially 'constructed', since so much activity is undertaken outside the official economy. Cf. Marer *et al.* 1992; Rose 2009: Pt I, and the footnotes to the annual statistical reports of the European Bank for Reconstruction and

effect of the immediate economic contraction due to the collapse of the command economy and the subsequent growth of the market economy, we use the cumulative economic growth over the time span of NEB surveys. However, this aggregate measure of economic growth has little effect on political trust and is less significant than the effect of individual evaluations.

Economic transformation had a much more extreme effect on the value of money than on the GDP. Whereas annual changes in GDP were almost invariably measured in single digits, the mean for annual inflation in the period covered here was 111 per cent. It was so high because of quadruple digit inflation in some countries in early years. Since inflation rates cumulate, the compound effect was to reduce the value of money by nine-tenths or more. At the height of economic transformation, when both inflation and unemployment were high, individuals were more likely to be worried by inflation (Rose 1998). This is consistent with the fact that in a money economy, inflation affects everyone, whereas unemployment can only affect those in the labour force or with no resources to fall back on in the unofficial and household economies. The more reason voters have to trust the stability of their currency, the more likely they are to trust their political institutions. Being satisfied with the economic situation at the micro-level of the household also has a positive effect on trust in political institutions. However, satisfaction with how one's household income has increased has tended to lag behind satisfaction with the national economic system.

The passage of time has a significant influence too on political institutions. However, the effect is negative (see Table 6.2). As post-communist citizens have learned more about the institutions of their new regime, they have become less trusting. Since the MLM analysis controls for all other influences, this cannot be explained away by reference to other negative developments. It could be a consequence of unrealistic expectations after the fall of the Berlin Wall about how trustworthy the new regime would be.

Thanks to the long time span covered by NEB surveys, we can also identify how the influence of individual attitudes is modified with the passage of time. The negative impact of corruption on political trust is increased and the positive impact of greater freedom is reduced. Time also increases the impact on political trust of evaluations of the national economy and confidence in being able to influence government (see Table 6.2).

As hypothesised, socialisation also has a significant and substantial effect on political trust. In post-authoritarian political systems, more educated people are less likely to trust political institutions. Trust is significantly higher among older people and among women. Since women tend to live longer and older women were at school when the state provided less education, their effects can be cumulative. It also implies that younger, more educated males will be less trusting of political institutions. The evaluation of the former communist regime is not included in Table 6.2 because preliminary analysis found that it was not significant.

Development.

Individuals approving of the old regime are no more or no less trusting of new institutions than those most alienated by it. The fact that none of the socialisation effects are mediated by any contextual variables means that the effects of socialisation are constant across countries and time.

The extent to which an individual does or does not trust political institutions reflects the combined effects of influences summarised separately above. While some combinations are positive, others are negative. Thus, while a government that is perceived as performing fairly and open to influence will thereby gain trust, there will be a negative counter-pressure if there is dissatisfaction with the economic system. Among socialisation influences, age and gender boost trust while education depresses it. Aggregate level indicators push in opposite directions too. Economic performance is distinctive in that its three significant influences all tend to boost trust in political institutions.

Performance: the key to trust

Trust or distrust in political institutions is principally determined by the political and economic performance of new democracies. Performance, however, is not a system-level attribute as macro-institutional theories suggest. The effects of macro-political and economic performance on trust are indirect and mediated at the micro-level by value-laden attitudes and perceptions of individuals. While individuals are unlikely to overlook either runaway inflation or their government having a reputation for corruption, they may discount or ignore many conditions at the national level according to their individual circumstances. The inevitably checkered performance of new democracies invites individuals to respond to those elements that each perceives, with predictable consequences for political trust.

The measurement of trust on a scale with an unambiguous mid-point has an important implication for public policy: it shows that a significant fraction of national publics are sceptical about whether their institutions are trustworthy. This may be due to a lack of knowledge or, alternatively, to conflicting experiences with an institution. In either case, their evaluation is open to change in a positive or negative direction through gaining more experience and understanding of political institutions.

Insofar as political institutions are uniform nationally, this encourages propositions that assume they stimulate a uniform response from citizens, an attitude that encourages a belief in quick technological fixes, i.e. changing how institutions operate will make them trustworthy in the eyes of all citizens. Our evidence shows that changes in trust do not require decades or generations of re-socialisation in order to transform a national political culture. This can occur relatively quickly because of citizens in new regimes re-learning attitudes as, with the passage of time, they accumulate experience in how they are governed. However, the effect of institutional changes on public opinion is contingent and problematic. Even if external observers certify that reforms have been substantially implemented, it remains an open empirical question as to what proportion of a country's population is of the same mind and how much and how little effect this has on trust.

The performance of trustworthy institutions can generate trust just as untrustworthy performance can generate scepticism and distrust. Elected politicians and public officials can increase public trust by rooting out corrupt practices and by protecting new freedoms; institutions can earn trust through policies that improve the state of the macro economy. The behaviour of citizens in Central and Eastern Europe thus confirms the wisdom of V. O. Key (1966) that 'ordinary people are not fools'.

Appendix A

NEB surveys in the analysis

	1993	1995	1996	1998	2000	2001	2002	2005
Belarus	2,067	1,000	–	1,000	1,090	–	–	1,000
Bulgaria	1,139	1,184	–	1,007	–	1,163	–	1,231
Croatia	1,000	1,000	–	1,000	–	–	1,000	1,017
Czech Rep.	1,167	978	–	1,017	–	1,101	–	1,071
Estonia	1,987	–	1,071	–	–	943	–	940
Hungary	1,060	1,067	–	1,017	–	1,577	–	992
Latvia	2,137	–	1,006	–	–	1,001	–	956
Lithuania	2,012	–	1,000	–	–	1,124	–	1,113
Poland	1,057	1,057	–	1,141	–	1,000	–	943
Romania	1,000	1,038	–	1,241	–	1,001	–	1,110
Russia	1,975	2,374	–	2,002	1,907	–	–	2,107
Slovakia	574	1,117	–	1,011	–	1,002	–	1,036
Slovenia	1,023	1,000	–	1,000	–	1,098	–	1,000
Ukraine	1,000	1,000	–	1,161	1,592	–	–	2,000
Total	19,198	12,815	3,077	12,597	4,589	11,010	1,000	16,516

Total: 80,802

For each round of surveys, dates of fieldwork varied between countries with their electoral calendar and other relevant factors, and a winter round sometimes ran into the following year. For precise dates for each country, see Rose (2009: 199–204). For the questionnaires for each round, see http://www.abdn.ac.uk/cspp/quest-index.shtml.

Appendix B

Coding of variables

I. INDIVIDUAL LEVEL VARIABLES		Mean	SD
Trust in political institutions	Mean score on 7-point scale of trust in parties, parliament, courts, police, and army.	3.47	1.2
Social trust	Mean score on 7-point scale of trust in most people in this country and most people that you know.	4.53	1.4
Education level	1=elementary; 2=secondary; 3=vocational; 4=university	2.28	1.02
Age	Age in years	44.8	16.8
Gender	1=female; 0=male.	.53	.49
Perceived corruption	Perceived number of corrupt public officials 0=almost none or a few; 1=most or almost all	.73	.44
Perceived freedoms	Mean score for extent individuals perceive greater freedom now than under communism re: freedom of speech, religion, association, and political involvement (1=much worse now; 2=a little worse now; 3=same; 4=a little better now; 5=much better now than under communism).	4.16	.69
Perceived fairness	1=much worse now than under Communism; 2=a little worse now; 3=same; 4=a little better now; 5=much better now.	2.78	1.22
Perceived influence	1=much worse now than under Communism; 2=a little worse now; 3=same; 4=a little better now; 5=much better now.	2.62	1.2
Pro authoritarian alternatives	Mean score measuring support for: return to communist rule, Army rule, Strong leader rather than Parliament (1=strongly disagree; 2=disagree; 3=don't know/na; 4=agree; 5=strongly agree).	1.90	.91
Current economy evaluation	21-point scale (-10 to +10) registering satisfaction/ dissatisfaction with current macro-economic system	–1.12	5.04
Current vs past family finances	Household finances today as compared to communism are: 1=much worse 2=somewhat worse; 3=same; 4=somewhat better; 5=much better than or before.	2.19	.77

II. AGGREGATE PERFORMANCE INDICATORS		Mean	SD
Year	Years Since 1993	5.84	4.02
Corruption Index	10-point Transparency corruption. (1 = lowest; 10=highest). For years before TI scores are available corruption coded equal to the first year of actual data. Source: Transparency International.	3.87	1.19
Freedom Index	7-point Freedom House score (7=Freest 1=Most unfree) measuring each country's civil and political liberties in 1998. Source: Freedom House (1998).	5.48	1.39
Change in GDP	Net change in gross domestic product since 1990 as reported by EBRD (2009).	87.66	24.95
Inflation	Annual inflation as reported by EBRD (2009)	110.91	337.95
Proportional representation	Coded 1 if electoral system fully proportional and 0 if hybrid or other. Source Pippa Norris, Democracy Timeseries Data, Release 3.0, January 2009	.642	.483
Electoral district magnitude	Mean Electoral District Magnitude. Source, Pippa Norris, Democracy Timeseries Data, Release 3.0, January 2009.	33.65	47.56

References

Almond, G. A. and Verba, S. (1963) *The Civic Culture,* Princeton: Princeton University Press.

Banfield, E. C. (1958) *The Moral Basis of a Backward Society,* Glencoe, IL: Free Press.

Berlin, I. (1958) *Two Concepts of Liberty: An inaugural lecture,* Oxford: Clarendon Press.

Churchill, W. (1947) 'Debate', House of Commons, *Hansard*, London: HMSO, 11 November vol. 206.

Coleman, J. S. (1990) *Foundations of Social Theory,* Cambridge, MA: Harvard University Press.

Dahl, R. A. (1971) *Polyarchy: Participation and opposition*, New Haven: Yale University Press.

Dalton, R. (2004) *Democratic Challenges, Democratic Choices: The Erosion of political support in advanced industrial democracies*, Oxford: University Press.

— (2008) *Citizen Politics: Public opinion and parties in advanced industrial democracies*, Washington, DC: CQ Press.

Dasgupta, P. (1988) 'Trust as a commodity', in D. Gambetta (ed.) *Trust: Making and breaking cooperative relations*, Oxford: Basil Blackwell.

Diamond, L. (1999) *Developing Democracy: Toward consolidation,* Baltimore: Johns Hopkins University Press.

Duch, R. and Stevenson, R. T. (2008) *The Economic Vote: How political and economic institutions condition election results,* New York: Cambridge University Press.

Easton, D. (1965) *A Systems Analysis of Political Life*, New York: John Wiley.

Eckstein, H. (1966) *Division and Cohesion in Democracy: A study of Norway*, Princeton: Princeton University Press.

Eckstein, H., Fleron, F. J., Hoffmann, E. P. and Reisinger W. M. (1998) *Can Democracy Take Root in Post-Soviet Russia? Explorations in state-society relations*, Lanham, MD: Rowman & Littlefield.

Flora, P. and Alber, J. (1981) 'Modernization, democratization and the development of welfare states in Western Europe', in P. Flora and A. J. Heidenheimer (eds) *The Development of Welfare States in Europe and America*, New Brunswick, NJ: Transaction Publishers.

Foley, M. W. and Edwards, B. (1999) 'Is it time to disinvest in social capital?', *Journal of Public Policy*, 19(2): 141–74.

Fortin, J. (2010) 'A tool to evaluate state capacity in post-communist countries, 1989–2010', *European Journal of Political Research*, 49(5): 654–86.

Fukuyama, F. (1995) *Trust: The social virtues and the creation of prosperity*, New York: Free Press.

Hedlund, S. (1999) *Russia's 'Market' Economy: A bad case of predatory capitalism*, London: UCL Press.

Inglehart, R. (1997) *Modernization and Postmodernization: Cultural, economic and political change in 41 societies*, Princeton: Princeton University Press.

Jackman, R. W. and Miller, R. A. (1996) 'A renaissance of political culture?', *American Journal of Political Science*, 40(3): 632–59.

Jowitt, K. (1993) *New World Disorder: The Leninist extinction*, Berkeley: University of California Press.

Keenan, E. (1986) 'Muscovite political folkways', *The Russian Review*, 45: 115–81.

Key, V. O. (1966) *The Responsible Electorate*, Cambridge, MA: Harvard University Press.

Kinder, D. and Kiewiet, D. R. (1979) 'Economic discontent and political behavior', *American Journal of Political Science*, 23(3): 495–527.

Kornai, J. (1992) *The Socialist System: The political economy of Communism*, Princeton: Princeton University Press.

Lambsdorff, J. G. (2007) *The Institutional Economics of Corruption and Reform*, Cambridge: Cambridge University Press.

Levi, M. (1996) 'Social and unsocial capital: A review essay of Robert Putnam's "Making Democracy Work"', *Politics and Society*, 24(1): 45–55.

McAllister, I. and White, S. (2009) 'Conventional citizen participation', in C. Haerpfer, P. Bernhagen, R. Inglehart and C. Welzel (eds) *Democratization*, Oxford: Oxford University Press.

March, J. G. (1988) *Decisions and Organizations*, Oxford: Blackwell.

Marer, P., Arvay, J., O'Connor, J., Schrenk, M. and Swanson, D. (1992) *Historically Planned Economies: A guide to the data*, Washington, D.C.: World Bank.

Mishler, W. and Rose, R. (1997) 'Trust, distrust and skepticism: Popular evaluations of civil and political institutions in post-Communist societies', *Journal of Politics*, 59(2): 418–51.

— (2001) 'What are the origins of political trust? Testing institutional and cultural theories in post-Communist societies', *Comparative Political Studies*, 34(1): 30–62.

— (2005) 'What are the political consequences of trust? A test of cultural and institutional theories in Russia', *Comparative Political Studies*, 38(9): 1050–78.

— (2007) 'Generation, age and time: The dynamics of political learning through Russia's transformation', *American Journal of Political Science*, 51(4): 822–34.

North, D. C. (1990) *Institutions, Institutional Change and Economic Performance*, New York: Cambridge University Press.

Pipes, R. (1974) *Russia Under the Old Regime*, New York: Charles Scribner's Sons.

Przeworski, A., Alvarez J., Cheibub, J. A. and Limongi, F. (1996) 'What makes democracies endure?', *Journal of Democracy*, 7(1): 39–55.

Putnam, R. D. (1993) *Making Democracy Work*, with R. Leonardi and R. Y. Nanetti, Princeton: Princeton University Press.

Raudenbush, S. W. and Bryk, A. S. (2002) *Hierarchical Linear Modelling: Applications and data analysis methods*, 2nd edn, Thousand Oaks, CA: Sage Publications Advanced Quantitative Techniques in the Social Sciences.

Rose, R. (1995) 'Russia as an hour-glass society: A constitution without citizens', *East European Constitutional Review*, 4(3): 34–42.

— (1998) 'What is the demand for price stability in post-Communist countries?', *Problems of Post-Communism*, 45(2): 43–50.

— (2009) *Understanding Post-Communist Transformation: A bottom-up approach*, London and New York: Routledge.

Rose, R., Mishler, W. and Munro, N. (2011) *Popular Support for an Authoritarian Regime: The changing views of Russians*, Cambridge: Cambridge University Press.

Rose, R. and Munro, N. (2009) *Parties and Elections in New European Democracies*, Colchester, Essex: ECPR Press.

Shlapentokh, V. (2001) *A Normal Totalitarian Society: How the Soviet Union functioned and how it collapsed*, Armonk, NY: M. E. Sharpe.

Steenbergen, M. R. and Jones, B. S. (2002) 'Modeling multilevel data structures', *American Journal of Political Science*, 46(1): 218–37.

Weber, M. (1968) *Economy and Society*, edited by G. Roth and C. Wittich, Berkeley: University of California Press.

chapter seven | corruption, the inequality trap and trust in government[1]

Eric M. Uslaner

Introduction

Corruption flouts rules of fairness and gives some people advantages that others do not have. Corruption transfers resources from the mass public to the elites – and generally from the poor to the rich (Tanzi 1998). It acts as an extra tax on citizens, leaving less money for public expenditure (Mauro 1997: 7). Corrupt governments have less money to spend on their own projects, pushing down the salaries of public employees. In turn, these lower-level staffers will be more likely to extort funds from the public purse. Government employees in corrupt societies will thus spend more time lining their own pockets than serving the public. Corruption thus leads to lower levels of economic growth and to ineffective government (Mauro 1997: 5).

Most accounts of the roots and remedies for corruption are institutional. Corruption, most academic and policy analysts argue, stems from bad governmental institutions – especially the lack of democracy, free and fair elections, and an ineffective judiciary. I argue that institutional accounts of the roots – and the solutions – to corruption are lacking (Uslaner 2008a). In an extensive six-equation model of corruption across a wide range of societies, I find little support for institutional accounts of corruption. Neither democracy, the structure of a country's electoral system, nor whether government is centralised or decentralised (measured by federalism or the share of a country's government expenditures spent at the local or national level) significantly shapes corruption.

I outline a different account of corruption here – what I call the 'inequality trap'. Corruption rests upon a foundation of unequal resources and it leads to greater inequality in turn. I first present my overall argument and then consider why transition countries at first seem to be exceptions, but then fit the thesis rather well. Next I argue that inequality and corruption both lead to lower levels of serv-

---

[1]. This paper derives from and extends Uslaner (2008a). I am grateful to the Russell Sage Foundation and the Carnegie Corporation for a grant on a related project that is encompassed in my work on the United States and to the General Research Board of the University of Maryland-College Park, for a Faculty Research Award in the Spring 2006 semester; and to Bo Rothstein, Mark Warren, Jong-sung You, Gabriel Badescu, Ronald King, Paul Sum, Kems Adu-Gyan, Michael Bratton, Nick Duncan, John Helliwell, Karen Kaufmann, Lawrence Khoo, Mark Lichbach, Anton Oleynik, Jon (Siew Tiem) Quah, Leonard Sebastian, and especially Marc Hooghe and Sonja Zmerli for helpful comments and discussions and to Mitchell Brown for research assistance. I am also grateful to the many comments I received as I presented my work at forums across the world.

ice delivery and that this effect exacerbates the inequality trap. I then show, using both aggregate and individual-level survey data, that service interruptions in transition countries reflect both inequality and corruption. Failures in public service in turn lead to reduced trust in government, higher tax evasion and a weaker infrastructure – which in turn exacerbates inequality.

The inequality trap thesis is a more encompassing thesis, where I argue that inequality leads to low levels of generalised trust, which in turn results in more corruption, and then to even more inequality (Uslaner 2008a: Ch 2). Inequality is particularly destructive of trust in people, but both corruption and inequality also lead to lower levels of trust in government (Uslaner 2008a: 176–8). The link between corruption and trust in government is straightforward: People are not likely to have confidence in leaders whom they believe to be dishonest. The link with inequality is less direct – through economic evaluations more generally. I examine survey data from the 2006 Life in Transition Survey (LiTS) conducted in twenty-eight transition countries (and Turkey) by the European Bank for Reconstruction and Development and the World Bank.[2]

Do perceptions of corruption, inequality, and service delivery shape people's trust in government? There is strong support for the direct connection between confidence in government and corruption. The tie between service delivery and trust in government is modest – and trust in government appears to thrive when there is *more* inequality, not less, and *lower* support for a strong government role in reducing economic disparities. After half a century (or more) of communist governments proclaiming to fight inequality but failing to produce prosperity, many people in transition countries seem to prefer governments that enhance the market rather than focus on inequities.

Inequality, corruption, and trust in government

The link between inequality and corruption seems compelling. Corruption is exploitive. Not all corruption is linked to inequality. 'Grand' corruption refers to malfeasance of considerable magnitude by people who exploit their positions to get rich (or become richer) – political or business leaders. Thus grand corruption is all about extending the advantages of those already well endowed. 'Petty corruption', small scale payoffs to doctors, police officers, and even university professors – very common in the formerly communist nations of Central and Eastern Europe (and many poor countries) – is different in kind, if not in spirit. Petty corruption, or 'honest graft' as New York City political boss George Washington Plunkitt called it (Riordan 1948), does not enrich those who practice it. It may *depend upon* an inequitable distribution of wealth – there should be no need to make 'gift' payments in a properly-functioning market economy.

Inequality promotes corruption in many ways. Glaeser, Scheinkman, and Schleifer (2003: 2–3) argue:

---

2. For details on the survey, see: European Bank for Reconstruction and Development (2007). The data are available for download at http://www.ebrd.com/country/sector/econo/surveys/lits.htm.

[...] inequality is detrimental to the security of property rights, and therefore to growth, because it enables the rich to subvert the political, regulatory, and legal institutions of society for their own benefit. If one person is sufficiently richer than another, and courts are corruptible, then the legal system will favor the rich, not the just. Likewise, if political and regulatory institutions can be moved by wealth or influence, they will favor the established, not the efficient. This in turn leads the initially well situated to pursue socially harmful acts, recognising that the legal, political, and regulatory systems will not hold them accountable. Inequality can encourage institutional subversion in two distinct ways [...] the have-nots can redistribute from the haves through violence, the political process, or other means. Such Robin Hood redistribution jeopardises property rights, and deters investment by the rich.

Similarly, You and Khagram (2005, italics in original) argue: 'The rich, as interest groups, firms, or individuals may use bribery or connections to influence law – implementing processes (*bureaucratic corruption*) and to buy favorable interpretations of the law (*judicial corruption*).' Inequality breeds corruption by:

1. leading ordinary citizens to see the system as stacked against them (Uslaner 2002: 181–3);
2. creating a sense of dependency of ordinary citizens and a sense of pessimism for the future, which in turn undermines the moral dictates of treating your neighbours honestly; and
3. distorting the key institutions of fairness in society, the courts, which ordinary citizens see as their protectors against evil-doers, especially those with more influence than they have (see also Glaeser *et al.* 2003; You and Khagram 2005).

Economic inequality creates political leaders who make a virtue out of patronage, since it provided jobs for ordinary citizens. These leaders *help* their constituents, but more critically *they help themselves*. Inequality breeds corruption – and a dependency of the poor on the political leaders. Inequality leads to *clientelism* – leaders establish themselves as monopoly providers of benefits for average citizens. These leaders are not as accountable to their constituents as democratic theory would have us believe.

There may well be the trappings of democracy, with regularly scheduled elections, so that the link between democratic and honest government may not be as strong as might initially be expected.[3] The political boss is well entrenched in his position. His party reigns supreme in the area. Potential opponents do not have the resources to mount a real challenge – and, even if they tried, the boss can count on the support of the legions whose jobs he controls through his patronage machine.

Unequal wealth leads people to feel less constrained about cheating others (Mauro 1998: 12) and about evading taxes (Owsiak 2003: 73; Uslaner 2003).

---

3. The r^2 between the 2003 Transparency International Corruption Perceptions Index and the trichotomised 2003 Freedom House index (not free, partially free, and free) is just .216.

Where corruption is widespread, people realise that they are not the masters of their own fate – and they lose faith that their future will be bright. People become resigned to their fate. In the World Values Survey waves 1–3 (1981, 1990, 1995–7), respondents who believed that corruption was widespread in their country were significantly less likely to believe that they could get ahead by hard work rather than by luck or having connections. The zero-order correlation is modest (as we might expect with a sample of almost 60,000, tau-b = .061) – but 34 per cent of people in societies where corruption was seen as widespread thought the only way you could get ahead was by luck, compared to 29 per cent in honest societies.

Economic inequality is not the only distributional issue affecting corruption; equality of treatment under the law also matters. If people feel that they have been treated unfairly by the police or in the courts, they are less likely to have faith in the legal system. The justice system is especially important for two reasons: a corrupt court system can shield dishonest elites from retribution; and the courts, more than any other branch of the polity, are *presumed to be neutral and fair*. We appeal 'unjust' decisions to the judiciary – and our vernacular includes the phrase 'court of last resort', suggesting that somewhere there must be justice. Rothstein and Stolle (2002) argue that there are two dimensions to the legal system: fairness and efficiency. Fairness is the key to the connection between law and corruption because it reflects the advantages that some people have over others. The efficiency of the courts should not matter so much for corruption – since rounding up the corrupt leaders and putting them in jail only makes room for a new group of miscreants, doing little to address the underlying causes of corruption. When the legal system is fair – when people see the courts in particular as fair – they will expect that the rich and poor will receive equal treatment and that corrupt officials will be unlikely to get away with their misdeeds.

As I argued above, the connection between trust in government and corruption is clear. Indeed, the standard trust in government scale used in the American National Election Studies includes an item asking respondents if they believe that 'quite a few of the people running the government are crooked'.[4] The connection between inequality and confidence in government is less clear. There are two paths to this linkage:

1. The direct path stems from a large body of research showing that trust in government – and indeed the evaluation of political leaders more generally – strongly depends on how well leaders manage the economy (Citrin 1974; Kinder and Kiewiet 1979; Lipset and Schneider 1983). Increasing inequality may be troubling to many voters – and a sign that the government is not performing well.
2. There may be an indirect link, especially in transition countries after the fall of communism. Rising levels of inequality in these polities (see below) led to increasing social strains and to perceptions of greater corruption.

---

4. For the items in the scale, see http://www.electionstudies.org/nesguide/toptable/tab5a_5.htm.

In transition countries, most people believe that the only way to get rich is by being corrupt (Uslaner 2008a: 102–3), so the link from inequality to corruption also leads to low levels of support for government officials, most notably those who are or are accused of being very wealthy (Uslaner 2008b).

Some preliminary evidence on the inequality trap

While the dominant explanations for corruption are institutional, there is at least one key reason why structural accounts are wanting. Institutions have been rather malleable across the world in recent decades as democratisation has spread across transition and developing nations. The r^2 for political rights using the Freedom House data from 1973 to 2003 is .165 and for civil liberties it is .263 (both N = 77). Even excluding countries that were communist in 1973, the respective r^2 values increase only to .264 and .375 (N = 67). More critically, changes in political rights and civil liberties from 1973 to 2003 are unrelated to changes in corruption from 1980–5 to 2004 (r^2 = .007 and .038 respectively, N = 38). Moving the democratisation measures forward to 1988 does not improve the fit with changes in corruption (r^2 = .004 and .0005 for political rights and civil liberties, N = 39).

The major components of the inequality trap – inequality, trust, and corruption – are rather sticky. They do not change easily because each breeds the other. The r^2 between generalised trust from the 1980 and 1990–5 World Values Surveys is .81 for the twenty-two nations included in both waves. Inequality, similarly, moves little over time. The r^2 for the most commonly used measures of economic inequality (Deininger and Squire 1996) between 1980 and 1990 is not quite as strong as the connection with trust over time, but it is still substantial at .676 for a sample of forty-two countries. A new inequality data base developed by James Galbraith extends measures of inequality further back in time and across more countries.[5] The r^2 between economic inequality in 1963 and economic inequality in 1996 is .706 (for thirty-seven countries). The r^2 between the Transparency International Corruption Perceptions Index for 2003 and the International Country Risk Guide measure for 1980–5 (even though they are not directly comparable) is .785 for forty-nine countries.

The linkage between corruption and inequality is not much stronger. The r^2 is a paltry .082 across eighty-five countries, suggesting no relationship at all between inequality and corruption. When the former and present communist regimes are removed, there is a moderate fit between the two indicators (r^2 = .246, N = 62). With a bivariate r^2 of this magnitude, it should not take much effort to see it vanish in a multivariate analysis. So I suggest that the relationship between inequality and corruption is indirect – through generalised trust, trust in strangers. Inequality is the strongest predictor of trust across nations without a legacy of communism, in the United States over time, and across the American states (Uslaner 2002: Chs 6,

---

5. The Galbraith data can be obtained at http://utip.gov.utexas.edu/data.html.

8; Uslaner and Brown 2005). And high levels of trust are strongly related to low levels of corruption (Uslaner 2008a: 45–53). Across nations, I thus suggest that the relationship between inequality and corruption is indirect.

I estimated a six-equation model of corruption, inequality, trust, regulation of business, the overall risk of a country's economy and polity, and a measure of government effectiveness (Uslaner 2008a: 63–74) and the fairness of the legal system is the only institutional variable that is a significant predictor of corruption. Legal equality is *not* the same as economic equality (the two are moderately correlated) nor the same as the efficiency or the size of the judiciary.

The transition countries stand out as the major exception to my argument linking high inequality through low generalised trust to much corruption. Yes, they have high levels of corruption – former and the handful of still communist countries on average are more corrupt than either the West (by far) or the developing nations. And yes, they have low levels of trust – slightly higher than developing countries, but much lower than the West. Yet, they have on average *the lowest levels of inequality* – marginally less than the West, but far lower levels than developing countries.[6]

However, there are many reasons to believe that the inequality trap argument fits transition countries well.[7] First, measures of economic inequality are based upon official statistics and do not take into account the great wealth of a handful of officials at the top, who had privileges unavailable to ordinary citizens. Secondly, while inequality has been historically relatively low in transition countries, there have been sharp increases in the uneven distribution of wealth since the communist regimes fell in the late 1980s. Two different data bases tell largely the same story: the Rosser, Rosser, and Ahmed (2000) data on income distribution show an increase in economic inequality from 1989 to the mid-1990s for every country save one (Slovakia). The more recent WIDER (World Institute for Development Economics Research) estimates indicate substantial increases in inequality – an average change of 78 per cent from 1989–1999 – for each of twenty-one countries.

The rise in inequality was accompanied by an increase in the shadow economy (Schneider 2003). Even the best-performing economies, Slovakia and the Czech Republic, had almost 20 per cent of their revenue off the books. Three countries had a majority of their revenue in the informal sector (Ukraine, Azerbaijan, and Georgia) and fifteen of twenty-one countries for which there are data have at least a third of their income in the shadow economy. Even more distressing is that sixteen of the eighteen countries for which there are data experienced increases in the

---

6. For the full set of nations ranked by Transparency International in 2005, former and present communist countries averaged 3.42 on the Corruption Perceptions Index, compared to 7.97 for the West and 3.50 for developing (other) nations (N = 29, 21, and 110, respectively). On trust (imputed), the East bloc averaged .234, developing nations .220, and the West .388 (N = 25, 39, and 30, respectively). For the World Bank Gini index, the present and former communist countries average .308, the West mean is .319, and developing nations average .443 (N = 23, 23, and 42, respectively).

7. This section is based upon Uslaner (2008a: 105–6).

shadow economy of at between 10 and 42 per cent; only one country (Hungary) had a (very slight) decrease while another (Slovenia) experienced no change. Not only did inequality increase, but more people had to rely upon the informal sector.

The greater the share of the economy beyond the reach of the state, the more difficult it will be for a government to marshal the resources to gain public confidence that the state can provide essential services. Overall, the average share of the shadow economy more than doubled from 1989 to 1999–2000 (from 17 per cent to 38 per cent) and the average increase in the Gini index of inequality was 33 per cent. The Gini coefficient is a measure of the inequality of a distribution, a value of 0 expressing total equality and a value of 1 maximal inequality.

Corruption is a persistent problem. In 2004, every transition country had a higher level of corruption than any Western country. The scores for 2005 show sharp leaps in honesty for Estonia and Slovenia (atypical for this index) – outranking Greece and Italy and tied with Israel among Western nations. However, excluding Estonia and Slovenia, the mean for East bloc countries is *lower* than for developing nations.

All of the eleven formerly communist countries ranked by Transparency International in 1998 had more corruption in 2004 (Uslaner 2008a: 105–6, 270). There is only a moderate amount of consistency from 1998 to 2005 ($r^2 = .543$, N = 12), but far greater for the larger sample between 1999 and 2005 ($r^2 = .832$, N = 24). The public in transition countries sees corruption as a long-term, insoluble problem. In a 2005 survey, just eight per cent of Russians held that corruption can be eliminated 'if dishonest leaders are replaced with honest ones', while 26 per cent hold that 'Russia has always been characterised by bribery and embezzlement, and nothing can be done about it' (Popov 2006; cf. Karklins 2005: 59 for a more general statement on transition countries).

Inequality seems to matter more for the transition countries as a determinant of corruption in more recent years. Inequality (together with perceptions that courts are not fair, GDP per capita, and the openness of the economy) is a significant predictor of corruption for the transition nations. There is a more powerful relationship between corruption and *change in economic inequality*: Corruption is also a significant predictor of increases in inequality in these nations (Uslaner 2008a: 108–11).

An unfair legal system predates the fall of communism in Central and Eastern Europe. Under communism, legal fairness was a vain hope. As corruption and inequality have increased, so have perceptions that the legal system is unfair (Uslaner 2008a: 97–8). The growth of the informal economy is a sign that the transition to a market democracy did not lead to a fairer legal system. At the top of the shadow economy, the rich evade taxes; at the bottom, the workers have no legal rights. Rising economic inequality makes people more sceptical of the fairness of the legal system. People see a clear connection between the maldistribution of both income and legal fairness and corruption and I find strong support for these linkages in surveys in Romania and Estonia (Uslaner 2008a: Chs 5, 6). Ordinary citizens (far more than elites) believe that you cannot get rich without being corrupt and that corruption plays a large role in promoting more inequality.

When Russian oil entrepreneur Mikhail Khodorkovsky confessed his sins of relying on 'beeznissmeny' (stealing, lying, and sometimes killing) and promised to become scrupulously honest in early 2003, Russians regarded this pledge as 'startling'. When he was arrested and charged with tax evasion and extortion under orders from President Vladimir Putin ten months later, the average Russian was unsurprised: about the same share of people approved of his arrest as disapproved of it (Tavernise 2003). The arrest of Khodorkovsky stands out as exceptional because corrupt officials and business people are rarely held to account. While crime spiralled in Russia after the fall of communism, conviction rates plummeted (Varese 1997).

Service failure, corruption and inequality

Corruption acts as a tax on the poor. Those in fortunate financial circumstances (the 'well-off') can afford bribes, but the poor often do without basic services. At the same time, corruption robs the state of resources for providing basic services to all citizens, but especially the poor. People who turn to the informal economy have few legal rights (their employment is not legal and there are no contracts or unions representing workers in the informal sector). Corruption is particularly rampant on those services the poor most depend upon such as the police, the schools and the medical sector. Countries with high levels of corruption have poor service delivery. The failure of corrupt states with rising inequality to provide basic services illustrates the inequality trap – but the wealthy have options to protect themselves against the failure of public services. They may bribe local authorities to ensure that their services are fixed first and they may not have to rely exclusively upon state-provided services. Compare this to the poor, who cannot afford bribes, nor do they have the option of using alternative services. When governments do not have the resources to provide services, the poor will suffer more.

I turn to three analyses to examine the connection between service interruptions in transition countries and both corruption and inequality. First, I examine the measure of public service deterioration in the Failed States dataset for 2007.[8] The Failed States index is a measure of the capacity of a polity to maintain order and to deliver essential services of the 'vulnerability to collapse or conflict'.[9] A key component of the index is the deterioration of public services, which is essential both for ordinary citizens and for businesses in a newly-privatised economy. Does the failure of a state to provide essential public services stem from corruption and inequality?

I also examine the 2005 Business Environment and Enterprise Performance Survey (BEEPS) of the European Bank for Reconstruction and Development and the World Bank. BEEPS 2005 is a survey of business people in twenty-six transition countries (all except Turkmenistan). It is *not* a survey of the mass public, but

---

8. http://www.fundforpeace.org/programs/fsi/fsifaq.php.
9. http://www.fundforpeace.org/programs/fsi/fsifaq.php.

it does focus on questions of service delivery and corruption, both of which are essential for the growth of business and the economy more generally. The survey asked respondents how many days a year they faced interruptions of service in water (low supplies), phones (no service), and electricity (power outages). I first estimate an aggregate regression model of levels of service interruptions. Then I turn to individual-level analyses of perceptions of poor service delivery in each of the three areas. For both the aggregate and individual-level models, my central focus is whether inequality and corruption – both the 'objective' perceptions measures of Transparency International and the 'subjective' perceptions of survey respondents – lead to higher levels of reported service interruptions.

First, consider the aggregate model for the State Failure measure of service deterioration, available for twenty-one countries. I present the model in Table 7.1. I use three predictors, which collectively account for almost 90 per cent of the variance:

1. the 2005 Transparency International Corruption Perceptions Index (higher scores mean less corruption);
2. the change in inequality from 1989 to 1999 as estimated by the United Nations University World Institute for Development Economics Research (WIDER).[10] (I chose the years 1989 and 1999 to get a measure of inequality at transition, first, and to maximise the number of available data points); and
3. the 2003 composite Freedom House democratisation index to test for institutional effects.

Table 7.1: Determinants of public service deterioration in transition countries: State Failure Data

Variable	Coefficient	Standard Error	t Ratio
Corruption (TI 2005)	-.418***	.130	-3.22
Change in Inequality (WIDER)	1.473**	.620	2.38
Democratisation (Freedom House 2003)	-.777***	.251	-3.09
Constant	4.973****	.964	5.16
R^2	.896		
S.E.E.	.480		

Notes: N = 21, * p < .10, ** p < .05, *** p < .01, **** p < .0001

---

10. Available at http://www.wider.unu.edu/research/Database/en_GB/database.

The story is simple: all three variables matter. While democratisation may not lead to less corruption, it does lead to better service delivery. But corruption and inequality change also have an impact. Countries with higher levels of corruption have worse service delivery; and increasing inequality is also significantly associated with deteriorating public services. What is notable is that inequality per se does not seem to matter, but *rising inequality* has a strong impact on service delivery. As countries become more corrupt, they have fewer resources to deliver these services. As states become more stratified economically, there seems to be a lack of will to provide public goods to all.

The pattern repeats itself in the aggregate model for the 2005 BEEPS data. There are three measures of service interruption: low water supply, lack of phone service, and power outages (see Table 7.2). I aggregated the survey data to the country level. I focus on three variables, one derived from the BEEPS data and indices of corruption and change in inequality.[11] From the BEEPS 2005 data, I aggregated the perception of confidence that the legal system will enforce contracts and property rights.

Across all three measures of service interruptions, change in inequality and corruption are significant. The most powerful effect of inequality appears to be for low water supply – though the simple regression coefficient for power outages is the greatest (but so is its standard error). Service interruptions are not very common for any of the three measures, but power outages are more frequent (6.1 days a year) with phone interruptions the least common (1.5 days) and low water supply in the middle (2.6). Reported telephone outages are relatively rare – with a mean number of days of only 1.24, compared to 4.72 for low water and 12.45 for power. Yet power outages are infrequent in most countries, with two outliers: Georgia at 57 days and Kyrgyzstan at 14.5. Of the three forms of service interruption, inequality matters least for telephone service – perhaps because telephones are not as ubiquitous as is reliance on water and power; it matters most for power.[12] Corruption seems to follow the same pattern: the greatest impact is on power, followed by water supply and phones. Regulating contracts and protecting property rights is only significant for power and water.

Service interruptions, even if uncommon, are more frequent where inequality has been rising, corruption is rampant and the courts do little to enforce rights. A weak legal system means that people have few opportunities to challenge service disruptions. Corruption robs the state of resources and provides for many opportunities for officials to withhold services unless they benefit from bribes. Rising inequality means that some people are better able to have services restored – or to go outside the grid – than others.

---

11. I use the 2004 Transparency International corruption ratings here rather than 2005 because the BEEPS data come from 2005 and a time lag is justified.
12. In Alex Dreher's globalisation data for 2003, the number of telephone main lines per 1,000 people in a country ranges from 1.04 for Albania to 5.10 for Slovenia among transition countries, compared to a range of 5.15 (Portugal) to 8.95 (Norway) for Western nations (Dreher *et al.* 2008). Dreher's data come from the World Development Indicators of the World Bank and are available at http://globalization.kof.ethz.ch/static/rawdata/globalization_2009_long.xls.

Table 7.2: Determinants of service interruption in transition: aggregate models from BEEPS 2005 (robust standard errors)

Variable	Low water supply			Lack of phone service			Power outages		
	b	S.E.	t Ratio	b	S.E.	t Ratio	b	S.E.	t Ratio
Change in Gini index (WIDER) 1989–1999	5.84****	1.371	4.25	1.520***	.619	2.45	15.220**	7.211	2.11
Confident legal system enforces contracts and property rights	3.026**	1.79	1.69	.476	.824	.58	19.893**	8.459	2.35
TI Corruption Perceptions Index 2004	-1.577****	.357	-4.20	-.484***	.199	-2.43	-5.998***	2.029	-2.96
Constant	-13.368**	6.308	-2.12	-1.497	3.054	-.49	-72.787**	30.177	-2.41
R^2	.684			.424			.535		
RMSE	2.030			.981			10.526		

Notes: * p < .10, ** p < .05, *** p < .01, **** p < .0001. N = 21

The aggregate results receive strong confirmation from the individual-level analysis of the survey data. I estimate a negative binomial model for the three forms of service disruption: the data are counts and there is substantial over-dispersion (confirmed by the significant alpha and ln alpha measures), so neither Tobit nor Poisson models are appropriate. I estimate two models for each form of service interruption. Common to the models are four measures from the survey:

1. whether courts are fair;
2. whether the Mafia is an obstacle to business;
3. whether economic instability is an obstacle to business; and
4. how often respondents have to make 'gift' payments to public officials to obtain routine services.

In the first set of models, I include the change in inequality and the change in the Transparency International Corruption Perceptions Index from 2002 to 2004 as country-level variables. In the second set of models, I replace these measures with an indicator of the size of the unofficial economy from World Bank economists (Johnson *et al.*1997: 184). The unofficial economy is strongly correlated with inequality change even in the survey data ($r = .766, N = 3,772$), so I estimate the models separately. I only report the coefficients for other variables in the first model, since there is not much difference for the other variables. I cluster the standard errors by country and report the results in Table 7.3.

There is much greater variation in reporting of service interruption in the individual level responses than in the aggregated data. Over 85 per cent of respondents never reported experiencing interruptions for either water or phones, though a handful (.67 per cent) said that they had 'interruptions' every day. 'Only' 58 per cent of respondents never had power outages, while 1 per cent lacked service every day. In the first set of models, there is clear support for the arguments that both change in inequality and change in corruption lead to more frequent reports of service interruption – for water, telephones, and power. Changes in corruption seem to matter more for low water supply and power than for phones – perhaps because the state has greater monopoly power over water and power than over phones. Change in inequality seems to affect phone service more – perhaps because telephone service may be less available to those at the bottom of the economic ladder.

People living in countries with greater informal economies are substantially more likely to report service interruptions – especially for water and power. A larger informal economy means more people living off the grid – the power grid as well as the legal one. Indeed, one of the key indicators of the size of the informal economy is the 'physical input' method, which compares the amount of electricity consumed with the amount billed (Schneider and Enste 2000). A large informal sector means that public utilities will be 'stressed' as people use more capacity than utilities routinely provide to their paying customers – and because there is no routine way for utilities to measure expected demand. People living off the grid but tapping into it may find their services 'interrupted' when utilities discover this

Table 7.3: Determinants of service interruption in transition: Individual-level models from BEEPS 2005: Negative binomial regressions with standard errors clustered by country

Variable	Low water supply			Lack of phone service			Power outages		
	b	S.E.	t Ratio	b	S.E.	t Ratio	b	S.E.	t Ratio
Change in Gini index (WIDER) 1989-1999	3.091***	1.287	2.40	1.340****	.355	3.77	1.809**	.920	1.97
Courts are fair	-.137***	.057	-2.43	-.095**	.056	-1.69	-.032	.067	-.08
TI Corruption Perceptions Index Change 2002-2004	-.514***	.190	-2.71	-.147**	.087	-1.69	-.537****	.115	-4.67
Make gift payments to public servants	.032	.107	.30	.187*	.137	1.36	.135**	.067	2.01
Mafia is obstacle to doing business	.161*	.103	1.56	.181	.144	1.25	-.113	.077	-1.48
Economic instability is obstacle to doing business	.157**	.091	1.73	.069	.128	.54	.088	.090	.97
Size of informal economy (World Bank)#	.068****	.013	5.19	.027***	.009	3.15	.066****	.011	6.21
Constant	-2.637	2.306	-1.14	-1.675*	.918	-1.82	.387	1.548	.25
alpha	27.156****	2.470		19.431****	2.142		6.200****	.571	
ln alpha	3.302****	.091		2.967****	.110		1.825****	.092	
Wald Chi square	51.61			46.28			60.26		
Log pseudolikelihood	-3717.96			-3832.64			-8722.76		
N	4,388			4,383			4,478		

Notes: * p < .10, ** p < .05, *** p < .01, **** p < .0001
Estimated in separate model without change in Gini index or change in Corruption Perceptions Index. Other coefficients show little difference

poaching and cut down their illegal lines. On the other hand, telephone service is less susceptible to the informal economy because it is so much easier to block service to people who try to tap into a phone line.

For two of the three measures, fair courts lead to fewer service interruptions. The exception is for power outages – with no obvious explanation except that this is the only service for which gift payments to public servants are significant. Petty bribes to public servants seem to reduce the level of power outages (which may reduce the need to go to court). They are not significant elsewhere. Organised crime leads to greater service interruptions only for low water supply. We see the same pattern for economic instability. It seems that low water supply may be a political and economic tool for corrupt leaders to ensure that business people make the expected payments. Power outages may simply reflect poor infrastructure that may be traceable to corruption and uncertain demand.

The larger story is that all three estimations point to the central role of both corruption and inequality in shaping poor service delivery. Corruption redistributes resources away from the poor to the rich and thus is a great source of envy, especially in the transition countries where egalitarianism has long been a widely held value.

Trust in government, corruption, inequality and service delivery

Do people who see government as corrupt and unable to deliver services lose faith in their government? Does inequality lead to a drop in confidence in leaders, just as it fosters low levels of social trust (Uslaner 2002: Chs 6, 8)? I use the Life in Transition Survey (LiTS)[13] of transition countries to examine trust in government and perceptions of service delivery for people living in regimes with high levels of corruption, rising inequality, and governments that did little to promote confidence among the citizenry.

LiTS surveyed 1,000 people in each of twenty-eight transition countries (as well as Turkey). The survey has good questions on trust in public officials, corruption, and satisfaction with the economic situation. But it is weaker on inequality and on service delivery. There are no questions on perceptions of inequality – only on what the state should do (be involved, stay out) regarding economic disparities. And the questions on service delivery are not ideal. LiTS asked respondents whether they were satisfied with a range of government services – police, road police, courts, the education system and social security – but only for those people who had direct exposure to each. I created revised scores assigning middling evaluations ('indifferent') to the large majority of respondents who did not have direct experience with each agent. This resulted in very limited impacts for all but one measure – satisfaction with the police.

LiTS also asked people about access to public services: tap water, electricity, telephone, heating, and gas. Access was almost universal in all of the transition

---

13. See footnote 2.

countries except for tap water – the only measure usable. Even here, the mean number of hours of access per day was 21.8.

I thus rely upon aggregate measures to tap inequality and service delivery. For inequality, I use a Gini index from the United Nations Development Program for 2003.[14] I also include a measure of the real growth rate of gross domestic product for 2005 from the International Country Risk Guide. For service delivery, I use two measures from the 2005 BEEPS aggregated to the country level: service interruption in power (as above) and perceptions by businesspeople that unreliable electricity sources are an obstacle to business. While these are perceptions by elites, if people in business find power unreliable, then ordinary citizens should do so as well – perhaps even more so.

Adding these aggregate measures reduces the sample size: the real growth measure is available only for twenty countries. I decided to restrict the analysis to a subset of countries because of anomalies or extreme values in two of the key indicators: trust in government and service interruptions. Trust in government is a factor score from a single dimension measure of confidence in the president, the cabinet, parliament, and political parties. Respondents in Azerbaijan, Kazakhstan, and especially both Tajikistan and Uzbekistan, were far more trusting than citizens in any other transition country. Their mean factor scores were .72, .66, 1.20, and 1.11. The next most trusting citizens came from Georgia (.29). Only three other countries had mean scores significantly above zero (Estonia, Kyrgyzstan, Mongolia, and Montenegro) and each of these means was about .15. All results for trust in government were driven by these outliers. These data may well be viewed as data anomalies – or perhaps as reflecting poor survey techniques in these countries or more simply as reflecting the dependence of people upon regimes that are still authoritarian.[15] There is little in our theories about confidence in government that would lead us to expect that people in these former Soviet nations should be more trusting than others – and plenty of reason to expect them to be *less* trusting: they rank *lowest* on service delivery. So I exclude respondents from these countries. This leaves two other countries with outlying values on service interruptions: Albania and Georgia. The values of Albania and Georgia on service delivery are hardly anomalies – but once I exclude Azerbaijan, Kazakhstan, Tajikistan, and Uzbekistan, the outlying values for Albania and Georgia drive the results of the analyses – leading to counterintuitive findings (as when all countries are included) that poor service delivery leads people to have more confidence in government.

This leaves us with respondents from Armenia, Bulgaria, Croatia, the Czech Republic, Estonia, Hungary, Kyrgyzstan (the only Asian republic included), Latvia, Lithuania, Moldova, Poland, Romania, Russia, Slovakia, Slovenia, and

---

14. The measure is available at http://www.jussemper.org/Resources/Economic%20Data/undphumandevelopment.html. I use this measure because it covers more countries than other available Gini indices for the transition countries.

15. The results may not be an anomaly: 92 per cent of Azerbaijanis said that they trusted the government in the 2001 World Values Survey, behind only Vietnam (97 per cent) and China (96 per cent).

Ukraine. Even so, preliminary analyses show little impact of either inequality or service delivery upon trust in government in models including variables measuring satisfaction with the economy and expectations for the future. It is hardly surprising that economic expectations would dominate evaluations of government performance and leaders. But it would be naive to assume that inequality and/or service delivery are unrelated to economic evaluations. So I estimated a two-stage least squares model, with measures of inequality and service delivery (and economic growth) as instruments for the level of economic satisfaction in 2006 compared to the economy in 1989 (the year of transition). This provides a more theoretically satisfying model that leads to support for most of the arguments I have presented. I present the equation for trust in government for the sixteen country sample in Table 7.4 and then estimate identical models for the top half and the bottom half of the income ladders.

The model for trust in government includes two measures of perceived corruption (has corruption got better or worse since 1989 and whether success in life depends primarily upon corruption rather than hard work or being smart or simply having connections), an aggregate indicator of service delivery (whether unreliable electricity is an obstacle to business, from the BEEPS 2005 survey), a question on whether the state should be involved in reducing inequality, and two measures of overall economic performance: whether the future for children will be better and whether the economic situation today (2006) is better or worse than that at transition (1989). I instrument the latter measure by a set of variables that are all either theoretically or empirically (or both) unrelated to trust in government: the number of hours per day a respondent has access to tap water, service interruptions for power (BEEPS 2005), the United Nations Gini index, real GDP growth, how often businesspeople had to make 'gift payments' to courts, the respondent's place on a 10-point income ladder (standardised across countries), and whether the respondent prefers a planned or a market economy. The reduced form equation predicts the perceived economic situation reasonably well ($R^2 = .30$) with powerful effects for income and support for a market economy.[16] More educated respondents also are more likely to see an improved economic situation. Respondents living in countries where more businesspeople perceived interruptions in electric power were less likely to see an improved economy, as were people living in countries where BEEPS respondents said that they did not have to make frequent gift payments to courts. Respondents living in countries with stronger growth in real GDP were more likely to evaluate the economy positively, but economic inequality was strongly linked to *more positive views on the economic situation.* More access to tap water led to more positive evaluations – while beliefs that success in life is due to hard work had no significant impact.[17]

The equation for trust in government shows considerable support for my

---

16. The 'power' of effects is roughly measured by the z ratios.

17. The coefficient is negative and the t ratio is -2.62, but the simple correlation is positive ($r = .057$), as expected.

overall argument, except inequality preferences are incorrectly signed (see Table 7.4). Service delivery matters most: Country-level perceptions of electricity as an obstacle to doing business have the strongest effect on trust. A respondent from Slovakia (with the lowest concern for power outages) will be far more likely to trust the government than one from Bulgaria (with the highest level of worry about power outages). The difference is 2.29 on a total range of 3.11 in confidence scores. Satisfaction with the police (at the individual level) leads to an increase of .27 on the trust scale. The next most important factors reflect perceptions of corruption, though their impacts are considerably smaller. People who perceive corruption as declining since 1989 have trust scores that are .32 greater, while respondents who say that success in life still depends upon corruption have trust scores .18 lower. The instrumented economic evaluations lead to greater trust in government, as do expectations for the future for children (.30 more trusting). The only anomaly is for inequality preferences: people who want the state strongly involved in reducing inequality are .15 *less trusting* of their governments.

Table 7.4: Determinants of trust in government (LiTS data): two-stage least squares estimates

Variable	Coefficient	Standard Error	z Ratio
Economic situation compared to 1989 (instrumented)	.127****	.023	5.55
Future looks bright for children	.076****	.011	7.03
Electricity obstacle to business (BEEPS)	-.450****	.043	-10.45
Satisfied with police	.067***	.028	2.42
Corruption better compared to 1989	.081****	.009	9.32
Success in life depends upon being corrupt	-.180****	.024	-7.39
Strong role for state in reducing inequality	-.074****	.015	-4.79
Constant	-.386**	.122	-3.16
R^2	.132		
S.E.E.	.741		

Notes: * $p < .10$, ** $p < .05$, *** $p < .01$, **** $p < .0001$, N = 8,524
All tests one-tailed except for constant and strong role for state in reducing inequality.

The results largely hold for both the relatively well-off and those with fewer resources. I divided the sample at the income ladder of .4 (where about half the cases fell above and half below) and estimated the same two-stage least squares regressions for each subsample. The results for the trust in government equation do not differ much between the two equations (results not shown) with three key exceptions, one of which seems distinctly counterintuitive. First, perceptions of corruption matter more for the well-off than for people with lower income. This is not surprising, since concern for reducing corruption is greater for the well-off and because the well-off are more convinced that corruption has declined since transition. Second, the coefficient for the instrumented measure of economic preferences is twice as large for those less well-off compared to the estimate for those with more resources. The latter coefficient is barely significant at $p < .10$ (one-tailed test). People who have fared worse since transition seem to place greater emphasis on changes in their economic situation in their trust in government judgments. These differences are not attributable to any divergences in the first stage estimates, which show few differences. Instead, as income increases, corruption becomes a stronger determinant of confidence in government and the economic situation less critical. The wealthy are more concerned with the honesty of regimes, perhaps because they are less dependent upon corrupt leaders for their livelihood and are more concerned with how well the government is handling economic issues (such as trade and growth) that touch the lives of the 'well to do' more than the poor.

Finally, the support for a strong role for the state in reducing inequality has a more powerful *negative* effect for lower-income than for higher-income people, with a coefficient almost twice as large. The mean score on the trust in government scale for low-income people who want the state to take a strong role is -.39, compared to -.21 for higher-income people. Lower-income people are more likely to favour a strong role for the state (74 per cent compared to 65 per cent), but this demand does not translate into positive support for the state – perhaps because people do not see post-transition regimes as very successful in combating economic disparities.

The negative impacts of inequality preferences on confidence in government may reflect a reaction against strong state control of the economy. This result is consistent with the powerful positive effect of inequality on perceptions of an improved economy since 1989. Yet, it is inconsistent with the inequality trap more generally – notably the strong negative effect of inequality on trust in other people, as opposed to trust in government, in transition countries as well as other nations (Uslaner 2002: Chs 4, 6; Uslaner 2008a: Chs 4–6). Trust in government is only modestly related to generalised trust – with correlations close to zero in the United States (Uslaner 2002: 148–58), but stronger in the transition countries ($r = .29$). Yet, support for a strong role for the state in reducing inequality is greater among people who *do not trust other people* rather than those who have faith in others. It may well be that these negative relationships indicate disappointment about rising inequality and a demand that government does more to reduce income disparities.

The service interruptions in transition countries (and elsewhere) are not simply a matter of going without basic amenities for a few days a year. Because they stem from corruption and inequality, they add to the mounting inequalities we see developing in these states. The wealthy are less likely to be affected by service interruptions and to be affected negatively by corruption overall.

Beyond increasing inequality, poor service delivery leads to a loss of faith in the political system and a greater likelihood of tax evasion. A principal cause of withholding tax payments is the belief that quality services from government are not forthcoming (Hanousek and Palda 2000; Torgler 2003; Uslaner 2010). In the 2005, BEEPS individual-level data, more frequent service interruptions are strongly related to tax evasion.

Respondents who reported more frequent low water supplies, lack of phone services and more frequent power outages were more likely to say that they paid taxes on less than 50 per cent of their income (r = .321, .474, and .386, respectively, N = 7,085). Ironically, the strongest zero-order correlation is for lack of phone service – which is the least likely of the three services to be provided by government. Many people may see it, especially in this day when communications are increasingly conducted by phone and online, as the most essential for a business. People may target their anger at government even when it is not the main culprit.

If people withhold their taxes, this adds to the burden of government in providing services. High levels of corruption may lead to poor services, but poor services lead to less confidence in government (Citrin 1974) and then to greater levels of tax evasion – and, in turn, to poorer levels of service and more inequality and more corruption – and to the never-ending inequality trap.

Reprise

Corruption and inequality both lead to lower levels of service delivery in transition countries. Corruption robs funds from the public treasury and leaves less money to invest in public services. Rising inequality means that the new wealthy class can afford to ensure that they receive public services –while those with fewer resources will be the victims of interrupted service delivery. Inequality thus has both direct and indirect effects on service delivery. The wealthy do not pay the price of corruption so directly. They can afford either to pay the bribes demanded by bureaucrats or they have sufficient connections so that they might avoid the bribes altogether; the poor often simply do without. The indirect effect of inequality stems from how corruption leads to poor service delivery. The wealthy can afford to go 'outside the grid', the poor cannot. Wealthy people may not worry about demands from doctors or teachers for extra payments by using private hospitals or sending their children to private schools. They live in areas where there is more reliable electricity and water.

Ironically, however, the wealthy judge government more by the level of corruption than do the poor. For elites, corruption is a sign of moral failure more than a barrier to accessing essential services (Uslaner 2008a: 173–6). The poor cannot afford such moral judgments so readily. Those who are less well-off want the government more involved in reducing inequality – and they judge government performance more by how well leaders have steered the economy rather than by how honest they are. While corruption is largely a tax on the poor, concern for corruption is mostly a cause for concern for the rich.

Overall, service delivery (cf. Citrin 1974) and corruption are the most critical factors people use in judging government performance in transition countries. When government does not deliver services, people are reluctant to pay taxes and this robs the state of even more resources to provide electricity, water, and other goods – and to less faith in government by both the poor (who do not get the services) and the rich (who will not pay their taxes). This cycle reinforces the inequality trap and the corruption-inequality nexus.

References

Citrin, J. (1974) 'Comment: The political relevance of trust in government', *American Political Science Review*, 68(3): 973–88.

Deininger, K. and Squire, L. (1996) 'A new data set measuring economic income inequality', *World Bank Economic Review*, 10(3): 565–92.

Dreher, A., Gaston, N. and Martens, P. (2008) *Measuring Globalization: Gauging its consequences*, New York: Springer.

European Bank for Reconstruction and Development (2007) *Life in Transition: A survey of people's experiences and attitudes*. Online. Available http://www.ebrd.com/pubs/econo/lit.htm (accessed 18 January 2010).

Glaeser, E. L., Scheinkman, J. and Schleifer, A. (2003) 'The injustice of inequality', *Journal of Monetary Economics*, 50(1): 199–222.

Hanousek, J. and Palda, F. (2000) 'Quality of government services and the civic duty to pay taxes in the Czech and Slovak republics, and other transition countries'. Online. Available http://home.cerge-ei.cz/hanousek/quality4b.pdf (accessed 10 December 2009).

Johnson, S., Kaufmann, D., Schleifer, A., Goldman, M. I. and Weitzman, M. L. (1997) 'The unofficial economy in transition', *Brookings Papers on Economic Activity*, 2: 159–239.

Karklins, R. (2005) *The System Made Me Do It: Corruption in post-communist societies,* Armonk, New York: M. E. Sharpe.

Kinder, D. R. and Kiewiet, D. R. (1979) 'Economic discontent and political behavior: The role of personal grievances and collective economic judgments in congressional voting', *American Journal of Political Science*, 23(3): 495–527.

Lipset, S. M. and Schneider, W. (1983) *The Confidence Gap: Business, labor, and government in the public mind*, New York: Free Press.

Mauro, P. (1997) 'Why worry about corruption?', *Economic Issues*, 6, Washington: International Monetary Fund.

— (1998) 'Corruption: Causes, consequences, and agenda for further research', *Finance & Development*, 35(1): 11–14, Washington: International Monetary Fund.

Owsiak, S. (2003) 'The ethics of tax collection', *Finance and Common Good*, 13/14: 65–77.

Popov, N. (2006) 'To give and take'. Online. Available http://www.indem.ru/en/publicat/Popov/Give&Take.htm (accessed 8 January 2008).

Riordan, W. (1948) *Plunkitt of Tammany Hall*, New York: Alfred A. Knopf.

Rosser, J. B., Rosser, M. V. and Ahmed, M. (2000) 'Income inequality and the informal economy in transition countries', *Journal of Comparative Economics*, 28(1) 156–71.

Rothstein, B. and Stolle, D. (2002) 'How political institutions create and destroy social capital: An institutional theory of generalized trust', Paper prepared for delivery at the Annual Meeting of the American Political Science Association, Boston, 29 August–1 September 2002.

Schneider, F. (2003) 'Shadow economies around the world: What do we know?', *CREMA Working Paper Series 2004–03*. Online. Available http://ideas.repec.org/p/ces/ceswps/_1167.html.

Schneider, F. and Enste, D. (2000) 'Shadow economies: Size, causes, and consequences', *Journal of Economic Literature*, 38(1): 77–114.

Tanzi, V. (1998) 'Corruption around the world: Causes, consequences, scope and cures', *IMF Staff Papers*, vol.45(4): 559–94.

Tavernise, S. (2003) 'Russia is mostly unmoved by the troubles of its tycoons', *New York Times*, Washington edition, 3rd November: A3.

Torgler, B. (2003) 'Tax morale in central and eastern European countries', Paper presented at the Conference on Tax Evasion, Trust, and State Capabilities, St. Gallen, Switzerland, 17–19 October 2003.

Uslaner, E. M. (2002) *The Moral Foundations of Trust*, New York: Cambridge University Press.

— (2003) 'Trust and civic engagement in East and West', in G. Badescu and E. M. Uslaner (eds) *Social Capital and the Transition to Democracy*, London: Routledge.

— (2008a) *Corruption, Inequality, and the Rule of Law: The bulging pocket makes the easy life*, New York: Cambridge University Press.

— (2008b) 'Coping and social capital: The informal sector and the democratic transition', in J. Lewandowski and M. Knoz (eds) *Trust and Transitions: Social capital in a changing world*, Newcastle upon Tyne, UK: Cambridge Scholars Press.

— (2010) 'Tax evasion, corruption, and the social contract in transition', in J. Alm, J. Martinez-Vazquez and B. Torgler (eds) *Developing Alternative Frameworks for Explaining Tax Compliance*, London, Routledge.

Uslaner, E. M. and Brown, M. (2005) 'Inequality, trust, and civic engagement', *American Politics Research*, 33(6): 868–94.

Varese, F. (1997) 'The transition to the market and corruption in post-socialist Russia', *Political Studies*, 45(3): 579–96.

You, J. and Khagram, S. (2005) 'A comparative study of inequality and corruption', *American Sociological Review*, 70(1): 136–57.

chapter eight | dissatisfied democrats, policy feedback and european welfare states, 1976-2001

Staffan Kumlin

Introduction

The 'welfare state' and 'political support' are among the more scrutinised topics in comparative research on advanced industrial democracies. However, while impressive bodies of work about each keep accumulating (Dalton 2004; Newton 2006; Carnes and Mares 2007), they have rarely been explicitly connected in empirical analyses. This is unfortunate as the two literatures are nevertheless linked by common patterns and themes. One of the most pervasive ones is the possibility of decline, i.e. simultaneously downward trends in certain aspects of political support as well as signs of welfare state retrenchment.

As for political support – or 'trust' as it is often called – times series including the 1980s indicated no universal and lasting trend (Klingemann and Fuchs 1995). But recent work on longer time-spans and more encompassing data suggest 'public scepticism about politicians and government officials is spreading to virtually all the advanced industrial democracies' (but see Torcal and Montero 2006; Dalton 2008: 243). At the same time, however, normative support for the idea of democracy with its attached norms, rights, and procedures has stayed strong. To capture this current ambivalence – endorsement of democratic principles but dissatisfaction with their implementation – scholars have coined expressions such as 'dissatisfied democrats' or 'critical citizens' (e.g. Klingemann 1999; Norris 1999).

Moving to welfare state research, scholars have addressed the nature and impact of 'permanent austerity' (Pierson 2001), a situation in which it is difficult to finance previous commitments to public services and income replacement systems. While the policy responses are unlikely to involve radical welfare backlash, moderate adaptation and cost containment efforts within existing systems now seem more common. As prophesied by Pierson (2001: 417):

> neither the alternatives of standing pat or dismantling are likely to prove viable in most countries. Instead, as in most aspects of politics, we should expect strong pressures to move towards more centrist – and therefore more incremental – responses. Those seeking to generate significant cost reductions while modernising particular aspects of social provision will generally hold the balance of political power.

Several policy changes have been registered. Korpi and Palme (2003) investigated net replacement rates in the public insurance systems for sickness, work accident and unemployment for eighteen OECD countries. They found that 'the long gradual increase in average benefit levels characterising developments up to the mid-1970s has not only stopped but turned into a reverse' (Korpi and Palme 2003: 445; cf. Allan and Scruggs 2004). Similarly, results indicating gradual service deterioration and increasing resource-scarcity (rather than radical system change) have been reported in comparative studies of public services such as education and health care (Clayton and Pontusson 1998). Finally, adding insult to injury, income inequality (Brandolini and Smeeding 2008) and unemployment rates (Cameron 2001) increased in many countries during this period, especially in Western Europe.

At the same time, support for welfare state policies appears rather stable at high levels (for recent overviews, see Kumlin 2007a; Svallfors 2010a), and is found to strengthen where unemployment and inequality are increasing (Borre and Scarbrough 1995; Blekesaune and Quadagno 2003; Finseraas 2009). This leads to the basic query dealt with in this chapter. Does less generosity in widely popular welfare state policies, and deterioration in the outcomes that they are meant to affect, generate dissatisfied democrats?

The next section reviews and critiques past research on 'government performance' and political support. Many studies have dealt with the apparently weak impact of macroeconomic performance. However, I argue that such negative results – and the explanations offered – are not automatically valid for welfare state-related outputs and outcomes. The subsequent section discusses a smaller accumulation of studies on welfare state performance and political support. These conclude that performance may affect political support. However, they also display various features calling for further investigation. For example, one strand of evidence comes from historical case studies; these are valuable, but cannot simultaneously gauge effects of, and interactions between, performance factors. Other studies examine effects of subjective dissatisfaction rather than 'actual/objective' performance; such analyses are worthwhile, but open to suspicions of endogeneity. Finally, few have simultaneously analysed welfare-related outcomes (such as inequality) and welfare state policies (such as benefit generosity). In contrast, drawing on the emerging literature on 'policy feedback' (e.g. Soss and Schram 2007), I raise the possibility that welfare state ramifications for democratic dissatisfaction may be driven by policies themselves, rather than to policy outcomes.

I then proceed to three-level analyses of Eurobarometer surveys across twenty-five years (Schmitt *et al.* 2005). These suggest generosity in unemployment benefits (but not pensions, sick pay or income inequality) helps explain over-time within-country variation in 'satisfaction with democracy', while controlling for macroeconomic factors. This positive effect is relatively stable across individuals with different interests and values, but is conditioned by unemployment rates. Specifically, the results support a 'visible costs hypothesis' predicting weaker generosity effects when more people are out of work.

Dissatisfied Democrats and macroeconomic performance: a weak relationship?

This study belongs to a broader theoretical family emphasising policy outputs and outcomes as explanations of general political support (shorthand: 'government performance') (Easton 1975). Most empirical studies have examined *macroeconomic* factors while ignoring other types of performance. However, far-ranging conclusions have been drawn, reflecting a general scepticism about the explanatory value of performance in established democracies. For example, Dalton (2004: 126–7) studied macroeconomic performance and political trust over time in a large number of advanced industrial democracies and concluded that:

> [t]he empirical analyses [...] demonstrate the limitations of the performance model [...] economic performance, whether measured in objective or subjective terms, does not seem to be a significant contributor to the long-term decline in political support during the later twentieth century (see also Listhaug 1995).

A common explanation for the relative unimportance of (macroeconomic) performance factors highlights repeated experiences of electoral accountability. Such experiences teach citizens the value of punishing and rewarding incumbents at the polls, rather than blaming the political system more generally. Further, essentially positive experiences of accountability generate affectively based 'diffuse support'. This type of support is by definition insensitive to short-term fluctuations in performance. In McAllister's (1999: 203) formulation:

> [t]he political economy of confidence of democratic institutions is [...] strictly limited. This conclusion underlies the gradual transformation that has taken place in the established democracies, where the frequency of national elections has slowly generated a reservoir of popular support for democratic institutions, with citizens drawing a clear distinction between the institutions of the state on the one hand, and the party and leaders elected to conduct public policy on the other.

Other political science subfields, however, increasingly see electoral accountability as fragile. Recent research on 'economic voting', for example, concludes that accountability is highly unstable and variant across time and space (for recent overviews, see Anderson 2007; Duch 2007; Lewis-Beck and Stegmaier 2007). Specifically, the economy has stronger effects on the vote under 'clarity of responsibility' (Powell and Whitten 1993; Anderson 2000; Taylor 2000; Bengtsson 2002; Nadeau *et al.* 2002) and strong 'competency signals' (Duch and Stevenson 2008). Unfortunately, most institutional and contextual conditions conducive to these values – such as single-party majority government, a long period of incumbency, clear government alternatives, centralised government, etc. – are unusual not least in Europe. Conversely, Taylor (2000) found that the economy has *weaker* effects on democratic dissatisfaction under the same rare conditions. Thus, citizens dissatisfied with government performance appear to value accountability, but get frustrated with the functioning of the democratic system when this value is obfuscated, i.e. when they cannot hold any specific actor to account.

Accountability may be particularly fragile in the welfare state domain. Several studies find that policymakers build blame-avoidance into the design of retrenchment policies themselves (e.g. Pierson 1994; Lindbom 2007). For example, retrenchment is more likely to occur in an incremental and hard-to-detect fashion, in areas where client organisations are weak, or where retrenchment can occur as the result of non-decisions (i.e. failing to adjust benefit ceilings and floors upwards with inflation) and opaque tinkering with eligibility criteria. Moreover, studies of voter behaviour conclude that accountability in this domain is (even) weaker and more variable than in the macroeconomic realm. One study finds that dissatisfaction with salient and supported services such as education and health care had significant effects on government voting in only four of nine analysed West European elections. These effects were systematically contingent on institutional clarity of responsibility, and usually weaker than the impact of macroeconomic perceptions (Kumlin 2007b). Similarly, actual cuts in replacement rates are inconsequential for government survival in Western Europe unless cuts are very large and recent, or extensively covered in election campaigns (Armingeon and Giger 2008).

In sum, then, it seems unsafe to simply assume positive experiences of well-functioning accountability in the welfare state domain. The clinical distinction between specific incumbents and 'politicians' and 'politics' more generally seems potentially problematic. Therefore, experiences of poor welfare state performance may be generalised beyond incumbents even in established democracies.

The next section reviews research on this particular topic.

Dissatisfied Democrats, policy feedback and the welfare state

Research into political behaviour is often divided into three paradigms. There is the 'sociological' tradition, focusing on group socialisation and communication; there is the 'psychological' tradition, looking more to individual values and identifications; and there is the 'economic' tradition, concentrating on self-interest and rationality. In spite of obvious differences, all three highlight factors largely exogenous to political institutions and public policies. There has been less room for 'policy feedback', i.e. the possibility that the groups, values, and interests, etc. are in turn shaped by results of previous democratic processes. As Mettler and Soss (2004: 1) argue in a programmatic article, 'aside from some notable exceptions, political science has had little to say about the consequences of public policy for democratic citizenship'. Quite such a harsh verdict may no longer be fair, however. Policy feedback ideas have recently been applied in empirical studies on political participation (e.g. Soss 1999; Mettler 2002; Campbell 2005; Soss and Schram 2007), welfare attitudes (e.g. Mau 2003; Jæger 2006; Larsen 2007; Svallfors 2010b), and social capital (e.g. Kumlin and Rothstein 2005).

However, only a handful of studies have examined how welfare state-related performance and policies affect general confidence in democratic processes and institutions. Interestingly, the studies that exist assign greater weight to 'performance' compared to the literature on macroeconomic variables. One line of inquiry is offered by case studies of specific countries and historical phases. These often conclude that dramatic increases in the proportion of 'dissatisfied democrats' is preceded by a whole package of poor performance involving a recession, rising unemployment and budgetary imbalances, unpopular public sector cutbacks, and rising inequality and poverty rates. Newton (2006: 860) examined the four most extreme cases of trust decline among established democracies – Finland, Sweden, New Zealand, and Japan. A careful analysis of sequences of events revealed that:

> [i]t is striking that all four countries experienced real problems of economic and political performance [...] real world problems caused citizens to revise their political opinions, and when these were (partially) solved in Finland, Sweden and New Zealand, the political mood became more positive and supportive. (c.f. Holmberg 1999)

Case studies are clearly valuable, but have difficulties disentangling effects of different kinds of performance. Are citizens reacting against macroeconomic problems per se, against welfare state retrenchment or against the social outcomes of recessions and retrenchment, such as growing inequality and poverty? Do such factors interact with each other so as to increase or suppress each other's impact? Moreover, case studies run the risk of over-emphasising the peculiarities of a situation. Dalton (2004: 46–7) notes that:

> [t]he national literatures often link the trends to the unique historical experiences of the nation. In Britain, for example, the decline is linked to economic struggles of the nation; in Canada, it is linked to the fractious regional conflict; in Austria to the collapse of the Social-Liberal consensus.

Case studies, then, may reveal the impact of a dramatic country-specific crisis, but may not do justice to performance factors understood in a more systematic sense.

Other studies have gauged the individual-level impact of subjective evaluations of performance. Analysing eight European countries, Huseby (2000) found that negative evaluations of performance in care of the elderly, health care, job- and social security all negatively affect attitudes towards the functioning of democracy, but not support for democratic principles (see also Miller and Listhaug 1999; Roller 1999).[1] Similarly, examining fifteen countries, Kumlin (2007b, 2009) reports that dissatisfaction with health and education services hampers national political trust in all examined countries, and breeds euroscepticism in most of them. Public service dissatisfaction has stronger effects in these regards than dissatisfaction with the economy.

Studies of subjective evaluations add pieces to the puzzle, but also leave questions open. Do performance evaluations really drive mistrust in a causal sense or are they merely projections of attitudes such as political mistrust? Are evaluations systematically driven by 'actual/objective' trends or best understood as 'construc-

---

1. Similar findings were reached by Miller and Listhaug using Norwegian and American data, and by Roller who found that former East Germans' comparisons between the communist and post-communist welfare state were unflattering for the latter, which in turn had negative consequences for political trust.

tions' inspired perhaps by political discourse and idiosyncratic interpretations with little basis in common patterns across time and countries?

Only a few studies have examined the impact of 'actual/objective' performance variables. Huseby (2000) found that actual performance plays a role, but was forced to use social spending indicators, which have serious and well-known drawbacks (Esping-Andersen 1990; for a recent discussion, see Scruggs 2008). Anderson and Singer (2008) reported that greater disposable income inequality affects trust negatively among countries from both western and central/eastern Europe, controlling for individual-level variables. They also controlled one type of macro performance (inequality) for another (macroeconomic conditions).[2] Interestingly, macroeconomic conditions came out as entirely insignificant once inequality levels were accounted for.

The latter study raises two final issues to be taken on board. A methodological remark is that cross-country variation at a single point in time introduces institutional, political, and cultural variation, much of which cannot be controlled for. There should be considerable leverage in analysing also within-country variation, especially as such variation can be substantial for welfare state outputs and outcomes (Brandolini and Smeeding 2008). The second issue is that past studies concentrate on policy outcomes rather than on politically-controlled instruments meant to affect such outcomes. This is true for studies of macroeconomic performance such as unemployment and growth rates as well as for Anderson and Singer's study of inequality. The latter scholars, however, touched on the distinction in choosing to study:

> [i]nequality in disposable incomes – that is, post-transfer incomes – rather than market incomes or wealth [...] because they are shaped by both the market and the state and thus should be closer to how voters evaluate democratic institutions than pretransfer levels of income would be (2008: 578).

Nevertheless, one may object that disposable inequality blurs market inequality and market-correcting policies. There remains the question: "Do citizens 'read off' welfare state arrangements by perceiving aggregated outcomes such as inequality" (Anderson and Singer 2008) or mainly by observing more directly the politically controlled policies that affect such patterns?

An answer was proposed by Soss and Schram (2007) in their case study of America's AFDC/TANF reform. This reform introduced, among other things, stronger work incentives and stricter eligibility criteria for recipients. Imagined 'policy feedback' effects on attitudes towards recipients and welfare were part

---

2. There are just a few other studies that simultaneously consider performance in several domains. Among them are Huseby (2000) and Kornberg and Clarke (1992). This is unfortunate as performance across different policy domains is likely to correlate. Thus, considering their effects under control for each other is necessary to avoid spurious interpretations and to reach a fairer verdict on the 'performance model'. For example, macroeconomic downturns are to some extent likely to be negatively correlated with many other types of government performance. Also, both welfare state generosity and income inequality are likely to be affected at least in severe recessions.

of its political rationale. However, '[w]ork requirements and time limits may be popular, but they did not generate more positive images of poor people, welfare recipients, or welfare itself' (Soss and Schram 2007: 120). The proposed explanation for absent feedback is that while policies received massive media attention at their inception, subsequent policy effects on recipient behaviour (viewed by many experts as a success) did not. Lacking attention to outcomes, the public was rather affected by information and symbols surrounding policies themselves, rather than by societal policy outcomes. This argument, then, reinforces the need to simultaneously consider distant policy outcomes as well as actual policies.

What now? Contribution, data and measures

This chapter sustains the emerging research programme on welfare state performance, while aiming at progress in several regards. It adopts a large-N approach that models over-time within-country variation and allows simultaneous consideration of different types of performance variables. We avoid subjective evaluations and employ measures of actual/objective welfare variables. Among these variables one finds policies as well as outcomes.

Specifically, I combine contextual data on performance with micro-level Eurobarometer surveys.[3] Data from the most often repeated survey items have been compiled in *The Mannheim Eurobarometer Trend File* (Schmitt *et al.* 2005). This data set is by far the most encompassing and suitable given our purposes, but it still only contains one indicator of democratic dissatisfaction: 'On the whole, would you say that you are very satisfied, fairly satisfied, not very satisfied, or not at all satisfied with the way democracy is functioning in [COUNTRY].' Critics of this ubiquitous item point out that its precise meaning is unclear. Does it measure overall democratic performance, trust in specific institutions, trust in politicians, support for democratic principles, or some mixture of these (Canache *et al.* 2001; Linde and Ekman 2003)? Its defenders agree, but maintain its usefulness as an overall measure of subjective political support (Klingemann 1999; Anderson 2002; Blais and Gélineau 2007). Given the interest here in broader generalisations to attitudes that transcend specific incumbents, my position is that finer distinctions would be desirable but are not absolutely crucial as long as the measure captures much of the broad category of general dissatisfaction with the functioning of politics and democracy.

---

3. Eurobarometer surveys are biannual opinion polls conducted on behalf of the European Commission in all member states. *The Mannheim Trend File* was provided by The Central Archive for Empirical Social Research (ZA) in Cologne.

The macro data were taken from the Quality of Government Institute's Social Policy Data Set (Samanni *et al.* 2008). In turn, this data set draws annual unemployment levels from OECD data as taken from the 'Comparative Political Data Set 1960–2006' (Armingeon *et al.* 2008), and GDP growth levels from Eurostat (http://ec.europa.eu/eurostat) and 'Penn World Table' (Heston *et al.* 2002). GINI coefficients measuring disposable income inequality come from the Luxembourg Income Study (http://www.lisproject.org; for an analysis, see Brandolini and Smeeding 2008).

Welfare state policies, finally, are represented by three variables from Lyle Scruggs' 'Comparative Welfare Entitlements Dataset' (Scruggs 2008). These variables represent perhaps the most ambitious attempt to track welfare state development across time and countries. They are available on an annual basis for eleven Eurobarometer countries (Austria, Belgium, Denmark, Finland, France, Germany, Ireland, Italy, the Netherlands, Sweden and the United Kingdom). Immediately inspired by Esping-Andersen's (1990) decommodification index, the three indices register a number of generosity aspects of unemployment benefits, sick pay and pensions. These aspects include replacement rates for different household types, qualifying period length, benefit duration, waiting days, coverage ratios, and (for pensions) minimum and standard replacement rates, as well as proportion of retirees receiving benefits. The resulting indices, displayed in Figure 8.1, take all such features into account (see Scruggs 2008 for details). The annual nature of these data allows us to take advantage of the over-time component of the Eurobarometer surveys in ways that are explained next.

Findings: the importance of unemployment benefit generosity

Table 8.1 displays estimates of multilevel models with three hierarchically nested levels: *individuals* nested in *years* nested in *countries*. The dependent variable is 'satisfaction with democracy', ranging from 1 to 4, with higher values indicating greater satisfaction. Model 1 is an 'empty' variance components model that lacks independent variables. Instead, it only estimates a universal intercept together with one random error term for each of the three levels (i = individuals, j = years, k = countries).[4]

Model 1: $\text{Satdem}_{ijk} = \alpha + e_{ijk} + u_{jk} + v_k$

Model 1 is interesting as the variation of the error terms hint at the hierarchical causal origins of satisfaction with democracy. Of course, a precondition for pursuing contextual effects is variation at the particular level in question. Characteristically for survey data, much of the overall variation can be attributed to individual-level factors (SD = .783). Still, there is significant variation across countries (.234) as well as across years within countries (.131). This three-level

---

4. Multilevel models were estimated using STATA's xtmixed command using the unstructured variance-covariance option.

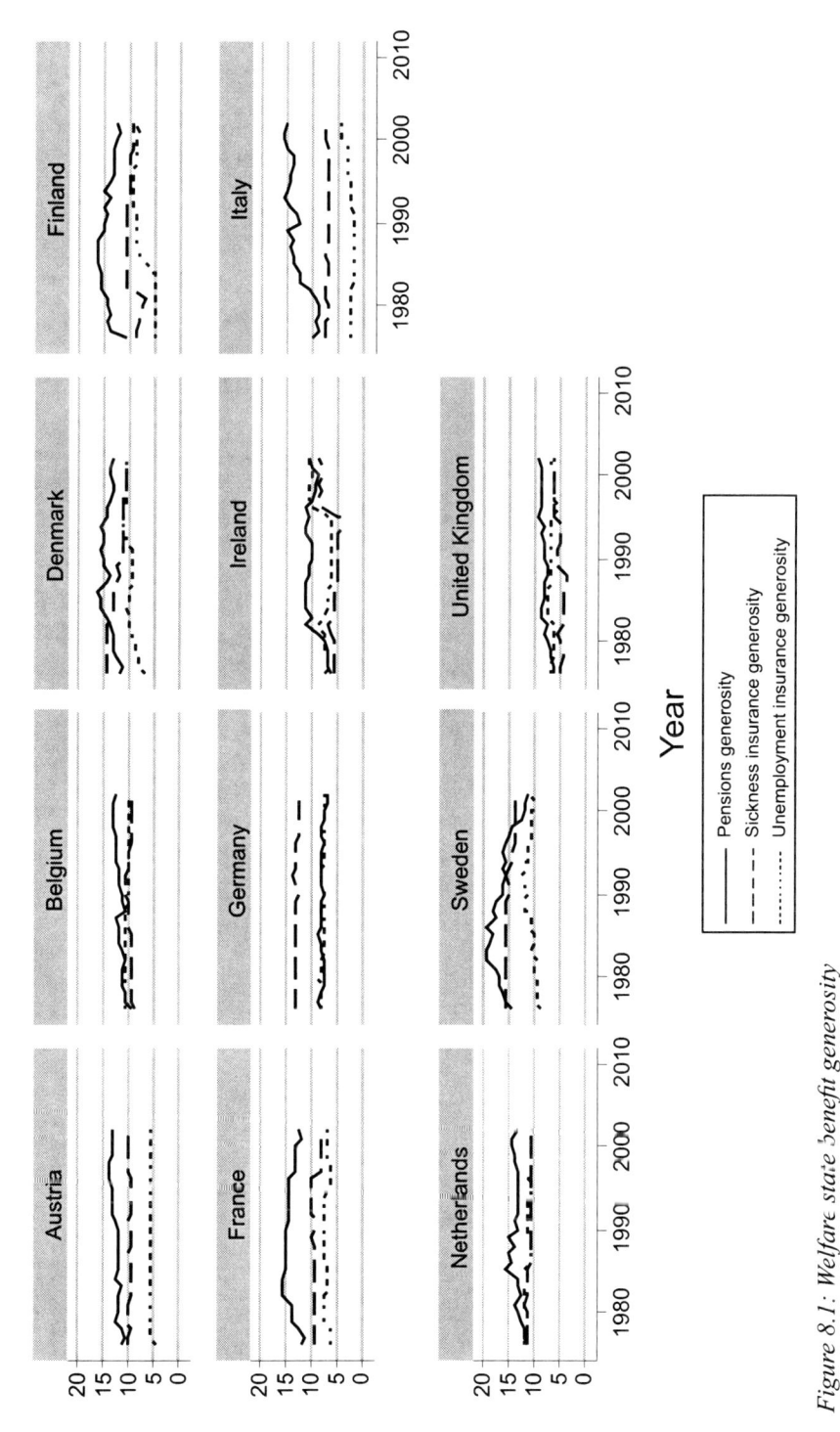

Figure 8.1: Welfare state benefit generosity

Note: Data from the Welfare State Entitlements Dataset (see Scruggs 2008)

nature of satisfaction with democracy means applying a 'flat' single-level OLS model might give biased coefficients and standard errors (Hox 2002; Steenbergen and Jones 2002).

Model 2 introduces independent variables, including individual-level controls, macroeconomic performance aspects such as unemployment rate and growth, as well as the welfare benefit generosity indices.[5]

Model 2: $\text{Satdem}_{ijk} = \alpha\ +$ Individual level controls$_{ijk}$
$+ \beta\ \text{Unemployment}_{jk} + \beta\ \text{GDPgrowth}_{jk} + \beta\ \text{GINI}_{jk} +$
$\beta\ \text{Year}_{jk}$
$+ \beta\ \text{Pension generosity}_{jk} + \beta\ \text{Sick leave generosity}_{jk}$
$+ \beta\ \text{Unemployment benefit generosity}_{jk}$
$+ e_{ijk} + u_{jk} + v_{k}$

A key observation is that unemployment benefit generosity, but not pensions and sick leave, has a significant positive effect on democratic satisfaction, even controlling for individual-level variables and macroeconomic performance. As for latter factors, Model 2 suggests both unemployment and GDP growth have significant effects in the expected directions.

Model 3 adds LIS data on disposable income inequality. This specification plays several roles. First, it tests if Anderson and Singer's (2008) cross-sectional relationship between income inequality and democratic satisfaction can be found also in over-time within-country variation. Secondly, we want to compare the impact of generosity policies with those of a central distributional outcome. Now, the prize to be paid for Model 3 is a reduction in the number of cases as the inequality data are not available for nearly as many time points as the others (beginning in the early 1980s in several countries).[6] To at least avoid losing countries, Model 3 drops the most unusual individual-level controls.[7]

---

5. As the units at level 2 are time points, I also include a linear time variable at this level.
6. Another point concerning number of cases is related to the fact that models 2–4 only contain eleven countries at the highest level. Admittedly, this is a bit on the low side, but should work as long as we are not interested in estimating effects of variables at this level. However, to be on the safe side, I have also estimated all models as two-level models (individuals in country-years) controlling for country dummies. This operation yielded the same main observations and conclusions.
7. Analyses including also these controls (based on nine countries; not shown here) indicate that results and interpretations remain largely the same. The exception is that the impact of unemployment level remains substantively strong, but drops below statistical significance.

Table 8.1: *Multilevel models of satisfaction with democracy (three levels; ML estimation)*

	Model 1	Model 2	Model 3
FIXED PART			
Individual level variables:			
Age_{ijk}		.0002**	-.0006***
$Woman_{ijk}$		-.017***	-.018***
Leftist ideology$_{ijk}$		-.225***	-.158***
Income$_{ijk}$ (country-year z-scores)		.048***	.058***
Unemployed$_{ijk}$		-.232***	-.237***
Political persuasion$_{ijk}$ (1–4)		-.016***	–
Political discussion$_{ijk}$ (1–3)		.067***	–
Low education$_{ijk}$		-.046***	–
Divorced/separated$_{ijk}$		-.098***	–
Urban resident$_{ijk}$		-.044***	–
Year level variables:			
Year$_{jk}$ (0=1980)		.008**	.007**
Unemployment rate$_{jk}$		-.015***	-.019**
GDP growth$_{jk}$		.010**	-.004
Pension generosity$_{jk}$		.002	-.003
Sick leave generosity$_{jk}$		-.012	-.012
Unemployment benefit generosity$_{jk}$		.044***	.053***
GINI$_{jk}$ (0–1)			-.692
RANDOM PART			
Individual level: Standard deviation of e_{ijk}	.783***	.771***	.768***
Country-year level: Standard deviation of u_{jk}	.131***	.105***	.135***
Country level: Standard deviation of v_k	.234***	.151***	.120***
No. of countries	11	11	11
No. of country-years	159	159	40
No. of respondents	226,236	226,236	69,442
Overall time frame	1976–2001	1976–2001	1979–2000

Notes: *p<.10, ** p<.05, *** p<.01

Unweighted data from *The Mannheim Eurobarometer Trend File*. The models also contain intercepts, as well as residual correlation between error terms at level 2, the estimates of which are not displayed here.

The results show that unemployment benefit generosity retains its effect also under control for income inequality.[8] Pensions and sick leave continue to be insignificant. Moreover, we see no significant effect of inequality. Thus, the negative effect reported by Anderson and Singer (2008) is not present here. Finally, their results suggested macroeconomic performance is wholly inconsequential under control for inequality. I find this to be the case for growth but not for unemployment which, if anything, takes on a slightly larger effect in Model 3. Thus, a higher unemployment rate negatively affects democratic satisfaction even controlling for whether the individual is unemployed or not.

Individual-level variation in contextual effects of generosity and inequality?

An objection to Table 8.1 is that overall contextual effects could mask variation among individuals. In fact, two studies do suggest that these could be contingent on *political values* as well as *economic interests*. As for values, Anderson and Singer (2008) uncovered a cross-level interaction between macro-level inequality and individual-level ideology, with political trust being more affected by inequality among leftist citizens; still, there was a significant negative effect also among non-leftists. General left–right position is relevant, not just for inequality, but for the evaluation of welfare generosity. Thus, below I follow Anderson and Singer's example and let this variable interact also with the impact of generosity on democratic satisfaction.

As for interests, Oskarson (2007) found that a simultaneous combination of high individual 'social risks' and welfare state retrenchment is especially conducive to 'political alienation'. Now, the Eurobarometer trend file does not allow tapping risks and interests with great precision. What we can do, however, is analyse interactions with broader demographic variables such as income (in the case of inequality), unemployment (for unemployment generosity) and age (for pensions).

It is possible to formulate different expectations on such interactions. On the one hand, large majorities in most of these countries have supported at least basic state responsibility for welfare policies throughout the studied period (Edlund 2009). This would imply that most groups react (more or less) positively to greater benefit generosity. On the other hand, issues of welfare benefits and income distributions also pit interests and ideologies against each other. After all, some groups benefit more than others and some support welfare policies more than others. Taken to its extreme, this could even imply that, say, unemployment generosity effects have different signs depending on interests or values, i.e. that more generosity simultaneously makes, say, beneficiaries or leftists more satisfied with democracy, and taxpaying non-beneficiaries, perhaps with a rightist value orientation, less so.

---

8. I have also estimated models including GDP/capita, but dropped this variable as it had no impact whatsoever controlling for the variables that are included in Table 8.1.

However, I find rather few traces of such empirical drama – effects are only inconsistently and very mildly structured by values and interests. This conclusion was reached by adding, one at the time, multiplicative cross-level interactions to Models 2 and 3 (not shown in tables, reported in text). The general form of the equations, which include level 2 variation in slopes of the level 1 interaction variable, can be expressed as follows:

Cross-level interaction models:
$$\begin{aligned}
\text{Satdem}_{ijk} = \alpha\ & + \text{Individual level controls}_{ijk} \\
& + \beta\ \text{Unemployment}_{jk} + \beta\ \text{GDPgrowth}_{jk} + \beta\ \text{GINI}_{jk} \\
& + \beta\ \text{Year}_{jk} + \beta\ \text{Pension generosity}_{jk} \\
& + \beta\ \text{Sick leave generosity}_{jk} \\
& + \beta\ \text{Unemployment benefit generosity}_{jk} \\
& + \beta\ \text{Individual-level variable}_{ijk} \times \text{Contextual variable}_{jk} \\
& + e_{ijk} + u_{jk} + v_k + u_{j;\ \beta\ \text{Individual-level variable}}
\end{aligned}$$

First, adding a cross-level interaction between leftist ideology and inequality to Model 3 yields no significant coefficient for this multiplicative term (p-value for $b_{\text{inequality x unemployed}}$ =.98). Neither is the impact dependent on the income of respondents (p-value for $b_{\text{inequality x income}}$ =.34). By the same token, the positive impact of unemployment generosity is stable across broad interest and value groups. For example, an interaction with leftist ideology to Model 2 yields nothing significant (p-value for $b_{\text{unemployment generosity x left}}$ =.42).[9] The same is true for being unemployed (p-value for $b_{\text{unemployment generosity X unemployed}}$ =.44) and for income (p-value for $b_{\text{unemployment generosity X income}}$ =.14).[10]

Moving to pensions, there is indeed a weak tendency for generosity to yield democratic satisfaction among leftists ($b_{\text{pension generosity X left}}$ =.022; p=.000). Thus, in this case the insignificant overall impact in Table 8.1 masks a positive effect among an important political subgroup. But even among leftists, the pension effect is only about half the stronger and more universal impact of unemployment generosity. Furthermore, there is not a more positive pension effect among the old.[11] Finally, for sick pay the data set does not contain proxies for health risks and individual sick leave. What we can do, therefore, is to investigate if sick pay generosity is more consequential among leftists. The results suggest this is not the case (p-value for $b_{\text{sick pay generosity X left}}$ =.30).

---

9. Consistent with Anderson's and Singer's (2008) coding, I use a dummy that takes on the value 1 if the respondent placed herself on one of the three first points along a 10-point left–right scale.

10. Here, there is in fact a very mild and non-significant tendency for higher-income groups to react somewhat more positively than others to greater benefit generosity ($b_{\text{unemployment generosity X income}}$ =.003; p = .13).

11. In fact, there is an unexpected but very mild tendency for pensions to matter less among the old ($b_{\text{generosity x age}}$ = -.0004; p = .000).

Unemployment rates and the benefit generosity effect: visible interests or visible costs?

Thus far we can conclude that especially unemployment generosity is a welfare state feature that has systematically affected democracy satisfaction across time and space in Western Europe. Moreover, the impact is rather similar across broad ideological and socio-economic groups. With so much time and space, however, it is still not necessarily the case that we have a contextually 'monolithic' causal factor at hand. Therefore, this section tests two hypotheses about a possible contextual source of variation in the effect.

Expressed generally, we are interested in how the prevalence of an underlying social problem/risk interacts with generosity in policies insuring citizens against it. Specifically, we pit two hypotheses concerning unemployment generosity against each other. The first one draws on the re-occurring finding that unemployment and crisis drives up support for unemployment protection. This has typically been explained by a mix of increasing salience of unemployment as a personal and societal problem, as well as increasing sympathy for the seeming victims of circumstance (Blekesaune and Quadagno 2003). All this would lead one to expect a positive interaction, with benefit generosity assuming a stronger positive effect on democratic satisfaction at higher unemployment rates. This prediction may be called the 'visible interests' hypothesis. Expressed generally, as a socio-economic risk becomes more common and visible, the benefits of social protection against it become more salient and visible, and appear more just.

But one may also imagine mechanisms working in the opposite direction. They can be summed up in a 'visible costs' hypothesis. The key here is that high unemployment may not only drive up welfare support and visibility, but also public expenditure and debt. This may, in turn, make different groups of citizens simultaneously perceive cause for dissatisfaction. Rightists and non-beneficiaries will complain about the state budget being in the red and fear realised or potential tax increases. Leftists and beneficiaries, on their part, will worry about potential cutbacks in terms of replacement rates or benefit eligibility. All can be united, however, in accusing politicians for creating a welfare system that currently seems unaffordable and less viable than under lower unemployment rates. Put differently, higher unemployment may prime citizens' attention to costs and problems associated with benefit generosity. Therefore, the normally positive effect of generosity may become weaker as unemployment rises.

Table 8.2 introduces a model containing a multiplicative interaction term between the unemployment rate and benefit generosity (Model 4). The key observation is the significantly negative coefficient for this term ($-.005$; $p = .001$). This is in line with the 'visible costs' hypothesis rather than the 'visible interests' hypothesis. Now, this does not exclude the possibility that also 'visible interests' mechanisms are at work. However, the negative interaction does suggest that the former process is on balance more powerful.

Table 8.2: *Multilevel model of satisfaction with democracy (three levels; ML estimation)*

	Model 4
FIXED PART	
Individual level variables:	
Age_{ijk}	.0002**
$Woman_{ijk}$	-.017***
$Leftist\ ideology_{ijk}$	-.225***
$Income_{ijk}$ (country-year z-scores)	.048***
$Unemployed_{ijk}$	-.232***
$Political\ persuasion_{ijk}$ (1 – 4)	-.016***
$Political\ discussion_{ijk}$ (1 – 3)	.067***
$Low\ education_{ijk}$	-.046***
$Divorced/separated_{ijk}$	-.099***
$Urban\ resident_{ijk}$	-.045***
Year level variables:	
$Year_{jk}$ (0=1980)	.008**
$Unemployment\ rate_{jk}$	-.010**
$GDP\ growth_{jk}$	.009**
$Pension\ generosity_{jk}$	-.008
$Sick\ leave\ generosity_{jk}$	-.006
$Unemployment\ benefit\ generosity_{jk}$	.053***
$Unemployment\ benefit\ generosity_{jk} \times Unemployment\ rate_{jk}$	-.005***
RANDOM PART	
Individual level: Standard deviation of e_{ijk}	.771***
Country-year level: Standard deviation of u_{jk}	.101***
Country level: Standard deviation of v_k	.157***
No. of countries	11
No. of country-years	159
No. of respondents	226,236
Overall time frame	1976–2001

Notes: *p<.10, ** p<.05, *** p<.01

Unweighted data from *The Mannheim Eurobarometer Trend File*. The models also contain intercepts the estimates of which are not displayed here. Unemployment rate and unemployment benefit generosity are centered over their means.

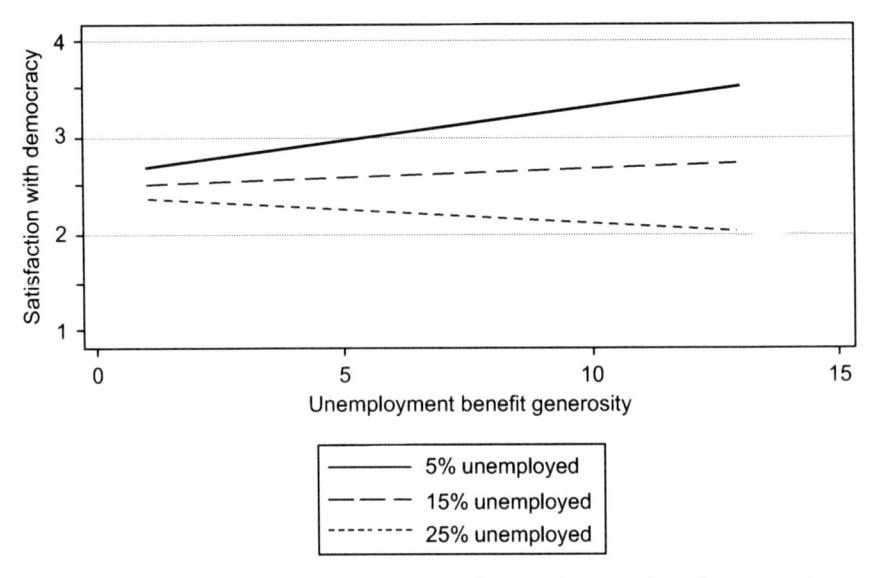

Figure 8.2: Satisfaction with democracy and unemployment benefit generosity at different unemployment rates

To facilitate interpretation of this interaction effect, Figure 8.2 plots the influence of unemployment level and benefit generosity with other variables at their means. First note the generally negative effect of unemployment. At mean levels of generosity, another 10 per cent of unemployment is predicted to reduce satisfaction by about .20 along the four-point scale. Judging from the tables, furthermore, this roughly equals the impact of becoming unemployed oneself.

Moving to the interaction, benefit generosity has a clearly positive effect at 5 per cent unemployment. At this level, moving from the lowest recorded generosity of around two (Italy during the 1970s and early 1980s) to the highest values of around thirteen (Scandinavia during early 1990s) is predicted to enhance democratic satisfaction by around one standard deviation (.80). As unemployment increases to crisis proportions of 15 per cent, however, the effect is predicted to have shrunk by around two-thirds. At the apocalyptic unemployment rate of 25 per cent, the effect of greater welfare generosity is even predicted to be slightly negative. Admittedly, this extrapolation is a bit of a stretch as Europe has mercifully experienced few such situations. But it is good for heuristic purposes as it illustrates the main point: the legitimacy-building role of welfare policies is found mainly when the problems policies alleviate stay within normal and affordable limits.

Conclusions: dissatisfied democrats and the nature of welfare state feedback

This chapter has linked research on the welfare state in general, and 'policy feedback' in particular, with research on political support. On the one hand, the findings confirm suspicions that welfare state variables can affect democratic dissatisfaction. On the other hand, the findings offer progress in several respects. By example, it is apparently not only possible to explain historically large confidence crises with reference to a time specific mix of poor performance (Newton 2006). One can apparently also explain general within-country over-time variation in democratic dissatisfaction using systematic measures of benefit generosity. This finding, moreover, supports the causal relevance of subjective evaluations of 'personal social protection', and the like (Huseby 2000). Perceived malperformance does not seem to be entirely endogenous to democratic dissatisfaction or only rooted in social constructions and idiosyncratic urban legends. At the same time, the results go some way towards specifying the aspects of actual social protection that are universally (un)important across time and space.[12] In particular, less generous unemployment benefits appear to be a universal generator of democratic dissatisfaction across broad groups in Western Europe.

All this is to say that studies on macroeconomic factors may have been too quick in dismissing performance-type factors more broadly conceived (McAllister 1999; Dalton 2004). The results suggest there is no simple master variable, or policy domain, that subsumes all relevant performance. Rather, what we need seems to be simultaneous consideration of several policy domains (i.e. macroeconomics and the welfare state). Part of this is the simple observation that different policy domains may have direct main effects. A finer case in point concerns the interactive interplay between social protection and the prevalence of underlying risks and costs. On the one hand, Figure 8.2 implies that one of the better vaccines against democratic dissatisfaction is a combination of generous unemployment benefits and low unemployment. On the other hand, generous benefits can lose their beneficial impact, or even contribute to a toxic mixture, if coupled with extreme unemployment and associated costs (the 'visible costs' hypothesis). Put differently, the long-term rise in unemployment in Western Europe has not only likely assisted in the birth of dissatisfied democrats directly, but also indirectly by disarming the previously legitimising force of unemployment benefits.

Findings such as these encourage more bridges between the vast welfare state and political trust literatures. Future studies may want to look at policy areas such as health care, care for the elderly and public education. Indeed, Huseby (2000) found that subjective evaluations of care for the elderly mattered more for political trust compared to several other subjective evaluations. Likewise, Kumlin (2007a) found that subjective evaluations of health care and education mattered more than economic evaluations.

---

12. This observation, it should be noted, is a contrast to the most serious worries about subjective performance evaluations that are sometimes voiced (van der Brug *et al.* 2007).

Finally, I was not able to echo Anderson and Singer's (2008) finding that disposable income inequality gives birth to dissatisfied democrats. The generality of their finding is thus an open question for future research. To be fair, the deviations could be partly due to the fact that these data cover Western Europe over a time span of several decades, whereas Anderson and Singer's cross-sectional results included only recent years and some central and eastern European countries. Perhaps inequality did play a genuinely causal role in those countries at that time?

But there is also methodological and substantive room for doubt. Beginning with methods, Anderson and Singer used cross-national variation across both old and new democracies. While this is a perfectly legitimate strategy, it is always hard to ensure that relevant spurious macro factors are controlled in a small but highly variable country sample. On a more substantive note, several studies cast doubt on the idea that 'policy feedback' in the welfare state domain is driven by citizens perceiving and drawing political conclusions from aggregated social policy outcomes (Soss and Schram 2007) such as overall inequality levels (Kumlin and Svallfors 2007). While citizens are by no means totally in the dark about things like wage differences (Aalberg 2003), the results reported here suggest they are better still at monitoring broad features of redistributive policies themselves (such as unemployment benefit generosity). This brand of policy feedback, then, may be an influential basis for citizens' reasoning about how 'fair', 'unequal' or 'satisfactory' their welfare state has become.

References

Aalberg, T. (2003) *Achieving Justice: Comparative public opinion on income distribution*, Leiden: Brill.
Allan, J. P. and Scruggs, L. (2004) 'Political partisanship and welfare state reform in advanced industrial societies', *American Journal of Political Science*, 48(3): 496–512.
Anderson, C. J. (2000) 'Economic voting and political context: A comparative perspective', *Electoral Studies*, 19(2–3): 151–70.
— (2002) 'Good questions, dubious inferences, and bad solutions: Some further thoughts on satisfaction with democracy', *Working Paper No. 116*, Binghamton, NY: Binghamton University, Center on Democratic Performance.
— (2007) 'The end of economic voting? Contingency dilemmas and the limits of democratic accountability', *Annual Review of Political Science*, 10: 271–96.
Anderson, C. J. and Singer, M. M. (2008) 'The sensitive left and the impervious right: Multilevel models and the politics of inequality, ideology, and legitimacy in Europe', *Comparative Political Studies*, 41(4): 564–99.
Armingeon, K., Gerber, M., Leimgruber, P. and Beyeler, M. (2008) *Comparative Political Data Set 1960–2006*, Berne: Institute of Political Science, University of Berne.
Armingeon, K. and Giger, N. (2008) 'Conditional punishment: A comparative analysis of the electoral consequences of welfare state retrenchment in OECD nations, 1980–2003', *West European Politics*, 31(3): 558–80.
Bengtsson, Å. (2002) *Ekonomisk röstning och politisk kontext. En studie av 266 val i parlamentariska demokratier*, Åbo: Åbo Akedemis förlag.
Blais, A. and Gélineau, F. (2007) 'Winning, losing, and satisfaction with democracy', *Political Studies*, 55(2): 425–41.
Blekesaune, M. and Quadagno, J. (2003) 'Public attitudes toward welfare state policies: A comparison of 24 nations', *European Sociological Review*, 19(5): 415–27.
Borre, O. and Scarbrough, E. (eds) (1995) *The Scope of Government*, Oxford: Oxford University Press.
Brandolini, A. and Smeeding, T. M. (2008) 'Inequality patterns in Western democracies: Cross-country differences and changes over time', in P. Beramendi and C. J. Anderson (eds) *Democracy, Inequality, and Representation*, New York: Russel Sage Foundation.
Cameron, D. (2001) 'Unemployment, job creation, and economic and monetary union', in N. Bermeo (ed.) *Unemployment in the New Europe*, Cambridge: Cambridge University Press.
Campbell, A. (2005) *How Policies Make Citizens: Senior political activism and the American welfare state*, Princeton, NJ: Princeton University Press.
Canache, D., Mondak, J. and Seligson, M. (2001) 'Meaning and measurement in cross-national research on satisfaction with democracy', *Public Opinion Quarterly*, 65(4): 506–28.

Carnes, M. E. and Mares, I. (2007) 'The welfare state in global perspective', in C. Boix and S. C. Stokes (eds) *The Oxford Handbook of Comparative Politics*, Oxford: Oxford University Press.

Clayton, R. and Pontusson, J. (1998) 'Welfare state retrenchment revisited: Entitlement cuts, public sector restructuring, and inegalitarian trends in advanced capitalist societies', *World Politics*, 51(1): 67–98.

Dalton, R. J. (2004) *Democratic Challenges, Democratic Choices: The erosion of political support in advanced industrial democracies*, Oxford: Oxford University Press.

— (2008) *Citizen Politics: Public opinion and political parties in advanced industrial democracies*, Washington, DC: CQ Press.

Duch, R. M. (2007) 'Comparative studies of the economy and the vote', in C. Boix and S. C. Stokes (eds) *The Oxford Handbook of Comparative Politics*, Oxford: Oxford University Press.

Duch, R. M. and Stevenson, R. T. (2008) *The Economic Vote: How political and economic institutions condition election results*, Cambridge: Cambridge University Press.

Easton, D. (1975) 'A re-assessment of the concept of political support', *British Journal of Political Science*, 5(4): 435–57.

Edlund, J. (2009) 'Attitudes towards state organized welfare in 22 societies: A question of convergence?', in M. Haller, R. Jowell and T. W. S. Smith (eds) *The International Social Survey Programme 1984–2009: Charting the globe*, London: Routledge.

Esping-Andersen, G. (1990) *The Three Worlds of Welfare Capitalism*, Cambridge: Polity Press.

Finseraas, H. (2009) 'Income inequality and demand for redistribution: A multilevel analysis of European public opinion', *Scandinavian Political Studies*, 32(1): 94–119.

Heston, A., Summers, R. and Aten, B. (2002) *Penn World Table Version 6.1*, Center for International Comparisons at the University of Pennsylvania (CICUP).

Holmberg, S. (1999) 'Down and down we go: Political trust in Sweden', in P. Norris (ed.) *Critical Citizens: Global support for democratic government*, Oxford: Oxford University Press.

Hox, J. (2002) *Multilevel Analysis*. Mahwah: Lawrence Erlbaum Associates.

Huseby, B. M. (2000) *Government Performance and Political Support: A study of how evaluations of economic performance, social policy and environmental protection influence the popular assessments of the political system*, Trondheim: Department of Sociology and Political Science: Norwegian University of Technology.

Jæger, M. M. (2006) 'Welfare regimes and attitudes towards redistribution: The regime hypothesis revisited', *European Sociological Review*, 22(2): 157–70.

Klingemann, H.-D. (1999) 'Mapping political support in the 1990s: A global analysis', in P. Norris (ed.) *Critical Citizens: Global support for*

democratic goverment, Oxford: Oxford University Press.
Klingemann, H.-D. and Fuchs, D. (eds) (1995) *Citizens and the State*, Oxford: Oxford University Press.
Kornberg, A. and Clarke, H. D. (1992) *Citizens and Community: Political support in a representative democracy*, Cambridge: Cambridge University Press.
Korpi, W. and Palme, J. (2003) 'New politics and class politics in the context of austerity and globalization: Welfare state regress in 18 countries, 1975–95', *American Political Science Review*, 97(3): 425–46.
Kumlin, S. (2007a) 'The welfare state: Values, policy preferences, and performance evaluations', in R. J. Dalton and H.-D. Klingemann (eds) *The Oxford Handbook of Political Behavior*, New York: Oxford University Press.
— (2007b) 'Overloaded or undermined? European welfare states in the face of performance dissatisfaction', in S. Svallfors (ed.) *The Political Sociology of the Welfare State: Institutions, social cleavages, and orientations*, Stanford: Stanford University Press.
— (2009) 'Blaming Europe: Exploring the variable impact of national public service dissatisfaction on EU trust', *Journal of European Social Policy*, 19(5): 408–20.
Kumlin, S. and Rothstein, B. (2005) 'Making and breaking social capital: The impact of welfare-state institutions', *Comparative Political Studies*, 38(4): 339–65.
Kumlin, S. and Svallfors, S. (2007) 'Social stratification and political articulation: Why attitudinal class differences vary across countries', in S. Mau and B. Veghte (eds) *Social Justice, Legitimacy and Welfare State*, Aldershot: Ashgate.
Larsen, C. A. (2007) 'How welfare regimes generate and erode social capital: The impact of underclass phenomena', *Comparative Politics*, 40(1): 83–101.
Lewis-Beck, M. S. and Stegmaier, M. (2007) 'Economic models of voting', in R. J. Dalton and H.-D. Klingemann (eds) *Oxford Handbook of Political Behavior*, Oxford: Oxford University Press.
Lindbom, A. (2007) 'Obfuscating retrenchment: Swedish welfare policy in the 1990s', *Journal of Public Policy*, 27(2): 129–50.
Linde, J. and Ekman, J. (2003) 'Satisfaction with democracy: A note on a frequently used indicator in comparative politics', *European Journal of Political Research*, 42(5): 391–408.
Listhaug, O. (1995) 'The dynamics of trust in politicians', in H.-D. Klingemann and D. Fuchs (eds) *Citizens and the State*, Oxford: Oxford University Press.
McAllister, I. (1999) 'The economic performance of governments', in P. Norris (ed.) *Critical Citizens: Global support for democratic government*, Oxford: Oxford University Press.
Mau, S. (2003) *The Moral Economy of Welfare States: Britain and Germany compared*, London: Routledge.
Mettler, S. (2002) 'Bringing the state back in to civic engagement: Policy feedback effects of the G.I. Bill for World War II veterans', *American Political*

Science Review, 96(2): 351–65.
Mettler, S. and Soss, J. (2004) 'The consequences of public policy for democratic citizenship: Bridging policy studies and mass politics' *Perspectives on Politics*, 2(1): 1–19.
Miller, A. and Listhaug, O. (1999) 'Political performance and institutional trust', in P. Norris (ed.) *Critical Citizens: Global support for democratic government*, Oxford: Oxford University Press.
Nadeau, R., Niemi, R. G. and Yoshinaka, A. (2002) 'A cross-national analysis of economic voting: Taking account of the political context across time and nations', *Electoral Studies*, 21(3): 403–23.
Newton, K. (2006) 'Political support: Social capital, civil society and political and economic performance', *Political Studies*, 54(4): 846–64.
Norris, P. (ed.) (1999) *Critical Citizens: Global support for democratic government*, Oxford: Oxford University Press.
Oskarson, M. (2007) 'Social risk, policy dissatisfaction, and political alienation: A comparison of six European countries', in S. Svallfors (ed.) *The Political Sociology of the Welfare State: Institutions, social cleavages, and orientations*, Stanford: Stanford University Press.
Pierson, P. (1994) *Dismantling the Welfare State?*, Cambridge: Cambridge University Press.
— (ed.) (2001) *The New Politics of the Welfare State*, Oxford: Oxford University Press.
Powell, G. B. and Whitten, G. D. (1993) 'A cross-national analysis of economic voting: Taking account of the political context', *American Journal of Political Science*, 37(2): 391–414.
Roller, E. (1999) 'Sozialpolitik und demokratische Konsolidierung: Eine empirische analyse für die neuen bundesländer', in F. v. Plasser, O. W. Gabriel, J. W. Falter and P. A. Ulram (eds) *Wahlen und politische Einstellungen in Deutschland und Österreich*, Frankfurt: Peter Lang.
Samanni, M., Teorell, J., Kumlin, S. and Rothstein, B. (2008) *The Quality of Government Institute Social Policy Data Set*, Gothenburg: University of Gothenburg. Online. Available http://www.qog.pol.gu.se.
Schmitt, H., Scholz, E., Leim, I. and Moschner, M. (2005) *The Mannheim Eurobarometer Trendfile 1970–2002. Data Set Edition 2.00*.
Scruggs, L. (2008) 'Social rights, welfare generosity, and inequality', in P. Beramendi and C. J. Anderson (eds) *Democracy, Inequality, and Representation*, New York: Russell Sage Foundation.
Soss, J. (1999) 'Lessons of welfare: Policy design, political learning, and political action', *American Political Science Review*, 93(2): 363–80.
Soss, J. and Schram, S. (2007) 'A public transformed? Welfare reform as policy feedback', *American Political Science Review*, 101(1): 111–27.
Steenbergen, M. R. and Jones, B. S. (2002) 'Modeling multilevel data structures', *American Journal of Political Science*, 46(1): 218–37.
Svallfors, S. (2010a) 'Public opinion', in F. G. Castles, S. Leibfried, J. Lewis, H. Obinger and C. Pierson (eds) *The Oxford Handbook of the Welfare State*,

Oxford: Oxford University Press.
— (2010b) 'Policy feedback, generational replacement and attitudes to state intervention: Eastern and Western Germany, 1990–2006', *European Political Science Review*, 2(1): 119–35.
Taylor, M. A. (2000) 'Channeling frustrations: Institutions, economic fluctuations, and political behavior', *European Journal of Political Research*, 38(1): 95–134.
Torcal, M. and Montero, J. R. (eds) (2006) *Political Disaffection in Contemporary Democracies: Social capital, institutions, and politics*, London and New York: Routledge.
van der Brug, W., van der Eijk, C. and Franklin, M. N. (2007) *The Economy and the Vote*, Cambridge: Cambridge University Press.

chapter nine | evaluations of welfare state reforms in germany: political trust makes a (big) difference

Eva-Maria Trüdinger and Uwe Bollow

Introduction

The recent economic crisis is not the only challenge the mature welfare states of Europe are confronted with. Demographic developments and budgetary constraints also put them under pressure to reform. Limited in their opportunities to expand and struggling to cope with permanent austerity (Pierson 2001), most European welfare states have been undergoing changes to adjust to the conditions of the post-industrial age, although no uniform path of retrenchment or dismantling can be observed (Allan and Scruggs 2004). This also applies to the German welfare state, which will be the focus of this chapter. Generally denoted as the reference case of the continental or conservative welfare regime type, which is often claimed to experience severe difficulties and to be in greatest need of transformation, it has undergone some major changes in recent decades (Esping-Andersen 1996; Palier and Martin 2007). Nevertheless, the German welfare still faces a demanding reform agenda.

Unless such adjustments and reforms are socially legitimised and widely accepted, governments risk punishment in subsequent elections by a disappointed electorate – especially in a climate of austerity when reforms often involve costs for certain groups of voters (Pierson 1994). In such a situation, resources to overcome public opposition to new welfare policies are essential. In this context, an important question to ask is whether political trust can enhance support for welfare policies in Germany. Considering that trust in the German Bundestag and the federal government has been declining since reunification (Gabriel and Neller 2010), the question is also whether public resistance to the reforms of the early twenty-first century can be explained with a lack of political trust.

In this chapter, we focus on the consequences of political trust – or the lack thereof. More precisely, we examine the effects political trust has on people's evaluation of reforms in three sub-domains of the German welfare state: pension, health care and family policy. Our *first assumption* is that political trust can promote support for policies and more or less unpopular welfare state reforms. Trustful people are assumed to be more supportive of the programmes and reforms that have been introduced in the past few years because they believe that the government will take their interests into account. On the individual level, political trust can serve as a heuristic in decision making with regard to the complex issue of welfare state reform. On the system level, it can be conceived as a resource providing government with flexibility in formulating and implementing reform policies.

Against the background of recent research this approach needs to be adjusted to incorporate the finding that the effect of political trust on people's evaluation of welfare state reforms can vary. For example, some analyses focus on the nature of a policy as a factor determining the influence political trust has on attitudes towards public policies (Hetherington 2005; Hetherington and Globetti 2002). However, the relevance of political trust as a rule of thumb in evaluating policies might depend on individual decision-making habits. Thus, it is worth taking a separate look at individual characteristics that are assumed to moderate the relationship between political trust and the evaluation of welfare state policies.

Previous research on various dimensions of government activity suggests that the political trust heuristic is more likely to be activated when individuals have to make financial or ideological sacrifices (Hetherington 2005; Rudolph and Evans 2005; Rudolph 2009; Rudolph and Popp 2009). In this chapter, we transfer these ideas to the context of policy evaluation. Our *second assumption* is that political trust is more consequential among potential losers of recent welfare state reforms – both in material and ideological terms. We thus need to identify categories of 're-form losers' in the German welfare state. Recent work emphasises the importance of perceived costs and ideological interests as factors moderating the influence of political trust. However, more research is required to specify the conditions under which the influence of political trust depends on perceived costs and/or ideological interests. In testing the assumptions with respect to pension, health care and family policy, we may provide further insights into the influence of political trust on policy evaluations.

The structure of this chapter is as follows: the second and third sections review previous work on welfare state support and particularly the effect of political trust on attitudes towards the welfare state. After developing our arguments and hypotheses on the conditionality of political trust we briefly illustrate our data and measures. Our assumptions are empirically tested and discussed in the final two sections.

Nature and relevance of political trust

Numerous empirical studies have investigated the determinants of attitudes towards the welfare state. Two major approaches to explain support for welfare state reforms can be identified (van Oorschot 2002; Blekesaune and Quadagno 2003):

1. The first approach is based on the self-interest argument and focuses on interest-orientations of recipients and contributors and on related sociostructural explanations. Net beneficiaries of the welfare state tend to prefer a tighter social security net than net contributors.
2. The second approach focuses on the effects of party-identification, values and orientations on the left-right axis and can be summarised as value-based approach. Ideological beliefs and values are considered to shape specific attitudes towards the welfare state.

Even if empirical analyses combine these two key approaches, their often moderate explanatory power indicates that this is only part of the story. One argument is that both approaches entail problems of conceptualisation and measurement (Ullrich 2000: 138). A better understanding of attitudes towards the welfare state might be gained by taking a closer look at the role of political trust as another potential explanatory variable. As long as thirty years ago, many researchers started to observe a decline in trust and associated it with a crisis of governability in Western democracies (see, for example, Crozier et al. 1975). Following this line of thought, a lack of political trust might be at the root of some governments' difficulties in implementing new policies. In other words, the less trustworthy citizens regard their government, the less likely they are to contingently consent to its policies (Levi 1997: 21). Before reviewing previous work on the relationship between trust and attitudes towards the welfare state, we will briefly introduce the concept of political trust.

Political trust is a well-established and widely-used concept in social science. According to Gamson (1968: 54), political trust implies that people expect the political system to produce preferred outcomes 'even if left untended'. It can be understood as a generalised affective evaluation of government performance, which shapes attitudes towards government action.[1] From a similar perspective, Easton (1975) describes trust as diffuse support for political authorities and institutions based on socialisation and generalised direct experience. As a form of political support it is thought to promote the persistence of political systems (Fuchs 1989). The importance of trust for democracy has been frequently pointed out by normative democratic theory: (a minimum of) trust is a key element of democracy. A society characterised by widespread distrust does not accord with a democratic self-image (Gabriel and Zmerli 2006). Finally, political trust also supports effective governance and benefits those being governed as it reduces transaction costs for all of the involved – for the government by ensuring support for its decisions even when they temporarily contrast with the interests of the trustees (Chanley et al. 2001); and for the citizens by eliminating the need to constantly monitor political actors because people trust their representatives and institutions to act in accordance with their interests (Easton 1975: 447). As Nye et al. (1997: 4) put it: 'If people believe that government is incompetent and cannot be trusted, they are less likely to provide [critical] resources.' This implies that trustful people tend to be more likely to provide support for public policy. When people are uncertain about the personal or public benefits of government action, trust might prove to be the critical resource for government.

Much research has been conducted on the determinants of political trust.[2]

---

1. We are aware that this view is not undisputed. However, it provides a basis for understanding the core of the concept. For an overview, see Newton (2007). Hardin (1999) understands political trust as 'encapsulated interest'; with reference to his concepts, Braithwaite (1998) distinguishes between communal trust and exchange-based trust.
2. Of the two key strands that emerge here (Denters et al. 2007), one is based on socio-cultural explanations stressing the importance of political socialisation in social networks (Almond and

The consequences of trust on attitudes towards certain policies, however, have received less attention. Chanley *et al.* (2000) analysed the influence of trust in government on policy preferences based on Stimson's (1999) measure of policy mood, which includes support for government spending and government activity. They found that in periods of declining trust, people are less willing to dedicate resources to public policy. In a comparative analysis, Svallfors (1999) did not find any evidence for a clear relationship between political trust and efficacy on the one hand and attitudes toward state intervention on the other. Similarly, Edlund's (1999) findings indicate only a weak correlation between political trust and public preferences for the welfare state. Svallfors (2002) assumed that cross-national differences in trust and efficacy account for variations in support for welfare state intervention. Since he found the effects on overall support of the welfare state to be weak and often insignificant, he focused on those domains where trust can explain attitudes.

On the whole, there are at least two major aspects that have not been sufficiently addressed by previous research on the effects of political trust on support for the welfare state and which we will focus on in this chapter. One is that most studies concentrate on the range and degree of government responsibility for welfare or simply introduce a measure of general support for the welfare state as the dependent variable. Specific policy fields and programs, however, receive only little attention. Addressing more concrete aspects of the welfare state seems to be a promising strategy (Svallfors 2002; Ullrich 2000).

The second aspect is that analyses of whether and how trust affects attitudes towards the welfare state mainly focus on demands for government action. However, it remains unclear why trust should be an important determinant of attitudes about the preferred range and degree of government activity rather than about its results. Svallfors (2002: 198), for example, points this out by stating that 'political trust does not influence how people view what the state *should* do, but it does influence how they perceive what the state is *actually* doing' (original emphasis). As a 'basic evaluative orientation toward the government' (Hetherington 1998: 791), it can encourage people to see government activities in a more favourable light. Trusting people might thus tend to evaluate past policies more positively.

In the next section, we first want to show why political trust can play a decisive role, particularly in the context of welfare state reforms. We then focus on the conditionality of political trust and take a more detailed look at evaluations of reforms in three separate branches of the German welfare state.

Political trust and evaluations of welfare state reforms

Even if the extent of the adjustments is frequently debated (e.g. see Pierson 2001;

Verba 1963; Putnam 1993, 2000; Klingemann and Fuchs 1995; Nye et al. 1997; Newton 2005) while the other suggests that experiences with government performance and responsiveness as well as orientations like party identification account for trust in government (Lipset and Schneider 1983; Citrin and Green 1986; Miller and Listhaug 1999; Newton 1999, 2005).

Palier and Martin 2007) and researchers do not always agree on how to characterise the reforms introduced in recent years, there are many studies on government activity in response to the challenges faced by the welfare state. However, only a few analyses deal with people's evaluations of recent welfare state changes and performance in specific welfare state domains. This is astonishing considering the fact that for new policies to work they must be perceived as legitimate by the population and that 'performance dissatisfaction is becoming increasingly salient in real-world politics' (Kumlin 2007: 366). Given these patterns of performance dissatisfaction, political trust may become an important resource for policy-makers. Trusting citizens will evaluate government decisions more positively because they are convinced that political authorities make apt use of their decision-making power, i.e. that they perform their duties with honesty, fairness and in reliable ways (Gabriel and Trüdinger 2011).

Political trust is relevant for evaluations of welfare state reforms for at least two reasons:

1. Citizens tend to know rather little about public affairs. They will rarely be able to fully comprehend the intentions and consequences of specific policies. The 'welfare state presents itself to the public as an extraordinary complex, diversified and unintelligible institutional arrangement' (Hinrichs 1997: 25). The consequences of welfare state reforms are particularly difficult to assess and might be felt only much later (Chanley *et al.* 2001). Under these conditions of uncertainty and risk, political trust can operate as a cognitive heuristic people may rely on when forming opinions about reform activities (Rudolph 2009: 146).

2. Welfare state reforms in periods of austerity can expose people to risks by cutting social expenditure in given arrangements or introducing new instruments that increase individual responsibility and contributions. 'Apprehensions about future uncertainties […] are becoming increasingly important' (Taylor-Gooby 2000: 1). Many citizens are aware that the level of protection might decline or additional contributions might have to be made. Welfare state reforms may thus generate an atmosphere of greater individual uncertainty[3] and risk. Moreover, future policies might conflict with the interests of the citizens, who widely benefit from the social security net today (Chanley *et al.* 2001). Under these circumstances, evaluations of welfare state reforms are assumed to depend heavily on trust in the capacity of the political system to manage existing challenges.

Both arguments suggest that trust is an important factor in explaining evaluations of welfare state reform. We derive our first and general hypothesis from these considerations and expect:

---

3. People may feel uncertain about possible outcomes due to the complexity of such policies and inconsistencies between political output and individual outcome of reforms. There may also be uncertainty about whether and how citizens are affected by changes at all because it takes time for the reform effects to take hold.

Hypothesis H1: People who place greater trust on political actors and institutions evaluate welfare state reforms more positively than people who tend to be less trusting.

Exploring the conditionality of political trust

Recent research findings suggest that the importance of trust as a determinant of attitudes towards the welfare state varies, depending on the demands the program or reform project in question places on people. Particularly, material and ideological interests may affect the extent to which people rely on political trust as a decision-making criterion. We will provide a brief overview of the arguments for material and ideological interests as moderators of political trust.

The hypothesis that material interests moderate the importance of trust in explaining citizens' evaluation of government action was first stated by Hetherington and his colleagues. Focusing on racial policy preferences, Hetherington and Globetti (2002) found that trust has a greater influence when the perceived costs of a policy are high and benefits are distributed to a small group of recipients. The effect is strongest when people bear the costs or reap the benefits directly. Hetherington (2005) refined this thesis by examining public support for different forms of government spending and distinguished programmes by how benefits are distributed (for redistributive policies, see also Rudolph and Evans 2005). The empirical results show that trust has a substantial effect on attitudes towards policies involving financial losses for citizens unless they belong to the group of beneficiaries of the respective program. In that case, the influence is negligible.

Rudolph and Evans (2005) expanded the idea of costs and benefits to include ideological orientations. They found that ideology conditions the relevance of political trust for attitudes towards government spending. As support for government spending implies higher ideological costs for right-leaning than for left-leaning individuals, political trust has a larger impact on attitudes towards public spending among the former, independent of the nature of the policy (Rudolph and Evans 2005: 668). The assumption of a moderating role of ideology on the relationship between political trust and attitudes towards certain policies is supported by further empirical evidence in studies on support for social security privatisation (Rudolph and Popp 2009) and on attitudes towards tax cuts (Rudolph 2009).

We apply these arguments about material and ideological costs to evaluations of recent welfare state reforms in three branches of the German welfare state that have been subject to transformation in recent years: health care, old-age pensions and family policy. We are going to focus on the following assumptions:

Hypothesis H2a: Political trust is more likely to affect an individual's evaluation of welfare state reform when the policy in question imposes material costs on him or her.

Hypothesis H2b: Political trust has a greater influence when the policy in question imposes ideological costs on the individual.

In the following, we will specify the concepts of material and ideological costs and then go on to determine for each domain under which circumstances certain groups are likely to incur material and ideological costs and who might therefore rely on political trust in evaluating reforms.

Recent reforms in health care, pension and family policy in Germany have neither raised social benefits nor provided greater social protection. On the contrary, not only do they involve losses but more often than not costs are distributed unevenly. Consequently, some citizens are made to pay disproportionately for new programmes and so for them political trust is of particular relevance. When speaking of costs, we first refer to direct and obvious costs incurred by parts of the population. But the term also refers to the greater future risks people might face and their perception of their situation as more insecure as a consequence of recent reforms (potential losses).

The material cost implications of welfare reforms are not the same for all three policy fields. Health care and pension policy cover so-called traditional risks, namely vulnerability in old age and health problems (Woods 2007). Changes in pension and health care policy thus tend to affect the material interests of the sick, who particularly depend on health care benefits, and of the elderly, to whom old age security is an immediate concern.

Family policy is an essential element of the modern welfare state. It develops strategies to deal with some of the so-called new risks: reconciliation of work and family life, need of care, and an ageing population (Taylor-Gooby 2004). Issues of child care and the need to invest in children have dominated recent welfare reform debates (Esping-Andersen *et al.* 2002). Reforms in this domain are intended to improve the (material) well-being of families, while people without children have to bear the costs without sharing the immediate benefits.

As we have stated above, people's ideological beliefs are an important determinant of their attitudes towards the welfare state. Leftist convictions imply a commitment to big government, a strong welfare state and the principle of equality (see, for example, Lipset *et al.* 1954; Knutsen 1995; Roller 1996). In contrast, right-wing attitudes are generally associated with preferences for little government interference and greater individual responsibility (for a discussion see Rudolph and Evans 2005: 662). The proposition that ideology moderates the effects of political trust makes sense when we consider evaluations of welfare state policies. For example, accepting a shrinking welfare state places higher ideological costs on people holding left-wing views and thus increases the importance of political trust for them.

Changes in health care and pension policy clearly touch issues on the traditional left-right axis of political preferences. Measures that promote private provisions or supplemental private health insurance go back to the polarised positions between socio-economic security and equality at the one end of the spectrum and individual freedom and responsibility at the other end. Family policy issues also represent both left- and right-wing positions, especially in the domain of child care. Rather than reflecting classic economic concerns, they pertain to socio-political components on the left-right axis, with a conflict between libertarian/self-enhancing and authoritarian/conservative positions (Inglehart 1984; Knutsen 1995). In the next section, we will describe the character of these welfare state policies to determine who might incur ideological and material costs.

Recent welfare state reforms in Germany – providing a context for the influence of political trust

Against the background of recent changes in health care, pension and family policy, we are going to take a closer look at certain subsets of the population that are likely to be adversely affected by recent reforms – both in ideological and material terms.

An ageing population, changes in the labour market and budgetary restrictions put considerable pressure on the German pension system. Old-age pensions in Germany are still based on a statutory pay-as-you-go defined benefit system financed through regular contributions. As a reaction to the above challenges, *pension policy* reform in Germany has for many years been driven by the need to contain costs (Pierson 2001). Pensions 'experienced continuous cuts in levels and annual adjustments with contributions rising until and including the 1990s' (Stiller 2007: 22).

However, the 2001 reform package marked a 'paradigmatic change' (Hinrichs and Kangas 2003: 580) by introducing a privately-financed pillar of provisions for old-age and providing incentives for voluntary private provision. Measures like raising the retirement age reflect efforts to stabilise contribution rates and pension levels. In the current situation, where 'the term pension reform is increasingly used as a synonym for cuts' (Bonoli *et al.* 2004: 30), people are aware of potentially higher costs. Furthermore, 'the expansion of private provision means that individuals will be more exposed to risks, such as those resulting from the market performance of their pension funds' (Bonoli *et al.* 2004: 47). So it may be argued that trust in the fairness and competence of political decision-makers is a critical factor for all citizens when evaluating pension reforms, especially if reforms are associated with the erosion of the insurance mechanism. Pensioners and people close to the retirement age are most likely to feel negatively affected by the new programmes intended to stabilise the German pension system. Most of the changes, such as the phasing in of a higher retirement age, do not apply to them, but those receiving pensions have not seen an increase in benefits in recent years. Under these circumstances, political trust seems to be an appropriate heuristic in evaluating pension reforms, particularly for older people.

At the same time, pension policy also takes a long-term perspective and the impact of many pension reforms is not always immediately visible (Clasen 2005: 16; Hinrichs and Kangas 2003: 574). Thus especially younger people tend to expect higher costs. More and more respondents believe that future pensions will be lower than current ones. This implies that the younger people are, the higher the potential financial burden on them and thus the greater the importance of trust in attitudes towards pension reform (Bonoli *et al.* 2004: 47). We therefore assume that the importance of trust in evaluating pension reforms is higher for younger people and for current pensioners than for people in the middle-age group. From an ideological perspective, we can assume that accepting reforms intended to expand private provisions and to raise the retirement age comes at higher cost for left-leaning individuals. Hence, political trust should play a more important role for these people.

German *health care policy* operates within the framework of a statutory health insurance system covering the large majority of the population. The principles of equality of treatment and progressive financing through contributions are important characteristics of this system (Stiller 2007: 29). In the light of rising costs, health care policy in Germany is largely driven by the search for effective cost-containment strategies. According to Bonoli *et al.* (2004: 37), recent health care reforms in Germany and other European countries mainly reflect attempts to encourage the more efficient use of resources, to control the prescription and cost of services and pharmaceuticals, and to shift some of the costs to patients. For example, the Health Care Reform Act of 2003 intended to raise individual cost awareness and to promote preventive behaviour. To some extent, recent reforms also involved risk-related individualised health care costs. When the range of medical treatments and services covered by social insurance shrinks, individuals are more likely to face higher costs. On the ideological level, this might strengthen the effect of political trust among left-leaning individuals. Financially, people of poor health and the chronically ill will have to bear most of the additional costs of recent reforms. We thus assume that political trust has a greater impact on the evaluation of health care reforms among sick people than among healthy ones.

Family policy reform in Germany is not characterised by cuts or cost-containment strategies, but rather by the realignment of government activities in response to emerging new needs and aspirations of families (Bonoli *et al.* 2004: 45). New initiatives to provide child care and parental leave schemes are intended to address demographic needs, economic pressures to retain female employees and changes associated with European integration (von Wahl 2008; Leitner *et al.* 2008: 175). These reforms focus on funding services and benefits for families to compensate them for their costs and efforts (Leitner *et al.* 2008: 177). Benefits are distributed widely among children and families, while childless people have to bear the costs of these policies, e.g. through taxes. Political trust should therefore have a significant and positive effect on the evaluation of family policies among those who do not have children because they are most likely to lose, or least likely to benefit, from recent reforms (Hetherington 2005: 87). Thus, we assume that for childless people, political trust matters more as a heuristic in evaluating recent family policies than for parents. At the same time, the shift of family policy towards balancing work and family life and providing child-care facilities challenges right-wing views (ideological costs). Consequently, political trust will have stronger effects on evaluations of recent family policies among citizens towards the right end of the political spectrum.

Data and analysis

The data we used for this article are survey data collected for a research project entitled 'Political trust and the support for welfare state reforms in Germany' run at the University of Stuttgart and supported by the German Research Foundation (Project no. GA 424/6–1). The survey contained various questions on attitudes towards the welfare state and political trust. It was conducted by Infratest Dimap from 12th November to 19th December 2007 and comprises data from 1,814 CAPI interviews. Citizens were asked to evaluate the direction of recent reforms in three domains of the German welfare state: health care, pension and family policy.[4]

In this analysis, 'political trust' is captured by an index consisting of nine variables that measure political trust towards federal political institutions and authorities. A principal component analysis suggested a one-dimensional solution for the index of political trust, and the reliability of the measure is high (Cronbach's alpha > .9). Apart from political trust as our main explanatory variable, other potential determinants have to be taken into account to statistically test our hypotheses. As stated previously, the 'self-interest argument' suggests that people evaluate policies in terms of the benefits they expect to receive, with personal benefits resulting in positive evaluations. Whether returns are considered positive is measured directly by data on subjectively perceived benefits of reforms and indirectly by people's social position as expressed by their income.[5]

We will also control for the effects of value orientations and ideological principles. Ideological orientations are conventionally measured by an individual's position on the left-right axis. Furthermore, we will consider the value dimension by measuring orientations towards general principles of the welfare state and distinguish between old principles ('social justice', 'protection') and new principles ('individual responsibility', 'personal provision') characterising welfare policies. A gap between individual preferences for these principles and the perception of how they are implemented will presumably reduce the acceptance of recent welfare state reforms. Due to the different logic of family policy, the respective attitudes are less likely to be determined by these old and new principles. Here, orientations towards the 'male breadwinner model' as an important frame of reference might be crucial for policy evaluations (Gabriel and Trüdinger 2011). As recent policies concerning family and child care in Germany turn away from this principle, its supporters will probably respond negatively to these reforms. We measure the acceptance of the 'male breadwinner model' by combining the replies to two statements on family life and child care. Other variables included in the models are: satisfaction with the current social security and family policy arrangements and the perceived justice of the German health care and pension schemes to control for assessments of the status quo. As research has shown that socialisa-

---

4. Detailed item wording underlying the trust variable and the other variables used in this study is reported in the Appendix.

5. Income is recoded into five same-size groups. As rates of item non-response were high, missing values are imputed on the basis of income grouped by education and age.

tion in the GDR still shapes expectations towards the welfare state, we include a dummy variable indicating whether the interview took place in East Germany or not. Additionally, we control for age[6] and educational effects.

To test the moderating effect of material and ideological costs on political trust we take a stepwise approach. First, we estimate the main effects of political trust for each branch of the welfare state investigated. The second step is to add the interactive terms: one between the left-right orientation and political trust to account for ideological costs, and one between a policy-specific variable for material costs and political trust. With regard to pension reform, we focus on age and introduce a group of younger people aged 16 to 39 and a second group aged between 40 and 59. Each group is coded as a dichotomous variable multiplied by political trust. People aged 60 and above constitute the reference category.[7] For evaluations of health-care reforms, we use a five-point scale of perceived state of health interacting with political trust. Finally, with regard to family policy, we use an interaction term between a dichotomous variable indicating whether the respondent has children or not and political trust.[8]

Empirical findings

To test the assumptions presented in the theoretical part of this chapter, we conducted binomial logistic regressions. This method allows for our dichotomous variables measuring general evaluations of recent reforms in the three domains to be regressed on a number of independent variables. Tables 9.1 to 9.3 contain the results of the logistic regressions listed separately for pension, health care and family policy, each with the interaction terms added in a second step (for an overview of logistic regression, see Menard 1995; for interpretations of interaction effects, see Jaccard 2005: 30 *et seq.*). We will first examine whether political trust does indeed promote support for recent welfare state reforms in Germany. For that purpose, we will interpret the Step 1 models (without the interaction terms). Then, we will analyse the conditionality of political trust and discuss the interaction between political trust and material and ideological interests in detail by examining the Step 2 models.

Overall, the explanatory power of our multivariate models is good. Political

---

6. Except for evaluations of pension policy; here, we expect the age variable to be responsible for the moderating effect.
7. Initially, we attempted to compare the middle age group (reference category) with the young and the elderly. As the differences between the middle-age group and the elderly and between the middle-age group and the young were insignificant, focusing on the middle-age group would mask substantial effects, so it is not suitable as reference category.
8. To reduce possible multicollinearity in the regression models, we z-standardised the metric variables included in the interaction terms. This z-standardisation was conducted separately for each model to account for different numbers of valid cases. The examined tolerance and VIF-values were within recommended parameters (cf. Menard 1995: 53 and 65). Cases with standardised residuals over 3 were excluded as outliers (cf. Menard 1995: 74). There was one outlier in each regression.

Table 9.1: Acceptance of welfare state reforms: old-age pensions

	Step 1				Step 2			
	B	Sig.	Exp(B)	Exp(B*s)	B	Sig.	Exp(B)	Exp(B*s)
Political trust (z-standardised)	0.62	***	1.86	0.62	0.86	***	2.36	0.86
Benefits from reforms – pensions	2.80	***	16.37	0.79	2.77	***	16.02	0.78
Ideological orientation (z-standardised)	0.07		1.07	0.07	0.04		1.04	0.04
Principle-policy gap old	0.36		1.44	0.09	0.39		1.48	0.10
Principle-policy gap new	-2.03	***	0.13	-0.58	-2.07	***	0.13	-0.59
Satisfaction with old-age insurance system	1.92	***	6.83	0.45	1.98	***	7.24	0.46
Justice of pension system	1.58	***	4.87	0.50	1.59	***	4.88	0.50
Income	-0.05		0.96	-0.02	-0.07		0.93	-0.02
Education	1.78	***	5.93	0.48	1.81	***	6.08	0.48
Aged 16–39	-0.40	*	0.67	-0.18	-0.22		0.80	-0.10
Aged 40–59	0.04		1.04	0.02	0.13		1.14	0.06
Place of interview: East Germany	-0.09		0.91	-0.04	-0.11		0.90	-0.04
Aged 16–39 x political trust (z)					-0.53	*	0.59	-0.28
Aged 40–59 x political trust (z)					-0.21		0.81	-0.13
Ideological orientation (z) x political trust (z)					0.09		1.09	0.10
Constant	-3.92	***	.020		-4.04	***	0.02	
-2LogLikelihood	1034.60				1029.59			
Chi²	514.60	***			519.61	***		
Δ Chi²	–				5.01			
Nagelkerke's R²	0.47				0.48			
Correctly classified cases	80.4%				80.7%			
Δ corr. classified cases: model – null model	11.3				11.6			
N	1,252							

Notes: * p<.05, ** p <.01, *** p<.001.
Standardised odds: Exp (reg. coefficient B * standard deviation).
Source: 'Political Trust and the Support for Welfare State Reforms in Germany', 2007.

Table 9.2: Acceptance of welfare state reforms: health care policy

	Step 1			Step 2		
	B	Sig.	Exp(B)	Exp(B*s)	B	Sig.	Exp(B)	Exp(B*s)
Political trust (z-standardised)	0.58	***	1.78	0.58	0.43	*	1.54	0.43
Benefits from reforms – health care	2.52	***	12.44	0.70	2.52	***	12.47	0.70
Ideological orientation (z-standardised)	0.14		1.15	0.14	0.18	*	1.20	0.18
Principle-policy gap old	0.67		1.96	0.18	0.61		1.85	0.16
Principle-policy gap new	-1.66	***	0.19	-0.48	-1.67	***	0.19	-0.48
Satisfaction with health insurance system	1.76	***	5.82	0.43	1.82	***	6.20	0.44
Justice of health care system	1.65	***	5.19	0.52	1.69	***	5.41	0.53
Income	-0.56	*	0.57	-0.20	-0.55	*	0.58	-0.19
Education	0.71	*	2.03	0.19	0.70	*	2.02	0.19
Age	0.01	**	1.01	0.21	0.01	**	1.01	0.21
Place of interview: East Germany	0.25		1.28	0.10	0.24		1.27	0.10
State of health	-0.57		0.57	-0.13	-0.65		0.52	-0.15
State of health x political trust (z)					0.43		1.54	0.20
Ideological orientation (z) x political trust (z)					-0.18	*	0.84	-0.19
Constant	-3.53	***	0.03		-3.53	***	0.03	
-2LogLikelihood	1127.97				1122.62			
Chi²	485.81	***			491.15	***		
Δ Chi²	–				5.35			
Nagelkerke's R²	0.44				0.45			
Correctly classified cases	79.6				79.4			
Δ corr. classified cases: model – null model	3.1%				2.9%			
N	1,280							

Notes: * p<.05, ** p<.01, ***= p<.001.
Standardised odds: Exp (reg. coefficient B * standard deviation).
Source: 'Political Trust and the Support for Welfare State Reforms in Germany', 2007.

Table 9.3: Acceptance of welfare state reforms: family policy

	Step 1				Step 2			
	B	Sig.	Exp(B)	Exp(B*s)	B	Sig.	Exp(B)	Exp(B*s)
Political trust (z-standardised)	0.52	***	1.68	0.52	0.18		1.20	0.18
Benefits from reforms – family policy	4.83	***	125.18	1.17	4.85	***	127.57	1.18
Ideological orientation (z-standardised)	0.12		1.13	0.12	0.20	*	1.22	0.20
Principle-policy gap old	-0.55		0.58	-0.14	-0.42		0.66	-0.11
Principle-policy gap new	0.11		1.11	0.03	0.03		1.03	0.01
Support of male breadwinner model	-1.64	***	0.19	-0.48	-1.64	***	0.19	-0.48
Satisfaction with family policy arrangements.	1.98	***	7.27	0.45	2.03	***	7.65	0.46
Income	-0.56	*	0.57	-0.19	-0.54	*	0.58	-0.19
Education	0.90	**	2.47	0.24	0.83	*	2.30	0.22
Age	0.01	*	1.01	0.20	0.01		1.01	0.15
Place of interview: East Germany	-0.18		0.84	-0.07	-0.17		0.85	-0.07
Children	-1.13	***	0.32	-0.49	-1.03	***	0.36	-0.45
Children x political trust					0.50	*	1.65	0.44
Ideological orientation (z) x political trust (z)					0.33	***	1.39	0.36
Constant	-1.19	*	0.30		-1.15	*	0.32	
-2LogLikelihood	1054.97				1034.18			
Chi²	469.46	***			490.25	***		
Δ Chi²	–				20.79	***		
Nagelkerke's R²	0.45				0.47			
Correctly classified cases	79.6%				80.8%			
Δ corr. classified cases: model – null model	12%				13.2%			
N	1,211							

Notes: * p<.05, ** p <.01, *** p<.001.
Standardised odds: Exp (reg. coefficient B * standard deviation)
Source: 'Political Trust and the Support for Welfare State Reforms in Germany', 2007.

trust, ideological beliefs and values, self-interest and general evaluations of the political and the social security system determine Germans' assessments of welfare state policies to a considerable extent. The chosen estimation model is slightly more suitable for evaluations of pension and family policy reforms than of health care reforms.

In hypothesis H1, we expected a positive influence of political trust on the attitudes towards the policies analysed here. The empirical results correspond with these expectations. We found significant effects of political trust in all of the Step 1 models when controlling for other potential determinants. Positive regression coefficients and odds ratios greater than 1 indicate that the effects follow the expected direction. That is, the more trust people place in political institutions and decision-makers in Germany, the higher the probability that they agree with the welfare state policies of the last few years. Moreover, comparing the standardised odds of political trust with those of the other determinants in each model, we found political trust to have the second strongest effect. Hence, political trust is one important motive for supporting welfare state policies and may promote the acceptance of reforms. Across all three policy fields, utilitarian considerations have the strongest influence on reform evaluations. People who believe to benefit from recent reforms are more likely to accept them. While attitudes regarding the respective branch of welfare state as just increase the probability of a positive evaluation of pension and health care reforms, inconsistencies between preferences for new principles of welfare policies and the perception of how they are implemented increase the likelihood of negative reform evaluations. In family policy, support for the male breadwinner model and dissatisfaction with the status quo negatively impact the respondents' opinion about recent reforms in addition to the effects of political trust and benefits. Contrary to popular assumptions, there is no significant difference between East and West Germans' evaluation of the welfare policies studied. Differences in socialisation and living conditions between East and West Germany might be covered by other factors such as socio-demographic variables or value orientations.

Our findings with regard to the relationship between ideological or material costs and political trust show that the ideological orientation of a person does not directly influence their acceptance of reforms in any of the three domains. Evidence for the influence of material costs is mixed. While people of both good and poor health evaluate health care policy in the same way, age is a differentiating factor. People placed in the younger group are 1.5 times less likely to evaluate pension reforms positively.[9] A considerable effect of the material cost variable can be reported in family policy. Here, parents are three times less likely to evaluate policies favourably than childless respondents. This is remarkable since it is the families who benefit from these policies. Rather than dissatisfaction with the direction of reforms, these results might also reflect the impression that reforms are

---

9. This value is obtained by computing the reciprocal value of the Exp(B). This procedure facilitates the interpretation of an Exp(B) value smaller than 1.

still falling short of expectations.

We now take a closer look at the conditionality of political trust and the moderating effects of individual circumstances that make people experience and evaluate recent policies in different ways. We identified material and ideological interests as critical to the opinions people form. To asses these moderators, we examine the interaction terms in the Step 2 models.

In *pension policy*, political trust was assumed to have a greater influence on whether reforms are approved of among the young and the elderly as they might face higher costs of future protection and reductions in current pension payments respectively. Moreover, political trust was thought to have the strongest impact, the further people place themselves on the left side of the ideological continuum. The empirical findings with regard to these assumptions presented in Table 9.1 are ambivalent. First, adding the interaction terms only marginally increases the explanatory power of the model, and the difference between Chi^2 in the Step 2 and in the Step 1 model is not significant. Most effects are stable, but some coefficients differ from the results of the first model. Particularly, adding interaction terms increases the main effect of political trust and the main effect of belonging to the younger age group loses significance. With regard to the main effect of political trust, our results show that an increase of this factor by one standard deviation raises the probability for a positive reform evaluation by 2.36 times compared to the mean. The reference group of the age variable are people aged 60 years and above. The interaction effect for younger people is significant and negative. The results indicate that the influence of political trust is 1.7 times smaller among the young than among the elderly. In contrast, the middle-age group does not differ significantly from the elderly. Therefore, the main effect of political trust does not vary for those belonging to the age group of 40–59 years.[10]

What are the implications of these results for our assumptions? Contrary to our expectations, it is not the elderly and the young who rely on political trust as a decision-making heuristic, but the elderly and the middle-aged. The younger the respondents, the less likely they are to accept recent pension reforms and to rely on political trust when evaluating these reforms. Younger people may still believe that future pensions will be lower than current ones and perceive the risk of material losses. But it seems that these uncertainties about the future directly affect their attitudes towards reforms and that political trust is not an adequate heuristic under these circumstances. Younger respondents are probably convinced that they have nothing to expect from politics concerning their statutory pension insurance. So, trust in political institutions and actors is not a suitable tool for guiding their decisions. So far, we have found only partial support for hypothesis H2a.

Our assumption of a greater importance of political trust when ideological

---

10. At this point we are able to explain why the main effect of political trust changes from Step 1 to Step 2. For younger people, the effect of political trust is less pronounced. As the first model does not analyse the interactions between age group and political trust, the influence of political trust was underestimated – and the original effect of belonging to the younger age group was overestimated.

costs are involved could not be confirmed empirically for pension reforms. The relevant interaction term is not significant,[11] so ideological costs do not moderate political trust in this domain.

In the field of *health care policy*, political trust was expected to be a more important heuristic in evaluating reforms for those who might incur additional costs because of their health status. We also assumed it to be of greater relevance for people holding left-wing views. As shown in Table 9.2, including the interaction terms improves the explanatory power of the regression models only minimally. Compared to the Step 1 model, most effects are stable, but the main effect of political trust decreases slightly and the influence of ideological orientation becomes significant. From this we can infer that in Step 1 the effect of political trust was overestimated and the effect of ideological convictions was underestimated.

With regard to hypothesis H2a on material costs, the data does not suggest that an individual's state of health moderates the use of the political trust heuristic. Sick and healthy people do not differ significantly in their reliance on political trust in evaluating recent health care reforms. Increasing political trust by one standard deviation raises the probability that recent reforms are supported by 0.5 in both groups. Ideological costs, however, do moderate the influence of political trust. The interaction effect is significant and negative, indicating that for respondents placing themselves one standard deviation to right of the sample mean the influence of political trust decreases by the factor 0.84. Conversely, the further people locate themselves to the left of the ideological spectrum (and the greater their ideological costs), the more they rely on political trust in evaluating recent health care reforms. In this case, the empirical findings support our ideological cost hypothesis H2b. As recent health care reforms directly refer to the ideological conflict between individual responsibility and collective solidarity, it seems that the conditionality of political trust is based on ideological factors rather than on material ones with reference to the groups we distinguished. Moreover, people of poor and good health probably do not differ in their perception of material costs as the risk of falling ill is universal. So evaluating health care reforms by relying on political trust does not depend on an individual's state of health at a given instant.

Finally, we come to the empirical findings on *family policy* evaluations. As specified above (see section on recent welfare state reforms in Germany), respondents without children are assumed to be net contributors to recent reform programmes. According to our application of the ideological cost hypothesis, recent reforms should prove ideologically more demanding for right-leaning individuals. As we can see in Table 9.3, the explanatory power improves significantly when the two interaction terms are included. Compared to the Step 1 model, most effects are stable, but the main effect of political trust is no longer significant. Ideological orientation, however, becomes a significant determinant of reform support in this

---

11. In this domain, ideological costs might also be expressed by the gap between new policy principles and recently implemented policies. Thus, a possible interaction between political trust and this factor was tested as well, but it was not significant either.

domain.[12] Interpreting the interaction terms, we conclude that both are significant and have a moderate to strong influence. With regard to the interaction between ideological costs and political trust, positive effects show that the relevance of political trust for the evaluation of reforms is greater the further people locate themselves to the right of the sample mean on the ideology scale. According to our interpretation, this means that people rely on political trust when their perceived ideological costs are high, as we assumed in hypothesis H2b.

While the interaction effect of ideology and political trust shows influence in the expected direction, the interaction effect between material costs and political trust points in the opposite direction. As the main effect of political trust is no longer significant, we can even state that the importance of political trust is completely conditioned by whether respondents have children. Political trust is of no relevance for those people we assumed to be affected by family policies on the material level (people without children), but only for respondents with children. For this group, the probability to support recent reforms is 1.65 times higher when political trust increases by one standard deviation.

A possible explanation of these findings is that the reforms of recent years imply potential material costs for families (if they do not benefit from the care infrastructure) and uncertainty about individual gains from new measures. People without children, on the other hand, might be aware that they bear these costs, but do not really perceive themselves as losers of policies in this domain. For parents, political trust might be of particular importance as these reforms entail not only financial risks, but can also affect their conceptions of family life. They 'directly alter the nature of the relationship among family members as well as between parents, children and the state, often in ways women and men will not yet have thought of, preferred or desired' (Ostner and Schmitt 2008: 13).

This last field of policy reform particularly demonstrates the conditionality of political trust, as it becomes relevant only when costs are involved, either material or ideological. If people do not fall into these categories, they do not rely on the political trust heuristic. In contrast to the other policy domains studied here, changes in family policy make political trust an important resource in evaluating those changes when material and/or ideological costs are incurred.

---

12. As well as in the previous models, changes in the effects between Step 1 and Step 2 have to be interpreted against the background of a statistical refinement of the model correcting an overestimated effect of political trust and an underestimated effect of ideological orientation in Step 1.

Concluding remarks

This chapter has presented a rather novel approach to analysing the role of political trust as a factor promoting positive evaluations of government activity. The empirical evidence presented supports the relevance of political trust for positive attitudes towards welfare policy changes. In line with our first assumption, we found it to have strong effects on evaluations of reforms in all three policy domains. This is an important finding in times of welfare state realignment. The greater the stock of political trust, the easier it is for the government to legitimise the implementation of new policies. The fact that political trust can be a general cultural resource to be developed and used by political actors in making decisions about and implementing new policies adds a further element to discussions on the relevance of trust. It actually increases the value of an important number of studies dealing with the determinants and development of political trust.

Apart from political trust, it is not only values and subjective self-interest that shape evaluations of welfare state policies, but also assessments of the status quo. Our results show that people evaluate reforms on the basis of their perception of the current situation. Interestingly, people who are satisfied with the current system are more likely to accept reforms in the three welfare state domains analysed here.

In a second step, we analysed whether the importance of trust as a promoter of positive evaluations of the welfare state varies among citizens with the demands recent reforms might have placed on them. Previous arguments in favour of a moderating effect of material and ideological costs on political trust were transferred into the context of welfare state policies in Germany. Our approach introduced some new elements to this research:

1. We looked at certain groups of the population separately to develop hypotheses about the relationship between costs and political trust – both in material and ideological terms.
2. We argued that material costs may also include risks or uncertainties about future benefits or losses associated with recent reforms.
3. We found empirical evidence that ideological and/or material costs do indeed moderate the influence of political trust on reform evaluations. Even if the results support the function of political trust as a general cultural resource, some people are more likely than others to use the trust heuristic in assessing political decisions. When they are asked to evaluate pension reforms, political trust is more influential among the elderly. In evaluating health care reforms it is the ideological rather than the material costs associated with health problems that moderate the role of political trust. With regard to family policy, the influence of political trust depends on whether the respondents have children and on their estimation of the ideological costs.

To summarise, we identified certain circumstances under which political trust is more likely to guide policy evaluations. These results not only provide further insights into how individual opinions are formed, but also indicate prerequisites for popular approval of welfare state reforms.

Appendix

Dependent variables

Evaluation of reforms:
Let us now talk about some individual aspects of social welfare and consider the health care system (the retirement pension system, family policy). All in all, how do you evaluate the reforms of the last few years in this policy area? Are these reforms headed in the right (1; positive answer) or wrong (0) direction?

Independent variables

Political trust:
I will now mention some political institutions and actors. I'd like you to tell me whether you trust them or not. Please use the scale (−2 'not trusting at all', −1 'rather not trusting', 0 'partly trusting/partly not trusting', +1 'rather trusting' +2 'completely trusting') again. What about: the German Bundestag, the Federal government, the federal chancellor, the minister of labour and social affairs, the health minister, the minister for family affairs, political parties, the supreme court, politicians in general. Index based on these items (to attribute unambiguous responsibilities to the various domains of welfare policies, each of the indices contains only the item on trust in the relevant ministry in addition to the core institutions). Scale values range from 0 'not trusting at all' to 1 'completely trusting'.

Benefits from reforms:
Have you benefited from recent health care reforms, do they involve disadvantages or have you not been affected by them?

Have you benefited from recent pension reforms, do they involve disadvantages or have you not been affected by them?

Have you benefited from recent family policy reforms, do they involve disadvantages or have you not been affected by them?

Justice of social security systems:
Do you consider the pension system just, rather just, rather unjust or unjust?

Do you consider the health care system just, rather just, rather unjust or unjust?

Index based on these items. Scale values range from 0 'social insurance systems are completely unjust' to 8 'social insurance systems are completely just'.

Satisfaction with democracy:
Generally speaking, how satisfied or dissatisfied are you with democracy as practiced in Germany? High values: Satisfaction with democracy.

Scale values range from 0 'completely unsatisfied' to 10 'completely satisfied'.

Ideological orientation:
Many people use the terms 'left' and 'right' when they want to describe political views. Here we have a scale ranging from left (1) to right (10). Thinking of your own political views, where would you place yourself on this scale?

New principles and welfare state reforms:
There are regular discussions about which principles should guide the reform of the social security system. In your opinion, how important should the following principles be? Principles: Individual responsibility, personal provision. Scale ranges from 0 'completely unimportant' to 10 'very important'.

And in your opinion, to what extent have these principles been realised by the recent reforms of the social security system? Scale ranges from 0 'not at all realised' to 10 'entirely realised'.

Index based on these items (Subtraction: principle minus realisation; folded scale to measure the principle-policy gap).

Old principles and welfare state reforms:
There are regular discussions about which principles should guide the reform of the social security system. In your opinion, how important should the following principles be? Principles: Maintaining social peace, protection against life risks, just and fair distribution of burdens. Scale ranges from 0 'completely unimportant' to 10 'very important'.

And in your opinion, to what extent have these principles been realised by the recent reforms of the social security system? Scale ranges from 0 'not at all realised' to 10 'entirely realised'.

Index based on these items (Subtraction: principle minus realisation; folded scale to measure the principle-policy gap).

Male breadwinner preferences:
Now let us talk about childcare, family and occupation. People can hold different sentiments. I'd like you to tell me whether you agree or disagree with the following statements:
Children under three should be cared for by their mothers at home.

All in all, family life suffers if the woman has a full-time job.

Index based on these items. Scale values range from 0 'opposing male-breadwinner model' to 1 'supporting male-breadwinner model'.

Satisfaction with compulsory health insurance, pension insurance, family policy:
Various fields of social security are listed below. In your opinion: On the whole, how well or badly managed are the following domains of social security? Please use the following scale: 0 means that overall you consider social security in this domain extremely badly managed. 10 means that overall you consider social security in this domain extremely well managed. Compulsory health insurance;

statutory pension insurance; benefits for families like child allowance or parental allowance.

Income:
Using this card, if you add up the income from all sources, which letter best describes your household's total net income? By this we mean the sum of wages, salaries, self-employment income and pensions after deducting tax, health insurance and social insurance. Please also consider income from rents, leases and funds as well as child benefits, housing subsidies, unemployment compensation, social benefits and other income. If you don't know the exact figure, your best estimate is fine. The scale measures income in 13 brackets from 500 euros to 6000 euros and more.

Education:
What is the highest level of education you have completed? Please indicate by using this list: (still at school [considered as missing value]), primary school, secondary school with eight or nine years of schooling (Hauptschulabschluss), secondary school with ten years of schooling (Mittlere Reife), extended secondary school, first stage of tertiary education.

Moderating variables

Age:
Open-ended question (year of birth)

State of health:
How is your health in general? Would you say it is:

very good (2), good (1), fair (0), bad (-1) or, very bad (-2)?

Children:
How many children do you have?

All scales are recoded to values ranging from 0 to 1. Metric moderating variables are z-standardised.

References

Allan, J. P. and Scruggs, L. (2004) 'Political partisanship and welfare reform in advanced industrial societies', *American Journal of Political Science*, 48(3): 496–512.
Almond, G. A. and Verba, S. (1963) *The Civic Culture: Political attitudes and democracy in five nations*, Princeton: Princeton University Press.
Blekesaune, M. and Quadagno, J. (2003) 'Public attitudes toward welfare state policies: A comparative analysis of 24 nations', *European Sociological Review*, 19(5): 415–27.
Bonoli, G., George, V. and Taylor-Gooby, P. (2004) *European Welfare Futures: Towards a theory of retrenchment*, Oxford: Polity Press.
Braithwaite, V. (1998) 'Communal and exchange trust norms: Their value base and relevance to institutional trust', in V. Braithwaite and M. Levi (eds) *Trust and Governance*, New York: Russell Sage.
Chanley, V. A., Rudolph, T. J. and Rahn, W. M. (2000) 'The origins and consequences of public trust in government', *The Public Opinion Quarterly*, 64(3): 239–56.
— (2001) 'Public trust in government in the Reagan years and beyond', in J. Hibbing and E. Theiss-Morse (eds) *What is it about Government that Americans Dislike?*, Cambridge: Cambridge University Press.
Citrin, J. and Green, D. P. (1986) 'Presidential leadership and the resurgence of trust in government', *British Journal of Political Science*, 16(4): 431–53.
Clasen, J. (2005) *Reforming European Welfare States: Germany and the United Kingdom compared*, Oxford: Oxford University Press.
Crozier, M., Huntington, S. and Watanuki, J. (1975) *The Crisis of Democracy: Report on the governability of democracies to the trilateral commission*, New York: New York University Press.
Denters, B., Gabriel, O. W. and Torcal, M. (2007) 'Political confidence in representative democracies', in J. W. van Deth, J. R. Montero and A. Westholm (eds) *Citizenship and Involvement in European Democracies: A comparative analysis*, London and New York: Routledge.
Easton, D. (1975) 'A re-assessment of the concept of political support', *British Journal of Political Science*, 5(4): 435–57.
Edlund, J. (1999) 'Trust in government and welfare regimes: Attitudes to redistribution and financial cheating in the USA and Norway', *European Journal of Political Research*, 35(3): 341–70.
Esping-Andersen, G. (1996) *Welfare States in Transition: Social security in a global economy*, London: Sage.
Esping-Andersen, G., Gallie, D., Hemerijck, A. and Myles J. (2002) *Why We Need a New Welfare State*, Oxford: Oxford University Press.
Fuchs, D. (1989) *Die Unterstützung des politischen Systems der Bundesrepublik Deutschland*, Opladen: Westdeutscher Verlag.
Gabriel, O. W. and Neller, K. (2010) 'Bürger und Politik in Deutschland', in O. W. Gabriel and F. Plasser (eds) *Deutschland, Österreich und die Schweiz im*

Neuen Europa, Baden-Baden: Nomos.
Gabriel, O. W. and Trüdinger, E.-M. (2011) 'Embellishing Welfare State Reforms? Political Trust and the Support for Welfare State Reforms in Germany', *German Politics*, 20(2): 273–92.
Gabriel, O. W. and Zmerli, S. (2006) 'Politisches Vertrauen: Deutschland in Europa', *Aus Politik und Zeitgeschichte*, 30–31: 8–15.
Gamson, W. A. (1968) *Power and Discontent*, Homewood, Ill.: Dorsey Press.
Hardin, R. (1999) 'Do we want trust in government?' in M. E. Warren (ed.) *Democracy and Trust*, Cambridge: Cambridge University Press.
Hetherington, M. J. (1998) 'The political relevance of political trust', *American Political Science Review*, 92(2): 791–808.
— (2005) *Why Trust Matters: Declining political trust and the demise of American liberalism*, Princeton: University Press.
Hetherington M. J. and Globetti, S. (2002) 'Political trust and racial policy preferences', *American Journal of Political Science*, 46(2): 253–75.
Hinrichs, K. (1997) 'Social insurances and the culture of solidarity: The moral infrastructure of interpersonal redistributions – with special reference to the German health care system', *ZeS-Working Paper* 3/97, Bremen: Centre for Social Policy Research.
Hinrichs, K. and Kangas, O. (2003) 'When is a change big enough to be a system shift? Small system-shifting changes in German and Finnish pension policies', *Social Policy & Administration*, 37(6): 573–91.
Inglehart, R. (1984) 'The changing structure of political cleavages in Western society', in R. Dalton, S. Flanagan and P. Beck (eds) *Electoral Change in Advanced Industrial Democracies. Realignment or dealignment?*, Princeton: Princeton University Press.
Jaccard, J. (2005) *Interaction Effects in Multiple Regression*, Sage University Paper Series on Quantitative Applications in the Social Sciences, 07–72, Thousand Oaks, CA: Sage.
Klingemann, H.-D. and Fuchs, D. (eds) (1995) *Citizens and the State*, Oxford: Oxford University Press.
Knutsen, O. (1995) 'Left-right materialist value orientations', in J. W. van Deth and E. Scarbrough (eds) *The Impact of Values: Beliefs in government*, 4, Oxford: Oxford University Press.
Kumlin, S. (2007) 'The welfare state: Values, policy preferences, and performance evaluations', in R. J. Dalton and H.-D. Klingemann (eds) *The Oxford Handbook of Political Behavior*, Oxford: Oxford University Press.
Leitner, S., Ostner, I. and Schmitt, C. (2008) 'Family policies in Germany', in I. Ostner and C. Schmitt (eds) *Family Policies in the Context of Family Change: The Nordic countries in comparative perspective*, Wiesbaden: VS Verlag für Sozialwissenschaften.
Levi, M. (1997) 'The contingencies of consent', in M. Levi (ed.) *Consent, Dissent, and Patriotism*, Cambridge: Cambridge University Press.
Lipset, S. M., Lazarsfeld, P., Barton, A. and Linz, J. (1954) 'The psychology of voting: An analysis of voting behavior', in L. Gardner (ed.) *Handbook of*

Social Psychology, vol. 2, Reading: Addison-Wesley.
Lipset, S. M. and Schneider, W. (1983) *The Confidence Gap: Business, labor, and government in the public mind*, New York: Free Press.
Menard, S. (1995) *Applied Logistic Regression Analysis*, Sage University Paper Series on Quantitative Applications in the Social Sciences, 07-106, Thousand Oaks, CA: Sage.
Miller, A. H. and Listhaug, O. (1999) 'Political performance and institutional trust', in P. Norris (ed.) *Critical Citizens: Global support for democratic government*, Oxford: Oxford University Press.
Newton, K. (1999) 'Social and political trust in established democracies', in P. Norris (ed.) *Critical Citizens: Global support for democratic government*, Oxford: Oxford University Press.
— (2005) 'Support for democracy: Social capital, civil society and political performance', *Discussion Paper SP IV, 2005–402*, Berlin: Wissenschaftszentrum Berlin für Sozialforschung (WZB).
— (2007) 'Social and political trust', in R. J. Dalton and H.-D. Klingemann (eds) *The Oxford Handbook of Political Behavior*, Oxford: Oxford University Press.
Nye, J. S., Zelikow, P. D. and King, D. C. (eds) (1997) *Why People Don't Trust Government*, Cambridge: Harvard University Press.
Ostner, I. and Schmitt, C. (eds) (2008) *Family Policies in the Context of Family Change: The Nordic countries in comparative perspective*, Wiesbaden: VS Verlag für Sozialwissenschaften.
Palier, B. and Martin, C. (2007) 'From "a frozen landscape" to structural reforms: The sequential transformation of Bismarckian welfare systems', *Social Policy & Administration*, 41(6): 618–37.
Pierson, P. (1994) *Dismantling the Welfare State: Reagan, Thatcher, and the politics of retrenchment*, Cambridge: Cambridge University Press.
— (2001) 'Coping with permanent austerity: Welfare state restructuring in affluent democracies', in P. Pierson (ed.) *The New Politics of the Welfare State*, Oxford: Oxford University Press.
Putnam, R. D. (1993) *Making Democracy Work: Civic traditions in modern Italy*, Princeton: Princeton University Press.
— (2000) *Bowling Alone: The collapse and revival of American community*, New York: Simon and Schuster.
Roller, E. (1996) 'Kürzungen von Sozialleistungen aus der Sicht der Bundesbürger', *Zeitschrift für Sozialreform*, 42(8): 777–88.
Rudolph, T. J. (2009) 'Political trust, ideology, and public support for tax cuts', *Public Opinion Quarterly*, 73(1): 144–58.
Rudolph, T. J. and Evans, J. (2005) 'Political trust, ideology, and public support for government spending', *American Journal of Political Science*, 49(3): 660–71.
Rudolph, T. J. and Popp, E. (2009) 'Bridging the ideological divide: Trust and support for social security privatization', *Political Behavior*, 31(3): 331–51.
Stiller, S. (2007) 'Surveying the German welfare state: Challenges, policy

developments and causes of resilience', *ZeS-Working Paper* 1/2007, Universität Bremen: Zentrum für Sozialpolitik.
Stimson, J. A. (1999) *Public Opinion in America: Mood, cycles and swings*, Boulder, CO: Westview.
Svallfors, S. (1999) 'Political trust and attitudes towards redistribution: A comparison of Sweden and Norway', *European Societies*, 1(2): 241–68.
— (2002) 'Political trust and support for welfare state: Unpacking a supposed relationship', in B. Rothstein and S. Steinmo (eds) *Restructuring the welfare state: Political institutions and policy change*, New York: Palgrave MacMillan.
Taylor-Gooby, P. (2000) 'Risk and welfare', in P. Taylor-Gooby (ed.) *Risk, Trust and Welfare*, Basingstoke: Macmillan Press.
— (ed.) (2004) *New Risks, New Welfare: The transformation of the European welfare state*, Oxford: Oxford University Press.
Ullrich, C. G. (2000) 'Die soziale Akzeptanz des Wohlfahrtsstaates. Ergebnisse, Kritik und Perspektiven einer Forschungsrichtung', *Soziale Welt*, 51(2): 131–52.
van Oorschot, W. (2002) 'Popular support for social security: A sociological perspective', in J. Clasen (ed.) *What Future for Social Security? Debates and reforms in national and cross-national perspective*, Bristol: The Policy Press.
von Wahl, A. (2008) 'From family to reconciliation policy: How the grand coalition reforms the German welfare state', *German Politics and Society*, 26(3): 25–49.
Woods, D. (2007) 'The welfare state and pressures to reform: A literature review', *WiP Working Paper 36*, Tübingen: Universität Tübingen.

index

Aalberg, T. 180
Aarts, K. 100
Aberbach, J. D. 15
Ahmed, M. 146
Albania 155
Alber, J. 131
Alesina, A. 69, 86
Allan, J. P. 164, 187
Almond, G.14, 17, 47, 63, 118, 190 n.2
  The Civic Culture 47
American National Election Studies
  13, 14–15, 144
American Political Science Review 14
Anderson, C. J. 13, 71, 100 n.6, 165,
  168, 169, 172, 174, 175 n.9, 180
Armenia 155
Armingeon, K. 166, 170
Australia 73, *88*
Austria 21 n.4, 27 n.9, *29, 34, 38, 113,*
  167
  welfare policy 170, *171*
authoritarian regimes 100, 102
  political trust and 2, 14, 100, 102
    n.9, 107–8, *109, 113*
  see also communist regimes; post-
    communist countries
Azerbaijan 146, 155

Bäck, M. 67
Bahry, D. 86
Balkenende, J. P. 52, 61, 97
Banducci, S. A. 99, 100
Banfield, E. 67, 86, 118
Bangladesh 73
Bélanger, R. 14
Belarus 122, *125, 135*
Belgium
  Dutroux affair 47, 62
  political trust, studies of 6, 21 n.4,

  27 n.9, *29*, 33, *34,* 56, 62, 73, *113*
  government satisfaction 33, *34,*
    35
  state benefits 170, *171*
  White marches 47, 62
Bengtsson, Å 165
Bentler, P. M. 18
Berlin, I. 128
Berlin Wall, fall of 119, 128, 132
Blais, A. 1, 169
Blekesaune, M. 164
Bobbio, N. 70
Bollow, U. 9, 10
Bonoli, G. 194, 195
Borre, O. 164
Bos, W. 52, 97
Bosker, R. 101
Bouckaert, G.
Bovens, M. 6, 28, 29, 33, 36, 59, 61,
  95, 99
Bowler, S. 48
Braithwaite, V. 97 n.1, 189 n.1
Brandolini, A. 164, 168, 170
Brehm, J. 69
British Economic and Social Research
  Council 117 n.1
Brown, T. A. 17, 18, 22, 24 n.6
Bryk, A. S. 127
Bühlmann, M. 67
Bulgaria 21 n.4, 22, 24, 35, *38, 88*
  political trust, studies 155, 157
    NEB political trust survey 122,
      128, *125, 135*
Business Environment and Enterprise
  Performance Survey (BEEPS)
  148–9, 150, *151, 153,* 155, 156,
  157, 159
Byrne, B. M. 22

Cameron, D. 164
Campbell, A. 166
Canache, D. 48, 169
Canada 167
Carnes, M. E. 163
Carter, J. 118
Catterberg, G. 13
Central Archive for Empirical Social Research (ZA) 169 n.3
Centre for the Study of Public Policy 122
Chanley, V. A. 61, 189, 190, 191
Chile *88*
China 73, 155 n.15
Chong, D. 71
Christensen, T. 57
Churchill, W. 119
Citrin, J. 14–15, 47, 49, 144, 159, 190 n.2
civic culture 63, 118
Clarke, H. D. 168 n.2
Clasen, J. 194
Clayton, R. 164
clientelism 143
Clinton, B. 59
Coleman, J. S. 119
communism *130*, 144, 145
    fall of 144, 147
communist regimes 104, 110, 117, 118, 119, 120, 122, 127, 130–1
    as welfare states 130–1
    corruption in 142, 146
    distrust, as foundation of 119, 122–3
    indoctrination in 122
    inequality levels and 146
    see also post-communist countries
Comparative Political Data Set 170
Comparative Welfare Entitlements Dataset 170
Confucius 67
Cook, K. S. 63, 97 n.1
Cook, T. 49, 57, 62
corruption 4, 8, 141–4
    as opposite of trust 98
    'grand' and 'petty' 142, 154
    'inequality trap' thesis 8, 141, 145, 148, 158, 159, 160
    legal system and 144, 148, 150
    political trust and 7, 8, 35, 37, 98, 107, 108, 129, 142, 143, 159
    parliamentary trust 98–9
    transition countries services interruption study 141, 142, 146–60
        crime and bribery 152, 154
        informal economies and 152, 154
        rising inequality and 150, 154, 155, 159
        trust in government analysis 155–159
    see also under inequality; post-communist countries
Corruption Perception Index (CPI) 102, 143 n.3, 145, 146, 149, *150*, 152, *153*
Costa, D. L. 86
Croatia 155
    NEB political trust survey 122, *125*, 127, *135*
Crozier, M. J. 36
Cuba 47
cultural theory 118
culture, political 4, 117
    political trust and 4–5, 27, 36, 118, 125, 133
Cyprus 21 n.4, n.5, *41, 88*
Czech Republic 21 n.4, 27 n.9, 146
    political trust studies 30, 34, *35, 113*, 155
    NEB surveys 122, *125, 135*

Dahl, R. A. 118, 120
Dalton, R. J. 13, 14, 36, 57, 117, 123, 163, 165, 167, 179
Dasgupta, P. 119
De Goede, P. 50
Deininger, K. 145
Dekker, P. 7, 59
Delhey, J. 67, 69, 72, 86, 101 n.7
Della Porta, D. 98

democracy 15–16, 47
　crisis of confidence and 13, 36
　distrust/mistrust, necessity of in 95, 122–3
　political support 163, 165
　'dissatisfied democrats' and 163, 164, 180
　　economy, role of in 165
　　political trust and 67, 189
　　decline, extreme cases of 167
Denmark 21 n.4, 27 n.9
　political trust studies 27, *28, 32,* 35, 56, *113*
　welfare policies 170, *171*
Denters, B. 95, 190 n.2
Diamond, L. 120
Dimitrova-Grajzi, V. 100
distrust 95, 96, 119
　corruption and 98
　former communist countries and 104, 122–3
　see also under post-communist countries
Dogan, M. 95
Dreher, A. 150 n.12
Drummond, A. J. 58
Duch, R. M. 119, 165
Durkheim, E. 67

Easton, D. 3, 13, 31, 47, 49, 120, 165, 189
　diffuse and specific support, trust as 13, 118, 189
Eckstein, H. 117, 118, 120
Edlund, J. 174, 190
education, provision of 164, 167
　voter behaviour and 166
Edwards, B. 118
Ekman, J. 169
electoral accountability 165–6
　'economic voting' 165
electoral systems, political trust and 7, 99–100, 107, *113*, 165
　majoritarian systems 99, 100
　proportional systems 99–100, 102

n.8, 107, 108, 110, 130
　political trust and 100, 130
Enste, D. 152
Esping-Andersen, G. 168, 170, 187, 193
Estonia 21 n.4, 27 n.9, 29, *30, 34, 35*
　corruption study 147, 155
　NEB political trust survey 122, *125, 135*
Eurobarometer surveys 6, 9, 15, 48, 50, 52–3, *54, 56, 59*, 123, 169 n.3
　political trust research 50, 123
　Mannheim Eurobarometer Trend File 169, *173, 174, 177*
　unemployment benefit generosity study 165
　welfare state development and 170
European Bank for Reconstruction and Development 125 n.5, 136 n.2, 142, 148
European Parliament (EP) 25, *26*
European Social Survey (ESS) 5, 7, 15, 101, 102, 107
　cross-cultural validity and 21
　political institutions, trust in (dataset analysis) 16, 17, 19–24, 27–37, 38–40, 111
　　Confirmatory Factor Analysis (CFA) *20, 21, 23, 39–40*
　　implementing and representative institutions 24–5
　　Multigroup Confirmatory Factor Analysis (MGCFA) 21, *23*
euroscepticism 167
Eurostat 102, 170
Evans, J. 188, 192, 193

Failed States index 148
Finland 21 n.4, 22, *23, 40, 41*
　political trust studies 27, *28, 32,* 88, *113,* 167
　welfare policy 170, *171*
Finseraas, H. 164
Fisher, J. 4, 14, 16

Flora, P. 131
Foley, M. W. 118
Fortin, J. 119
Fortuyn, P. 62
France 21 n.4, *88*
  political trust studies 27 n.9, *29, 34,* 56, *113*
  welfare policy 170, *171*
Franklin, M. 1, 61
Freedom House Index (FHI) 17 n.3, 128, 130, 143 n.3, 145, 149
Freitag, M. 67
Fuchs, D. 13, 27, 31, 95
Fukuyama, F., theory of trust 124

Gabriel, O. W. 100, 187, 189, 191
Galbraith, J. 145
Gamson, W. A. 189
Gélineau, F. 169
Georgia 146, 150, 155
German Research Foundation 196
Germany *88*, 102
  Bundestag 187
  political trust, studies of 6, 21 n.4, 27 n.9, *29*, 33, *34,* 47, 73, 101, *113,* 196
  government trust decline 187
  reunification 47
  welfare policy 170, *171*
Germany, welfare state reform study 9–10, 187–8, 192, 193, 194–206
  austerity climate and 187
  data and analysis 196–206
    conditionality and 197, 202
    political trust, measurement of 196
    variables in 196–7, 206
  family policy 187, 188, 192, 193, 195, 201, 203–4
    effect on the childless 195–6, 201, 203, 204, 205
    male breadwinner model, use of 196, 201, 207
    reform acceptance table *200*
  health care 187, 188, 192, 193, 195, 196, 203, 205
    Health Care Reform Act 2003 195
    reform acceptance table *199*
  pension reform 187, 188, 192, 193, 194–5, 196, 197, 201, 202, 203
    age and 201, 202, 205
    reform acceptance table *198*
    2001 reforms 194
  political trust, role of 187–8, 194–5, 197
    ideological costs and 188, 193, 195, 197, 201, 202, 203, 204
    material costs and 188, 192, 193, 197, 201, 202, 204
  socialisation, effect of 197, 201
Germany, East 47, 101, *113,* 196
  welfare state reform study and *198, 199, 200,* 201
Giger, N. 166
Glaeser, E. L. 86
Glanville, J. L. 67
globalisation 150 n.12
  political effects of 6, 58
Globetti, S. 188, 192
Goldstein, H. 103
Greece 21 n.4, 102
  corruption study 128, 147
  political trust studies 27, *28*, 31, 36, 47, 108, *113*
  government satisfaction 31–2, *33,* 56
Gronke, P. 49, 57, 62
Gross, K. 31
Guillory, C. A. 100 n.6
Gutmann, A. 86

Hanousek, J. 159
Hardin, R. 3, 48, 50, 97, 189 n.1
Harles, J. C. 86
Hay, C. 50, 56, 56, 58, 62
health care 164, 167, 179, 193, 195
  political trust studies and 102, *106,* 107, *109,* 187, 188, 192, 195
  voter behaviour and 166

see also under Germany, welfare state reform
Heath, J. 86
Hedlund, S. 118
Helliwell, J. F. 82
Hendriks, F. 28, 50, 55 n.6
Hero, R. E. 69, 86
Heston, A. 170
Hetherington, M. J. 2, 14, 27, 31, 50, 59, 61, 188, 190
Hibbing, J. R. 14, 61, 95
Hinrichs, K. 191, 194
Hix, S. 59, 61
Hobbes, T. 67
Holmberg, S. 27, 167
Hooghe, M. 2, 13, 14, 17, 24 n.6, 141 n.1
Hox, J. 172
Hu, L. 18
Hungary 21 n.4, *23*, 24
 corruption study 147, 155
 political trust studies 24, 27 n.9, 30, 34, 35, 36, 37, *113*
 NEB survey 122, *125, 135*
 government satisfaction in 34, 35, 37
Huseby, B. M. 167, 168, 179

IMF 102
India *88*
inequality
 as predictor of trust 145–6
 clientelism and 143
 corruption, link with 8–9, 142–3, 145 6, 159 60
 economic 143, 144, 154, 159
 political patronage and 143
 government trust and 86, 142, 154, 158, 159, 167
 left-right position and 174, 193
 of income and 174, 180
  increase in inequality and 164, 168
 transition countries and 144–5, 150, 154, 158–9
'inequality trap' thesis and 146 n.6, 147, 158, 159, 160
 LitS survey 154–5, *157*
 state role, support for 158, 159
 under the law 144
 World Bank Gini index 146
 see also under corruption; welfare state research
Infratest Dimap 196
Inglehart, R. 2, 18, 70, 117, 118, 194
 index *78, 79, 80, 81, 82, 83, 90*
institutional performance, theories of 108, 111, 119, 121
institutional trust 14, 36, 113
 citizen evaluation 7, 16, 121–2
 cross-cultural equivalence and 14, 21–2, 24, 30 n.10
 new/established democracies and 24, 25, 29–31, 35, 36, 37, 117, 124, 132
 Northern/Southern Europe and 27–8
 definition of 16
 implementing and representative institutions and 24–5, 36
 multilevel model of 125, *129*
 political trust research and 7, 14, 16, 18–23, 119–20, *123*
  NEB data 117, 122–5
 see also political trust; post-communist countries
International Country Risk Guide 145, 155
internet, political effects of 6, 59, 60
Ireland 27 n.9, *29, 35,* 73, *113,* 170
 political trust studies 56
Israel 16 n.3, 101, 147
Italy *88, 113*
 corruption study 147
 political culture 118
 political trust studies 56, 128
 welfare state policy 170, *171,* 178
Jaccard, J. 197
Jackman, R. W. 118
Jæger, M. M. 166

Jagodzinski, W. 67
Japan 167
Johnson, S. 152
Jones, B. S. 103, 127
Jowell, R. 16
Jowitt, K. 118
Jukam, T. 49 n.1

Kaase, M. 67
Kahn, M. E. 86
Kangas, O. 194
Karklins, R. 147
Karp, J. 48
Kasperson, R. 97
Kawachi, I. 70
Kazakhstan 155
Keefer, P. 86
Keele, L. 99
Keenan, E. 118
Kestilä, E. 67
Key, V. O. 134
Khagram, S. 143
Khodorkovsky, M. 148
Kiewiet, D. R. 131, 144
Kinder, D. 131, 144
Klesner, J. L. 98
Klingemann, H.-D. 13, 16, 27, 31, 36, 163, 169, 190 n.2
Knack, S. 86
Knutsen, O. 193, 194
Kornai, J. 119
Kornberg, A. 169 n.2
Korpi, W. 163, 164
Korsten, A. 50
Kumlin, S. 9, 164, 166, 167, 179, 180, 191
Kymlicka, W. 86
Kyrgyzstan 150, 155

La Ferrara, E. 69, 86
Laegreid, P. 57
Lambsdorff, J. G. 128
Larsen, C. A. 166
Latvia 21 n.4, 155
    NEB political trust survey 122, *125*, *135*

legal system, trust in (ESS dataset analysis) 19, *20*, 22, *23, 26,* 27, *39*
Leitner, S. 195
Lenard, P. T. 95
Levi, M. 49, 55, 56, 97 n.1, 189
Lewis-Beck, M. S. 165
Life in Transition Survey (LiTS) 8, 142, 154–5, *157*
Lindbom, A. 166
Linde, J. 169
Lindström, M. 2
Lipset, A. M. 13, 27, 144, 190 n.2, 193
Listhaug, O. 50, 95, 99, 101 n.7, 165, 167, 190 n.2
Lithuania 155
    NEB political trust survey *122, 125, 135*
Locke, J. 67
Lockerbie, B. 31
LoTempio, A. J. 71
Luxembourg 21 n.4, 27 n.9, *29*, 31, *34, 113*, 170
    political trust studies 56

McAllister, I. 99, 100, 128, 165, 179
McClosky, H. 71
Macedo, S. 36
Magalhaes, P. 100
Magone, J. M. 32
Manabe, K. 67
March, J. G. 119
Marer, P. 131 n.5
Mares, I. 163
Marien, S. 2, 5–6, 14
Martin, C. 187, 191
Mau, S. 166
Mauro, P. 141, 143
Mavrogordatos, G. T. 32
media
    as intermediary mechanism 111
    bias in 50
    political trust, role in 6, 48, 49, 57, *58*, 59, 62, 111
Menard, S. 197
Mettler, S. 166

index | 219

Mexico *88*
Mill, J. S. 67
Miller, A. H. 14–15, 50, 99, 101 n.7, 167, 190 n.2, 211
Miller, R. A. 118
Mishler, W. 8, 67, 100, 117, 119, 123, 124, 131
Misztal, B. 67
Moldova 155
Mongolia 155
Montenegro 155
Montero, J. R. 163
Moreno, A. 13, 95, 100
Morris, S. D. 98
Mueller, J. 61
Muller, E. 49 n.1
Munro, N. 130, 131
Muste, C. 49
Mutz, D. 61

Nadeau, R. 14
Nannestad, P. 49, 50, 67
Neller, K. 187
Nelson, M. 31
Netherlands, The *88*
  Belevingsmonitor Rijksoverheid 51–2
  democracy, attitudes to 53, *54*, 55
    consumer confidence and 59, *60*
  Dutch Parliamentary Election Studies (DPES) 48, 52, 53, *54*, 55 n.5
  overheid (government) 48, 50, *51, 52*, 55
  political trust, studies of 6, 21 n.4, 27 n.9, 28–9, 31, 47, 49, 50, 55, 57–8, 59–60, 95, 99
    aspects of trust 97–8
    economy, state of and 59–60, 61, *62*, 99
    government satisfaction 33, *34*, 47
    trust, decline/fluctuation in 47–8, 50, 51, 55, 57–8, 59, 61, 62, 98, 99

  politicians/parties, attitudes towards 53, *54*, 55
  regering (cabinet) 48, 50, *51*, 52, 53, 55
  Social and Cultural Planning Office (SCP) 50–1, 52
    Continue Onderzoek Burgerperspectieven (COB) 52
New Europe Barometer surveys (NEB) 8, 116–17, 121, 122, 124, *127,* 132, *135*
  corruption rating 122
  post-communist countries 117, 122, 123, 128, 130, 131
  trust measurement 116–18
New Zealand *88,* 167
Newton, K. 2, 6–7, 21 n.4, 59, 67, 68, 69, 70, 72, 73, 78, 81, 86, 102 n.7, 163, 167, 179, 189 n.1, 190 n.2
Norris, P. 2, 15, 56, 57, 67, 69, 100, *137,* 163
North, D. C. 119
North Korea 47
Norway 21 n.4, 150 n.12
  political trust studies 25, 27, *28,* 31, *32*
Nye, J. 36

Obama, B. 2
OECD 102, 164, 170
Orren, G. 67
Oskarson, M. 174
Ostner, I. 204
Owsiak, S. 143

Pakistan 73
Palda, F. 159
Palier, B. 187, 191
Palme, J. 163, 164
parliament, trust in *26*, 48, 96, 99, *123,* 126
  aspects of 96, 110
  cross-national differences 95, 104
  ESS dataset analysis 19, *20,* 22, *23*
  objective criteria/subjective evalua-

tion study 96, 97–114
  corruption hypotheses 99, 102, 104, *105, 106,* 107, 108, 110, 111, *113*
  country level characteristics 102, 107–8, 110–11, *113*
  economic development (competence test) 99, 102, 103, 104, *105, 106*, 101, 111, *113*
  ESS 2002/3 cross-national data, use of 101, 102, 111
  multilevel modelling, use of 101, 103, 110
  proportional electoral systems and 99–100, 104, *105, 106,* 107, 108, 110, *113*
  regime type and 100, *105, 106*, 108, 110, 111, *113*
  World Values Survey 73
  see also European Parliament (EP)
parties, political
  ESS data analysis 19, *20*, 22, *23, 26, 39*
  identification with 70, 71
  trust in 48, *123,* 126
Patterson, O. 69
Paxton, P. 67, 69
Pelligra, V. 70
Peru *88*
Pharr, S. J. 57
Pierson, P. 163, 166, 187, 191
Pipes, R. 118
Plunkitt, G. W. 142
Poland 21 n.4, 27 n.9, 30, *88,* 155
  government satisfaction 34, *35*
  NEB political trust survey 122, *125, 135*
police, trust in 6, 18, 19, 69, 81–2, *123*
  ESS data analysis 19, *20*, 21, 22, 23–4, 25, *26, 27, 39, 40–2*
  'policy feedback' research 164, 166, 168–9, 179, 180
  see also welfare policy performance research
political economy, theories of 130, 131

political leaders, trust in 142, 143, 144
  clientelism and 143
  economic management and 144
  inequality and 143
  patronage 143
  transition countries and 145
political support 163, 189
  democratic dissatisfaction and 165, 166
  macroeconomic performance research and 165, 166
  welfare state performance and 164, 166, 179
political trust 2, 15–16, 48, 95, 191
  concept of 3, 5, 48, 49–50, 68, 129, 189
    as a rational evaluation 97
    as relational 95, 96–7
    definition of 47, 49–50
    one-dimensionality and 4, 5–6
  conditionality of 188, 190, 192–3, 204
  determinant characteristics of 95 96, 129, 189–90
    attitudes, perceptions and evaluations, link with 95, 188, 190, 192
    economic performance and 99, 118, 120, 121, 131–2, 133–4, 135, 165
    education level and 2, 71, 77, 103, 133
    ideological interests and 188, 189, 192, 193
    policy evaluation and 188, 190, 192
      cost/benefit analysis and 192
    political/social culture and 4–5, 14, 17, 190 n.2
    role of 189
    support for unpopular reforms and 187–8, 189
    social trust, relations with 67, 69–70, 72, 77, 80, 84–6, 126
  see also institutional trust; political support

political trust research 13, 14
  conceptual and empirical gap 50
  contextual characteristics affecting 7, 96
  cross-national studies 95, 110, 111, 119, 168
  decline/fluctuations of trust analysis 50, 56, 57, 59, 60, 62, 190
    case studies, difficulties with 167
    consumer confidence and 59, 60
    cross-national gradual erosion 57
    international crises and drama, effect on 61–2
    media, role of 57, *58*, 59
    short/long term explanations for 57–8, 59, 63
    welfare state reform and 187–90
  measurement of 14–15, 48–9, 57
    macroeconomic performance factors and 165, 166, 167, 168, 179
    surveys, use of and 15, 48–9, 50
  Mokken scale analysis 68, 73–4, *75*, 76, 77, 79, 84
  Multilevel Modelling (MLM) use of 101, 103, 104, *105*
  qualitative research and 111
  subjective evaluations, studies of 167, 169, 179
  trends in 14, 15, 24–31, 50
  'winner hypothesis' 68, 69, 71, 84
  see also 'policy feedback' research; political support
politicians, trust in 13, 15, 16, 48
  ESS data analysis 19, *20,* 22, *23, 26, 27, 28,* 47
  media, role in 59
Polity IV project 73
Pontusson, J. 164
Popov, N. 147
Popp, E. 188, 192
Portugal 21 n.4, 102, 150 n.12
  political trust studies 25, 27, *28,* 40
    government satisfaction and 32, *33*

post-communist countries 102, *105,* 111, 130–4
  corruption, levels of 8, 104, 108, 122, 133, 134, 144–5, 147, 154
    as measure of political performance 129
    inequality as a determinant 147
    shadow economy and 146–7
    see also corruption, transition countries study
  distrust in 122, 123, 125, 128, 130, 133, 134
  economic performance and management 121, 131, 133, 154
  fairness, perception of 131, 147
  Freedom House liberty rating 128, 130
  freedom, perception of 120, 128, 130
  inequality in 144, 146, 147
  political trust analysis 8, 100, 104, 108, 110, 119–137, 167 n.1
    cross-national comparisons *126*
    democratic expectations and 120
    institutional performance and 119–20, 123
    national culture and 120, 126
    New Europe Barometer surveys (NEB) 117, 122, 123, 128, 131
    passage of time and 117, 119, 121, 125, 127–8, 130, 131, 132, 133
    political and economic evaluations 121, 131–2, 135
    research methodology 129–30
    socialisation and 120, 122, 127, 128, 132, 133
  social services in 130–1
Powell, G. B. 100, 165
Przeworski, A. 119
public services
  corruption and 142, 148
  deterioration and political trust 142, 148
  see also corruption; post-communist

countries
Putin, V. 117 n.1, 148
Putnam, R. D. 57, 69, 70, 86, 118, 124, 190 n.2
  social capital theory 118

Quadagno, J. 164, 176
Quality of the Government dataset 102, 170

Rahn, W. M. 69, 103
rational choice theory 130
Raudenbush, S. W. 127
Reagan, R. 59
Reeskens, T. 17, 24 n.6
Reeves, B. 61
Riordan, W. 142
Roller, E. 167, 193
Romania 88, 147, 155
  NEB political trust survey 122, *125, 135*
Rose, R. 8, 67, 100, 117, 118, 119, 120, 123, 124, 130, 131, 132, *135*
Rosenberg, M. 71
Rosenvallon, P. 2, 58
Rosser, J. B. 146
Rosser, M. V. 146
Rothstein, B. 18, 67, 70, 81, 144, 166
Rudolph, J. 86
Rudolph, T. J. 50, 59, 61, 104, 188, 191, 192, 193
Russell Sage Foundation 97 n.1, 141 n.1
Russia 117 n.1, 118
  Freedom House rating 128
  NEB political trust survey 122, *125, 135*
    corruption study 128, 147, 148, 155

Samanni, M. 170
Scarbrough, E. 164
Scheinkman, J. A. 142
Schleifer, A. 142
Schmitt, C. 204
Schmitt, H. 164, 169

Schneider, F. 146, 152
Schneider, W. 13, 27, 144, 190 n.2
Schram, S. 164, 166, 168, 169, 180
Scruggs, L. 164, 168, 170, *171*
Shlapentokh, V. 118
Simmel, G. 67
Simon, E. 100
Singer, M. M. 168, 172, 174, 175 n.9, 180
Slovakia 21 n.4, 22, 24, 27 n.9, 30, 146, 155, 157
  government satisfaction 34–5
  NEB political trust survey 122, *125, 135*
Slovenia 21 n.4, 27 n.9, 30, 34, 35, *88, 113,* 150 n.12, 155
  corruption study 147
  NEB political trust survey 122, *125, 135*
Smeeding, T. M. 164, 168, 170
Smith, A. 67
Snijders, T. 101
Sociaal en Cultureel Planbureau 49 n.2
social capital theory 67, 70, 85, 126, 166
social security systems 2
social trust 2, 6, 7, 67–8
  family trust and 76
  forms of 72, 76
  general and particular 68, 69, 72, 77–83, 89
    Mokken scale analysis, use of 74, 76, 79, 84
  relation with political trust 67, 69–70, 72, 77, 80, 84–6
  'winner hypothesis' and 68, 69, 70, 77, 78, 79, 80, 84
  cross-national analysis 76, 84
  see also political trust; trust
socialisation
  political trust and 50, 120, 189
    post-communist countries and 120, 122, 127, 128, 132, 133
  theories 114, 115, 126
Soss, J. 164, 166, 168, 169, 180

South Africa *88*
Soviet Union 117
  culture, authoritarian character of 118
  see also post-communist countries
Spain 21 n.4, 22, *88*
  Madrid bombings 2004 and 31
  political trust studies 27, *28*, 31, 47, 108, *113*
    government satisfaction 31, *33*
Squire, L. 145
State Failure survey 149
Steenbergen, M. R. 103, 127, 172
Steenvoorden, E. 111
Stegmaier, M. 165
Stevenson, R. T. 119, 165
Stiller, S. 194, 195
Stimson, J. 57, 63, 190
Stoker, L. 49, 55, 56, 57
Stolle, D. 18, 70, 81, 144
Sullivan, J. L. 70
Svallfors, S. 164, 166, 180, 190
Sweden *88, 113*
  elections 2010 1
  political trust research 21 n.4, 27, *28*, 31, *32,* 167
  Swedish Democrats 1
  welfare policy 170, *171*
Switzerland 21 n.4, *88, 113*
  political trust studies 25, 27 n.9, *29*, 31, 33, *34*
  welfare policy 170, *171*

Tajikistan 155
Tanzania 73
Tanzi, V. 141
Tavernise, S. 148
Tavits, M. 34
Taylor, M. A. 165
Taylor-Gooby, P. 191, 193
Teorell, J. 102
Theiss-Morse, E. 14, 61, 95
Thomassen, J. J. 100
Tiemeijer, W. 59
Tocqueville, A. de 67, 70
Toennies, F. 67

Tolsma, J. 103
Torcal, M. 163
Torgler, B. 159
Transparency International (TI) 101, 128, 143 n.3, 145, 146 n.6, 147, 149, 150 n.11, 152, *155*
Transue, J. E. 70
Trüdinger, E.-M. 9, 10, 191
trust 6–7, 69–70, 158
  as rational evaluation 96
  four aspects of 96–8, 102
  cultural theory and 118
  education and 2, 70, 71, 77, 133
  Fukuyama's theory of 124
  notion of 3, 45–6, 67
  social capital theory and 124
  socialisation, role of 50, 120
  three forms analysis 67–87
  see also institutional trust; political trust; social trust
Turkey 142, 154
Turkmenistan 148

Uganda 73
Ukraine 17 n.3, 27 n.9, 29, 30, 35, 36
  corruption study 146, 156
  government satisfaction in 34, 35
  NEB political trust survey 122, *125*, 128, *135*
  corruption rating 122
  Orange Revolution 34
Ulbig, S. G. 100 n.6
Ullrich, C. G. 189, 190
unemployment 9, 121, 126, 164, 179
  benefit generosity study 9, 164, 169, 170, *171*, 175, 176–9
  democratic satisfaction and 164, 172, *173*, 174, 176, *177*, *178*, 179
  visible costs hypothesis 9, 164, 176, 179
United Kingdom *88*
  elections 2010 1
  Labour Party 1, 33
  political trust studies 21 n.4, 27 n.9,

29, 73
  government satisfaction 33, *34*
  trust decline 167
United Nations 25, *26,* 149, 155
  Gini index 146 n.6, 147, *152, 153,* 155, 156, 170, *172, 173, 175*
  see also World Institute for Development Economics Research (WIDER)
United States *88*
  AFDC/TANF reform study 168
  health care reform 2
  inequality in 145
  legal system in 19
  political trust 73, 145, 158
    Congressional approval and 61
    decline/fluctuation of 1–2, 6, 13, 27, 61
    economy, link with 59
    research 14–15, 56
    September 11th 2001 attacks 56, 61
    voter turnout 1
Uslaner, E. M. 8, 9, 50, 67, 69, 70, 71, 74, 86, 96, 141, 142, 143, 145, 146, 147, 154, 158, 159
Uzbekistan 155

van de Walle, S. 13, 47, 48, 50, 55, 56, 59, 61, 63
van der Brug, W. 55 n.6, 179 n.12
van der Meer, T. W. G. 7, 69, 95, 96, 97, 99, 100, 104
van Oorschot, W. 188
van Praag, P. 55 n.6
van Schuur, W. H. 74
Varese, F. 148
Verba, S. 14, 17, 47, 63, 118, 190 n.2
  The Civic Culture 47
Vietnam 73
von Wahl, A. 195

Walter-Rogg, M. 100
Weber, M. 67, 118
welfare state performance research 163–4, 166–8, 169, 191
  benefit generosity study 9, 164, 170–80
    unemployment benefit 170, 172, 175, 176, *178*
  data sets, use of 169–70
  democratic (dis)satisfaction and 164, 167, 169, *173*, 174, *177*, 178, 179, 191
  left-right position and 174–5, *177*
  'permanent austerity' and 163
  policy changes and 163–4, 168
  political trust and 5, 9
welfare state reform 187
  ideological beliefs and 192, 193–4, 197, 203–4, 205
  measurement of 196
  material costs and 10, 192, 193, 197, 201, 203, 204, 205
  policy evaluation and 188, 190, 192, 205
  political trust, role in 187–8, 190, 191, 205
    as cognitive heuristic 191, 195, 205
    as support for reform 190, 192, 205
    conditionality of 190, 192, 203, 204
    opinion formation and 191
  research approaches to 189–90
  self-interest and 188, 196
  value-based explanations 188–9, 196
  uncertainty, risk and 191, 193
  see also Germany, welfare state reform

Welzel, C. 70
White, S. 128
Wilkenfeld, B. 13
Wille, A. 6, 28, 29, 33, 36, 59, 61, 95, 99
Woods, D. 193
World Bank 102, 142, 146 n.6, 147, 150 n.12, 152, *153*

World Institute for Development
    Economics Research (WIDER) 146,
    149, *151, 153*
World Values Survey 6, 67, 68, 72, 73,
    84
    corruption analysis 144, 145
    political trust questions 72–3, 81

You, J. 143

Zaller, J. R. 58
Zmerli, S. 6–7, 21 n.4, 67, 68, 72, 73,
    78, 96, 189
Zussman, D. 58, 59

Lightning Source UK Ltd.
Milton Keynes UK
UKOW031937291111

182869UK00001B/8/P